2/12

The Human Condition

The Human Condition

John Kekes

CLARENDON PRESS · OXFORD

OXFORD
UNIVERSITY PRESS

Great Clarendon Street, Oxford OX2 6DP

Oxford University Press is a department of the University of Oxford.
It furthers the University's objective of excellence in research, scholarship,
and education by publishing worldwide in

Oxford New York

Auckland Cape Town Dar es Salaam Hong Kong Karachi
Kuala Lumpur Madrid Melbourne Mexico City Nairobi
New Delhi Shanghai Taipei Toronto

With offices in

Argentina Austria Brazil Chile Czech Republic France Greece
Guatemala Hungary Italy Japan Poland Portugal Singapore
South Korea Switzerland Thailand Turkey Ukraine Vietnam

Oxford is a registered trade mark of Oxford University Press
in the UK and in certain other countries

Published in the United States
by Oxford University Press Inc., New York

British Library Cataloguing in Publication Data
Data available

Library of Congress Cataloging in Publication Data
Data available

Typeset by Laserwords Private Limited, Chennai, India
Printed in Great Britain
on acid-free paper by the
MPG Books Group, Bodmin and King's Lynn

ISBN 978–0–19–958888–6

10 9 8 7 6 5 4 3 2 1

for J.Y.K

Contents

Acknowledgments   xi

Introduction   1

1. The Question   7
    1.1 The Question   7
    1.2 Two Interpretations of Contingencies   12
    1.3 The Possibility of Control   16
    1.4 Practical Reason   19
    1.5 Toward an Answer   23

2. Increasing Control   26
    2.1 A Case in Point   27
    2.2 The Question of Significance   28
    2.3 The Variable Approach   33
    2.4 Objections Considered   38
    2.5 Loose Ends   46

3. Correcting Attitudes   47
    3.1 Values   48
    3.2 Limits   53
    3.3 Commitments   56
    3.4 Critical Reflection   63
    3.5 Corrected Attitudes   64

4. Aiming at Well-Being   67
    4.1 Mistakes about Well-Being   68
    4.2 Coherence   72
    4.3 Coherence is Not Enough   76
    4.4 Realism   81
    4.5 Obstacles to Well-Being   86

5. Dimensions of Value   88
    5.1 The Human Dimension   89
    5.2 The Cultural Dimension   91
    5.3 The Personal Dimension   96
    5.4 Conflicts   97
    5.5 Right vs. Wrong Approaches
         to Conflict-Resolution   103

6. The Human Dimension and Evil   114
    6.1 What is Evil?   114
    6.2 The Secular Problem of Evil   119
    6.3 Inadequate Explanations   122
    6.4 Toward an Adequate Explanation   127
    6.5 Evil and the Human Condition   135

7. Responsibility for Evil   138
    7.1 The Reflexivity of Evil   139
    7.2 Intention and Responsibility   146
    7.3 The Standard   149
    7.4 Excuses   153
    7.5 Weakening the Reasons for Evil-doing   160

8. The Cultural Dimension and Disenchantment   162
    8.1 Disenchantment   163
    8.2 Modes of Evaluation   166
    8.3 Exemplars   171
    8.4 The Quest for an Overriding Mode of Evaluation   177
    8.5 Modus Vivendi   182

9. The Personal Dimension and Boredom   185
    9.1 Boredom   186
    9.2 The Thrill of Evil   189
    9.3 Unassuagable Boredom?   194
    9.4 The Burden of Reflection   199
    9.5 Overview   204

10. Secular Hope   207
     10.1 Depth   207
     10.2 Modest Hope   211
     10.3 The Illusion of Autonomy   216
     10.4 The Illusion of the Categorical Imperative   219
     10.5 Secular Hope without Illusions   225

Conclusion   232

Notes   246

Works Cited   262

Index   271

Acknowledgments

Chapter 1 was published as "The Human World" in *Ratio* 22 (2009): 137–56. Chapter 5 is a substantial revision of Chapter 6 in *Enjoyment: The Moral Significance of Styles of Life* (Oxford: Clarendon Press, 2008). Chapter 7 includes parts of Chapter 13 in *The Roots of Evil* (Ithaca: Cornell University Press, 2005). I thank the original publishers of these works, Wiley-Blackwell, Oxford University Press, and Cornell University Press for permission to use here a revised version of these writings of mine.

I owe special gratitude to Thaddeus Metz who was one of the, then anonymous, referees consulted by Oxford University Press. His criticisms and suggestions were exceptionally helpful. The final version has been greatly improved by his comments. James Ryan and Lucas Swaine read and most helpfully commented on an earlier form of the first five chapters. Their comments have led to numerous revisions. I am grateful for the time and attention each of them devoted to my work.

Peter Momtchiloff, my editor at Oxford University Press, has once again most helpfully guided the transformation of the typescript into a book. I acknowledge his midwifery with pleasure and gratitude.

John Kekes

Ithaca
Charlton
New York

Introduction

The central argument of this book is that the secular view of the human condition is the most reasonable approach to our well-being. Secular views are united by doubting that there is a supernatural realm, but they differ, because they understand our condition and well-being in different and often incompatible ways. My view is pluralist, not absolutist; rationalist, not relativist; fallibilist, not skeptical or dogmatic; realist, not optimist or pessimist; particular and concrete, not general and abstract; and it aims to understand our lives humanistically from our perspective, not from an external perspective that transcends our own. These components are complex and controversial. The reasons for them is what this book is about.

Secular doubts call into question all religious views about the human condition that assume the existence of a supernatural realm. The arguments for and against belief in such a realm are familiar and endlessly debated. What I would say in support of secular doubts has been said many times, and it would be pointless to repeat it. In doubting supernaturally based religious views, however, I do not mean to deny that religious reflection often has the great merit of raising deep questions about the meaning of life, the basis of morality, the contingencies of human lives, the prevalence of evil, the nature and extent of human responsibility, and the sources of the values we prize. These are among the questions to which I hope to give reasonable answers. The aim of the book may be characterized, then, as giving secular answers to religious questions.

I draw on the resources of our system of values to provide the answers we need.

From a religious point of view, our system of values is inadequate, unless it reflects, or at least conforms to, a moral order that is supposed to permeate the scheme of things. Its defenders may acknowledge the waning of religious belief and the spread of secular doubts about it, but they lament this state of affairs and blame on it the growing disenchantment with contemporary life and the unsatisfied yearning for the forsaken religious inspiration and consolation. I agree that the disenchantment and yearning are felt, but I deny that they follow from the spread of secular doubts. They follow, rather, from ignorance about the resources of our system of values; from the failure of nerve of jaded savants in the face of primitive, regressive challenges; from the knowingness of cynics who suppose that to see is to see through; and from the iconoclastic efforts of ideologues of various persuasion to undermine the system of values on which our well-being largely depends. I will argue that the yearning for inspiration and consolation can be satisfied by our system of values without appealing to a supposed supernatural moral order.

The version of the secular view I defend differs in significant respects from other versions. One of these differences is that it does not share the optimism about human perfectibility and progress that several secular views derive from the Enlightenment. Optimists assume that human beings are basically reasonable and good. They explain the plentiful manifestations of unreason and evil by attributing them to corruption by bad social conditions, but they do not face the obvious question of why social conditions are bad. Social conditions are human creations. If they are bad, it is because those who create and maintain them are unreasonable, bad, or both. A realistic view of the human condition must recognize that our basic dispositions are ambivalent toward reason and goodness. Our efforts to improve social conditions, therefore, are handicapped by the same ambivalence that makes the conditions bad. This is an obstacle to progress and perfectibility that seems to be built into the human condition.

Another difference has to do with science. In contrast with several versions of the secular view, I do not suppose that all genuine understanding is scientific. Science is undoubtedly one of the greatest human achievements, the key to our understanding of the nature of the world. But not even scientific omniscience, were it possible, would give us all we need. We also need to understand how we should live, given what science tells us about the world. Understanding that, however, involves judging the significance of the facts from the point of view of human well-being. This is an evaluative and anthropocentric point of view, in contrast with the scientific one, which is neither. To suppose, as some defenders of secular views do, that all genuine understanding must be scientific is to mistake an impossibility for a desirable goal. That scientific understanding is not evaluative and anthropocentric is no more a defect of science than it is a defect of art, history, literature, morality, philosophy, politics, or religion that they provide no understanding of quarks or of the biochemistry of the brain. And, of course, scientists may be dedicated to human well-being. *Qua* scientists, they have other interests, but *qua* human beings, they may be as concerned with our well-being as anyone else.

A further difference has to do with conflicting views about the nature of reason involved in our pursuit of well-being. Theoretical reason aims at true beliefs. If a belief is true, it is true universally, always, everywhere. We may be ignorant of it or of the evidence for it, we may doubt or dislike it, but that reflects only on us, not on the truth of the belief. Practical reason aims at action that succeeds in furthering human well-being. Human well-being, however, varies, because we have different characters, circumstances, experiences, preferences, hopes, fears, values, and we rank the relative importance of our values differently. Successful action varies accordingly. It may follow from practical reason that we must act in a particular way or be unreasonable. But it does not follow that any other person, let alone everyone, in a similar situation must also act that way or be unreasonable. Theoretical reason is universal, but practical reason often is not, and none the worse for that. Nevertheless, some defenders of the secular view suppose that practical reasons must be universal or fail as reasons. This is as mistaken as the supposition that understanding must be scientific or fail to be genuine. Both mistakes stem from the same source: misunderstanding the nature of human well-being. A defensible secular view must avoid these and other misunderstandings of practical reason.

All secular views face a problem that has been recognized at least since the ancient Greeks struggled with it. If human beings are part of nature, then we are subject to the laws of which science aims to provide ever deeper understanding. But then it depends on the laws what we do and what happens to us, and we are not in control of how we live. One consequence of our embeddedness in nature is the fact, obvious to anyone who cares to look, that there is only a contingent connection between the life we have and the one we deserve to have. Our well-being does not reflect our merits or demerits. How well life goes for each one of us is, at least partly, a matter of luck—of *tuche* in Greek, *fortuna* in Latin, or *contingencies* as I will call it.

Our system of values should be understood, among other things, as our attempt to cope with contingencies by making the connection between our well-being and actions less contingent and more within our control. We do have some control over how we live, because there is a gap between the necessities to which we are subject and the possibilities we might try to realize. This gap is not mysterious. It is the outcome of the evolutionary process that has endowed us with more abundant capacities than we need for viability. The importance of our system of values is that it guides us to use excess capacities to increase the control we have and thereby decrease the extent to which we are subject to contingencies.

A preliminary indication of the emerging secular view of the human condition is as follows. The world is indifferent to human well-being. How good or bad our lives are depends in part on how well or badly we cope with the conditions to which we are subject. In order to cope with them, we rely on our system of values to guide how we live. Being guided by it requires us to increase our control. One way to increase it is by critical reflection, which is the use of practical reason for the betterment of human lives. The objects of this kind of critical reflection are the natural and social conditions external to us and the beliefs, emotions, and motives that are part of the internal conditions of our lives. The most formidable obstacles to increasing our control are the contingencies of life that affect both our external and internal conditions and our all too frequent failures in critical reflection. We aim to cope with these obstacles, but we cannot free ourselves from them, because our attempts to do so are handicapped by the very problems we are trying to overcome. How well we succeed in coping with them depends on the correction of mistakes we make in responding to contingencies and on critical reflection on how we live.

According to the secular view I defend, human well-being is individually variable; values are plural; and successful critical reflection must be concrete and particular. Critical reflection is necessary for some conceptions of well-being, but it is not sufficient for them. All this requires explanation and supporting argument, and I aim to provide them in what follows. But I aim also to work out some of the many implications of this secular view about values, evil, responsibility, disenchantment, boredom, the meaning of life, hope, the relation between individuals and society, and, of course, about the human condition.

Lastly, this book is about our prospects of well-being, not about what others have written about our prospects of well-being. I have, of course, read and learned from the works of others, but I have decided, for better or worse, not to engage in detailed discussions of what is called "the literature." Such discussions are important, but, I concluded, not without hesitation, that they are best conducted in specialist journals. I wanted to make what I have to say accessible to non-specialist readers who are likely to be interested in human well-being, rather than in how I arrived at my views about it. This has led me to avoid detailed discussions of the works of others. I came to think of such discussions as the scaffolding without which no structure can be built, but which should be removed once the structure is completed. I hope that the end product will be judged on the basis of its merits, not on the basis of the scaffolding necessary for building it. I want to acknowledge, however, that its design has been shaped, through agreement and disagreement, by the lasting influences of Aristotle, Montaigne, and Hume.

1

The Question

1.1. The Question

> . . . do we, holding that the gods exist,
> deceive ourselves with unsubstantial dreams
> and lies, while random careless chance and change
> alone control the world?

Euripides posed this good and deep question 2,500 years ago.[1] The unsubstantial dream is that the scheme of things is governed by a moral order. The dreamers may acknowledge that we daily experience senseless inhumanity, conflict, unreason, and the tendency of even the best laid plans to go wrong. But they explain all that by our willful or ignorant deviation from the moral order on which our well-being depends. What Euripides regards an unsubstantial dream is, in fact, the venerable assumption on which the great religions and most metaphysical systems rest.

As Euripides makes clear in his tragedies, he thinks that careless chance and change control the world. We do not have to agree, of course. We may believe that the unsubstantial dream is true, or accept it for reasons other than its truth. I think Euripides is right to reject it, but he is wrong to conclude that we must believe, then, that chance and change alone control the world. There are good reasons for rejecting the dream and I will not repeat them here.[2] What I hope to do is to avoid the dilemma that we must either deceive ourselves and accept the dream even though it is not credible, or resign ourselves to the senselessness of the world. Opting for either has destructive implications for human well-being. If we deceive ourselves with the dream, we forfeit responsibility and control over how we live. If we accept that the world is senseless, we must abandon the belief that being guided by our reason and values is better than ignoring them. The unwholesomeness of these alternatives is a good reason for looking for another possibility, which is what I will now do.

To begin with, Euripides' question is too crude. Even if we disbelieve the dream, we do not have to regard it as completely false, nor hold that the only alternative to it is a senseless world. If the dream were completely false, there would be no order at all and random chance and change would rule the world. The dream, however, may be only partly false: there is order in the world, but it is not moral. This is not to say that it is immoral, for it may be non-moral and uncaring. It may hold regardless of what happens to anything subject to it, including ourselves.

To say that the world is uncaring is misleading, because it leaves open the possibility that the world may change its mind and start caring. But this verges on absurdity. Only sentient beings can care, and the world is not a sentient being. It is better to say, therefore, that the order in the world is indifferent. Of course, we are sentient, part of the world, and we care about our well-being. What is true of a minute part, however, need not be true of the whole. There is caring in the world, but no caring by the world. This leaves room for the possibility that, although the world's order is indifferent, we care about what happens in it, especially to us.

It is not clear, however, that this possibility is anything more than an idle thought we should reject as having no application to the real world. For our caring may be just an illusion we nourish to avoid the unpleasantness of facing the futility of caring about anything. The truth may be that it is our caring that is senseless, not the world. Our beliefs about facts and things may be true, but our beliefs about values may be false. If this were so, I would have clarified a little Euripides' question, but would not have avoided his answer that it is an illusion to suppose that being guided by reason and values will make our lives better. Avoiding it depends on further clarifications about the supposed indifferent order and the illusoriness of caring about anything.

I start with the indifferent order. Let us understand by the world absolutely everything that exists: objects, processes, energy, human constructions, and organisms; ideals and mistakes; acts and omissions; microscopic and macroscopic systems; beliefs and feelings; viruses and galaxies; rainbows and shadows; works of art and inflation. Given this understanding, there can be nothing outside the world. The physical and biological sciences have given us ample reasons to believe that a causal order permeates the world, so I will say that the world is law-governed. We are, of course, part of the law-governed world and subject to its laws. But the laws are indifferent to our well-being.

As Bernard Williams put it: "The world was not made for us, or we for the world . . . our history tells no purposive story, and . . . there is no position outside the world or outside history from which we might hope to authenticate our activities. . . . There is no redemptive Hegelian history or universal Leibnizian cost-benefit analysis to show that it will come out well in the end." It is an unsubstantial dream that "somehow or other, in this life or the next . . . we shall be safe; or if not safe, at least reassured that at some level of the world's constitution there is something to be discovered that makes ultimate sense of our concerns." We can rely only on ourselves as we are "dealing sensibly, foolishly, sometimes catastrophically, sometimes nobly, with a world that is only partially intelligible to human agency and in itself not necessarily well adjusted to ethical aspirations."[3] I think this is the human condition. The question, then, is what we can do to make our lives better.

The beginning of the answer is that the indifferent law-governed world allows us some control over how we live. Its laws hold under certain conditions, and we can sometimes change the conditions. We cannot alter the effect of sub-zero temperature on human bodies, but we can dress in protective layers, or stay inside a heated house. Furthermore, although we are always subject to its laws, we can sometimes choose the one to which we are subject. If we want to lose weight, we can fast, diet, exercise more, or have subcutaneous fat surgically removed. Laws will govern each possibility, but we can opt for the possibilities we want to pursue and accept limits that go with them. The laws establish the possibilities and limits of our various endeavors, but they leave us with some control. Necessities do not exhaust our possibilities. We may regard whatever control we have as reward for having done well in the relentless course of evolution.

The fact remains, however, that we cannot completely free ourselves from the laws, partly because we often cannot change the conditions in which we must act or choose the laws to which we are subject. And even when we have some control over them, we have it only because preceding laws had made it possible. This is true of everything we do or might do, including the evaluations we make. Ultimately, therefore, we have no control over how much control we actually have. Since the law-governed world is indifferent and our control limited, there is apparently little we can do to direct our lives. This is part of what concerns me.

Another part is the supposed illusoriness of our evaluations. Why might it be an illusion that the rule of law, enjoyment, and kindness are good and lawlessness, misery, and cruelty bad? The answer often given is that from the point of view of the law-governed world, nothing matters. If looked at with complete detachment from human concerns, then how it goes for humanity as a whole or for particular individuals has no more or less significance than how it goes for distant galaxies, colonies of ants, or cancelled streetcar tickets. This is not because everything matters equally but because nothing at all matters. In the vastness of the law-governed world, things happen, processes unfold and come to an end, change is ceaseless. There are only things, processes, and facts devoid of meaning, significance, or value.

We need not, of course, ignore our concerns and view what happens with complete detachment. We can recognize that what happens matters, because it affects our well-being. The world may not care, but we do. We evaluate facts by asking how they affect us collectively or individually. Such evaluations may be true or false. Everyone may believe that in the long run all manner of things will be well, or that prosperity is good, or that humility is a virtue, and everyone may be wrong. What is good or bad for us does not depend on what we think or hope; it depends on how it affects our well-being. Our evaluations, therefore, are not detached. They proceed from the point of view of our well-being, and express our beliefs and emotions about what contributes to or hinders it. These beliefs may be mistaken and the emotions may be misplaced or inappropriate. Euripides is right in this: if we approach our evaluations from the point of view of the indifferent law-governed world, we will be driven to conclude that nothing matters. But this is a reason for not approaching them from that point of view, not a reason against taking the human point of view from which many things matter a great deal. Not the least reason for this approach is that our well-being depends on it.[4]

Doubts, however, may persist. It may be granted that evaluations need not be illusory, but it may still be thought that they are futile. For the law-governed world is what it is, the facts are what they are, and how we evaluate them changes nothing. What, then, is the point of evaluations? Why should we care, if caring makes no difference? Is the preoccupation with things mattering not a pointless exercise that wastes time and energy? The answer, as we have seen, is no, for two reasons.

One is that we can sometimes change the conditions in which an adversely evaluated law holds in favor of another set of conditions in which a law more favorable to us prevails. We need not always freeze in sub-zero weather and, if we must lose weight, we can sometimes choose between the fastest, or the safest, or the least painful way of doing so. Another is that even when we cannot change the facts, we can change our attitude toward them. We can respond to the unalterable conditions we face with despair, hope, indignation, irony, rage, resignation, self-deception, surprise, and so forth, and the attitudes we cultivate and those we wean ourselves from have much to do with the quality of our lives.

For these reasons, we need not agree with Euripides that if we reject the unsubstantial dream, then we must accept that being guided by reason and values is futile, evaluations are pointless, and we have no control over how we live. Even if the law-governed world does not allow us to have complete control, it allows us to have some control. And we can use that control in better or worse ways.

Given these clarifications, can we say that we have found a defensible alternative to Euripides' clarified view that the law-governed world is indifferent to our well-being, that deceiving ourselves with unsubstantial dreams is to forfeit responsibility and control, and that it is illusory to rely on reason and values? We cannot. For even if we have some control over how we live and our evaluations may make our lives better, we must recognize that we do not have adequate control either over the extent to which we can control how we live, or over the conditions that influence the evaluations we make. Whether we have the small amount of control I have insisted we have partly depends on the indifferent law-governed world. Euripides' view, then, may be restated in a clarified and sharpened form as claiming that our control is an illusion, because indifference rules the law-governed world and we are unavoidably subject to it. I will now argue that this view is mistaken.

1.2. Two Interpretations of Contingencies

Consider a commercial jet with many people on board flying over the ocean. It runs into a freak storm, lightning strikes, its engines catch fire, the electronic system is disabled, and crash is imminent. One scenario is that it crashes and everyone dies. This may be described as bad luck for those who died, for their families and friends, and for the airline. Another scenario is that there is a nearby island with a short runway and the pilot manages to land the plane, because he has had much experience in the air force landing and taking off from aircraft carriers. Everyone is saved. This may be described as good luck for everyone concerned. Such things happen, of course. One interpretation is that contingencies are matters of luck. Bad luck harms us, good luck benefits us, but we cannot control either. If we could, it would not be bad luck, but negligence or laziness; nor would it be good luck, but deserved benefit.

Describing anything as luck is a loose shorthand. It stands for various causal chains that intersect and whose intersection we can neither predict nor explain, because we lack the relevant knowledge. In the case of the jet, weather predictions are imperfect, the skill of pilots varies, we cannot make planes safe enough. We are vulnerable, because we are ignorant. And even if we knew enough, we might still not be able to prevent being harmed or to gain benefits. Viruses may assail us, meteorites may destroy us, earthquakes may bury us, or extraterrestrials may tell us about an unlimited source of energy, mutation may make us invulnerable to cancer, and the next great scientific discovery may already be cooking in someone's unusual mind. Luck does not describe how things are; it describes how things seem to us when we are handicapped by ignorance, incapacity, or self-deception. If we were omniscient and omnipotent, or if there were no human beings, there would be nothing describable as luck. Or, to put it differently, in the law-governed world there is no luck; there is luck only from the limited and fallible human point of view.

If we interpret contingencies as luck, then control is an illusion, because how much control we have is a matter of luck: our knowledge and capacities are limited and what we do not know and cannot alter may affect us in ways we cannot predict, explain, or control. If this is how we understand the lines of Euripides that "careless chance and change alone control the world," then Euripides is right.

On another interpretation, however, contingencies are avoidable, at least to some extent, and on that understanding of what Euripides says, he is wrong. Consider again the stricken jet. Among the hundreds of people on it, there is a torturer going to ply his trade, a pedophile in search of children for rent, and a serial murderer who judged it prudent to change location for a time. There is also a physician on his way to work without pay in Africa, a diplomat returning home after having negotiated the end of a murderous civil war, and a policeman escorting the kingpin of a drug cartel he arrested and persuaded to testify against the corrupt government that allowed him to function. This time, however, there is no convenient island, the pilot cannot land, and they all die.

A widely shared reaction to this scenario is likely to be that life should not be like that. Good people deserve good things, bad people bad things, but contingencies prevented this from happening. Because the law-governed world is indifferent, everyone fell afoul of the same fate, and this offends our sense of what the world ought to be like. What we find offensive are contingencies, interpreted as the normative indifference of the law-governed world: the laws to which we are subject affect us without regard to our merits or demerits. We do not want the world to be like that. We agree with Hume's lament that "such is the disorder and confusion in human affairs, that no perfect or regular distribution of happiness and misery is ever, in this life, to be expected. Not only the goods of fortune, and the endowments of the body (both of which are important), not only these advantages, I say, are unequally divided between the virtuous and the vicious, but even the mind itself partakes, in some degree, of this disorder. . . . In a word, human life is more governed by fortune than by reason."[5] This is not sentimental hand-wringing but a realistic description of the human condition. Nevertheless. it does not follow from it that we are helpless and cannot do anything about it. We can and have done so.

We have created and we maintain a system of values. Although the system is part of the law-governed world and subject to its laws, the values of our system guide us in deciding how to use the limited control we have. And one of the important ways in which we can use it is to make benefits and harms as proportional to the merits or demerits of their recipients as the contingencies of life allow.

Our values are many and varied: among them are aesthetic appreciation, literary classics, moral exemplars, philosophical depth, and political and religious ideals. They may be universal, cultural, or personal; enduring or changing; deeply serious or entertaining; some no society can do without, others vary with contexts; they may be products of reflection, disciplined feeling, or creative imagination; they may be accessible to any moderately intelligent person or only to those with rigorous training of their intellect, character, perception, or taste. Corresponding to these values, there are kitschy imitations, as well as disvalues that are impoverishing or demeaning in the same dimension as the values are enriching or ennobling. Values give meaning, purpose, and significance to what we do or try to do once our physical needs are satisfied. They civilize our experiences and responses to the indifferent law-governed world, when necessity does not compel us to eat, drink, breathe, sleep, or cope with dangers.

The great difference between the small segment of the law-governed world that contains our system of values and the vast rest of it is that values exist only in our small segment and there are no values outside of it. The values inform our beliefs, emotions, and motives, desires and goals, the capacities we prize and the decisions we make. I will refer to these psychological states and processes jointly as our attitudes. Our conception of well-being, then, is constructed out of our values and attitudes.

One reason why many lives are bad is that many of these attitudes are mistaken. There are also other reasons, and we may or may not be able to alter them. Correcting mistaken attitudes, however, is something we can do. The proof is that we have done it in the past about slavery, the divine right of kings, the persecution of witches, the sinfulness of charging interest for money lent, and stoning adulterers. I stress this as a significant possibility, without wishing to suggest that self-congratulation is warranted. Mistaken attitudes abound, and they may do so, because we have not discovered that they are mistaken. The mere possibility that we can correct mistaken attitudes, however, is not enough to warrant optimism about the human condition. But the possibility of correction exists. It is significant, because it shows that we have some control over how we live and we are not totally at the mercy of contingencies. We can do something to increase our control and make us less vulnerable.

1.3. The Possibility of Control

It will be said that control is an illusion, because, as I have repeatedly acknowledged, we lack adequate control over how much control we have. I acknowledge it once more, but I deny that it makes the control we have illusory. Consider a more personalized example than the stricken jet. A man has accepted a much better job than what he had and his family and he must relocate to take it up. Assume that the family is loving, its tensions are normal, and there are no hidden crises, hatreds, or deep resentments lurking under the placid surface. They must decide whether to live in town or country, in a house or an apartment, close to schools or spend time commuting; how much they should spend on housing; weigh the preferences of everyone in the family; consider how new surroundings might change their customary lives; take into account crime, pollution, likely neighbors, the proximity of stores; try to imagine how life would be if they opted for various possibilities; and so forth. They think, talk, weigh, and arrive at decisions they can all live with. The decisions may still turn out to be mistaken, because they have not foreseen everything, what they have imagined may be unrealistic, they were guided by wishful thinking, or they did not think hard enough.

Decisions like this are ubiquitous. Most of us make them about marriage, family, job, money, health, housing, education, love affairs, politics, and we make them even if those who are immediately affected are not as idyllically related as in my example above. Through such decisions we exercise some control over how we live and reduce the extent to which contingencies rule our lives, even if we have not escaped them altogether.

Contingencies, of course, may still interfere with our control either by external causes that seem to us to be accidents, disasters, emergencies, epidemics, and so forth, or by internal causes, such as genetic predispositions; internalized early training and education; repressed traumas; blind obedience to religious, political, or nationalistic authorities; or the unquestioned influence of advertising, propaganda, or charismatic figures.

One of the many objections to what I have been saying is that what appears to us as control is always the effect of internal causes of whose nature and influence we may be unaware. This is what many psychologists, sociologists, deconstructionists, ideologues, and other unmaskers are claiming. They think that what is on the surface is a misleading indication of depths below; and that appearances systematically misrepresent reality.

I reply with Oscar Wilde that "it is only shallow people who do not judge by appearances."[6] This is not just a witticism. Appearances normally reflect what they are appearances of. What seems red is normally red; the bacon that seems salty is normally salty; the voice on the phone that seems to be my wife's is normally hers; the anger I seem to feel is normally anger; and when it seems to me that I have made a considered decision, I have normally done just that. We may suspect that in any particular case an appearance is misleading. But the suspicion is reasonable only if we have some reason for it. That what we suspect is an appearance is not a reason. The reason must be some ground for supposing that the appearance is misleading.

The unmaskers who refuse to take any appearance at its face value often endeavor to offer as such a ground a theory about the supposed deep structure of psychology, sociology, history, language, or whatever. What needs to be said about these theories is what G.E. Moore had said in another context. He held up his finger and said: "This, after all, you know, really is a finger: there is no doubt about it: I know it and you all know it. And I think we may safely challenge any[one] . . . to bring forward any argument in favour . . . of the proposition that it is not true, which does not at some point rest upon some premise which is, beyond comparison, less certain than is the proposition which it is designed to attack."[7] Even Freud conceded that a cigar is sometimes just a cigar—especially when he smoked it.

Moore's robust common sense is refreshing and only a little overstated. Obviously, there are theories that explain why appearances in some areas of life are always misleading: why the Earth seems flat, the Sun rising and setting, the phantom limb aching, and so forth. What Moore should have insisted on is that there could not be a reasonable theory that explains why all appearances are always mistaken. There could not be such a theory, because all theories take for granted some appearances, such as their initial data, confirming or disconfirming observations, instrument readings, the accuracy of their measurements, surprising findings, or the cogency of their quantifications. If they were to deny the reliability of all appearances, they would have to reject the basis on which they rest. If the unmaskers merely said that we are sometimes mistaken when we think that we have achieved some control over our lives, they would be right. But that would not be an adequate reason for doubting the appearance that we have constructed a system of values and that we can sometimes control at least to some extent whether we live according to it. Our well-being, therefore, is not entirely subject to contingencies.

I will assume, then, that we have some control over how we live. But this will not take us very far. For the control we have is the outcome of contingencies beyond our control: of inherited capacities, education that favors their development, and circumstances in later life that provide opportunities for their exercise. These conditions vary with persons and contexts. Whether and how fully they are met in any particular case is beyond our control.

The mere possibility of control, therefore, leaves open the question of whether it is possible to increase the control we happen to have. Our well-being depends on increasing it, because the more control we have the less vulnerable we will be to contingencies. And we can increase it by relying on practical reason.

1.4. Practical Reason

Reason has many forms, interpretations, and uses. Practical reason is only one of them, but that one is centrally important for us, because it is the use of reason to enhance human well-being. Practical reason also has other uses, and the non-practical uses of reason may also enhance our well-being, but, if they do, it is a welcome by-product of the pursuit of other ends, such as scientific or historical understanding, not the end they directly aim at. Practical reason aims directly at human well-being. It is concerned with understanding what fosters or hinders it and with motivating us to act on this understanding. This kind of understanding is partly of the best means and partly of the end, well-being itself. The end is complex, because human well-being takes many different forms and depends on the realization of many different values. But in one form or another, understood in terms of one or another set of values, we all aim at it, unless contingencies prevent it. Part of the motivational force of practical reason derives from this natural aim that all normal human beings in normal circumstances have.

One important use of practical reason, then, may be regarded as our attempt so to arrange matters, insofar as we can arrange them, that when we act by using reasonable means to realize reasonable ends we reasonably think are required for our reasonable conception of well-being, then our actions will be successful. And practical reason enables us to distinguish between more and less reasonable means, ends, and conceptions of well-being.

Consider what I have called earlier an attitude. I am hungry, want to eat, decide to go home for lunch, and I walk there. Implicit in the sequence is that I have a desire (to eat), a set of beliefs and emotions (my house is nearby, there is food in the fridge, I love the walk home, I enjoy the privacy of eating alone) and I have the required capacities (I can walk, rely on my memory, estimate distance), I have a goal (to satisfy my desire), and these components of the attitude give me a motive to act accordingly. The attitude that precedes action, then, has the following elements: desire, belief, emotion, capacity, goal, and motive. Each may be defective: desires may be irrational, beliefs false, emotions misdirected, capacities inadequate, goals unattainable, and motives too strong or too weak. Suppose, however, that they are not defective and I perform the action the attitude prompts. I expect, then, that my action will be successful, that it will achieve its goal. We have normally good reason to suppose that such attitudes are mistake-free and no reason to doubt it. Our ordinary expectation that our routine actions will be successful is generally reasonable. If it were otherwise, we would long ago have gone the way of dinosaurs. Our well-being requires that such reasonable expectations be most of the time met.

It would be comforting if such attitudes were adequate for the business of living, but they are not. Complexities unavoidably arise, because it is often difficult to tell whether a component of an attitude is defective. Desires conflict and we constantly have to make decisions about which of them we should try to satisfy. We routinely have to evaluate the reliability of our beliefs and emotions on the basis of imperfect knowledge and insufficient evidence. Our capacities are always limited and we have to estimate whether they are adequate for the achievement of difficult goals. We usually have several incompatible goals and must decide about their relative importance, but what seems important at one time may become less so at another. The world changes, we change, and we have to make guesses about how these changes might affect our goals. The motives we have depend on understanding our circumstances and what we want, all things considered, out of life, and both may be unclear at the time we have to decide, and it may be even more unclear how they might be in the future. Coping with complexities requires, therefore, in addition to getting the facts right, also judging their significance. Good judgment about such matters is difficult.

Suppose I act on the basis of a mistake-free attitude. Might I reasonably expect, then, that my action will be successful? No, because even if I act as reasonably as anyone in my position could, I may fail, because others justifiably prevent my success. Most of the time my success depends on the cooperation of others, and they may have more important concerns; or they may also want what I want and are better at getting it; or what I want may run counter to their interests or to the interests of an institution, cause, or collectivity they wish to protect. More is needed, therefore, before I can reasonably expect to get what I want, and the same, of course, is true of everyone else. We all have to take into account that we live in a society and depend on the cooperation of others. The terms of cooperation, therefore, have to be set. In the vast majority of complex sequences, we can get what we want only on the prevailing terms. These terms may be more or less adequate to the purpose of maintaining the optimum conditions in which as many of us as possible can go about getting what we want.

Can we reasonably expect that our actions will be successful if they are based on mistake-free attitudes and conform to the prevailing terms of cooperation? The answer is still no, because the prevailing terms may be defective. But even if they are adequate, our expectation of success may be premature, because adequate terms cannot eliminate competition. We may fail to achieve our goals, although we have good judgment and conform to the adequate terms, because we lose out in a competition with others whose judgment is also good and who also conform to the terms. Only one person can win the race, get the job, be the first to make the discovery, and only a few can make the best-seller list, get elected, add to the canon, or make a lasting contribution to science. For each of those who succeed, there are many who try and fail. Not all goals are competitive, of course; having a good marriage, enjoying nature, developing a historical perspective, listening to music are not. But many are, and because of them we may have mistake-free attitudes, conform to the terms of cooperation, and still fail to achieve our goals.

Putting all this together, the following requirements of successful action emerge: acting on mistake-free attitudes, conforming to adequate terms of cooperation, and, if our goals are competitive, prevailing in the competition. These requirements are the requirements of practical reason, and we want a world in which we can expect that our actions will be successful if we are guided by practical reason. The actual world, of course, is not as we want it to be. Our reasonable expectations are often frustrated, because contingencies over which we have no control stand in our way even if we conform to the requirements of practical reason. One main reason for needing and prizing practical reason is that it motivates us to increase our control by correcting our mistaken attitudes, making the prevailing terms of cooperation less inadequate and conformity to them more likely. The more we succeed, the less we will be subject to contingencies and the more we will be in control of our well-being.

No matter how well we succeed, however, contingencies will unavoidably doom to imperfection our control over our well-being and make it impossible for our reasonable expectations to succeed. The most obvious way in which this may happen is the insufficiency of available resources. If there is not enough money, food, medicine, prison space, police protection, or hospital care, then some of us cannot have what we have good reason to expect. It is not only material resources, however, that may be insufficient but also the expertise needed to create and deliver them. Physicians, teachers, administrators, or research scientists may be as scarce as food, shelter, and medicine. The distribution of insufficient resources among those who reasonably expect them may unavoidably fall short of what we aim at, because it forces on us decisions that deprive some people of what they reasonably expect to have.

It is useless to try to overcome this by distributing insufficient resources equally, because the equal distribution of insufficient resources may result in the even worse outcome that no one's reasonable expectation is met. If there are not enough oxygen tanks, it does not help to ration the suffocating to the same brief periods of breathing. Furthermore, there are numerous insufficient resources whose equal distribution is impossible. Medical specialists, inspiring teachers, or first-rate administrators must restrict their activities to particular contexts, but if there are not enough of them, people outside of those contexts will not get the treatment, education, or efficient service they reasonably expect.

Even if the adverse effects of contingency can be corrected in some cases, in many others correction is impossible. Nothing can be done to undo or minimize the damage done to those who sacrificed their lives for a noble cause, or were forced to spend the best years of their lives in concentration camps on trumped-up charges, or contracted AIDS through blood transfusion. It is often impossible to arrange the world so that what people reasonably expect to have is what they actually have. Hume is right: "no perfect or regular distribution of happiness and misery is ever . . . to be expected." Perfection is unattainable, but imperfection can be diminished, and that is one main aim of practical reason. When we use it well, we improve the human condition by increasing our control, reducing our vulnerability to contingencies, and making room for our values in the indifferent law-governed world. In the chapters that follow, I will discuss in detail what is involved in increasing our control.

1.5. Toward an Answer

In this chapter I have taken the first step toward answering Euripides' question. The dilemma he posed is too stark. The human condition does not force us to choose between deceiving ourselves with unsubstantial dreams and accepting that careless chance and change rule the world. We have constructed a system of values, and it guides our efforts to increase the control we have over our lives. This is an alternative to the choice Euripides believes is forced on us. But the first step toward an answer is not an answer. A proper answer must spell out the possibilities and limits of our control in much greater concreteness and detail than I have done so far. What I have said about control, values, understanding, attitudes and their correction, and practical reason is only a sketchy first approximation. In the rest of the book I will deepen and broaden it.

We have, however, made some progress. There is good reason to think that our well-being is essentially connected with increasing our control. For it enables us to sustain the system of values that gives meaning and purpose to our lives. We could live without its values, but we could not live well. The values exist, however, only because we have made them. They are the ways in which we humanize a small segment of the law-governed world. Our values and attitudes are fallible and we continually revise them in the hope of making them less fallible. They are also unavoidably reflexive, because we are both the valuing and attitude-forming subjects and the objects of our evaluations and attitudes. Our fallible and reflexive attitudes and our forever changing values are genuine characteristics of the law-governed world. Although we have made them and we are perpetuating them, they really do exist.

If we lost them, we would lose our humanity. We would still have some control over how we live, but we would not know how to exercise it. Beyond the satisfaction of basic needs, we would have no conception of what is better or worse, nor of what to make of our evolutionary advantages. Our system of values, therefore, is not a dispensable luxury parasitic on the physical and biological elements of the human condition but an essential part of it. The system is causally dependent on our biological consti-tution, which, in turn, is causally dependent on our physical constitution, which, in turn, is causally dependent on subatomic particles and forces, or on whatever are the ultimate constituents of the law-governed world. The fact that effects are dependent on causes, however, does not make the effects less real than the causes. Our system of values is the effect of causes, but it is an effect that enables us to interpret both its causes and itself, and therein lies its importance. For such interpretations guide the control that we may wrest from the contingencies of the world. Or, so I have argued.

I have not argued and I do not think that we can or should view the law-governed world only from our parochial point of view. It is important to cultivate also as much detachment as we can. Science is the most obvious attempt in that direction. Even science, however, is done by us and we do it partly because we care about the significance its findings have for us. Perhaps their significance is that human concerns are puny and unimportant in the scheme of things. But the aspirations of science are among those concerns and cannot transcend them. The impulse to go beyond the familiar segment of the world and explore what lies outside of it is probably irresistible, and I certainly do not think we should try to resist it. The results of scientific explorations, however, can only alter but not transcend human concerns. Any attempt to do more is a dangerous denial of our humanity. I share Montaigne's sentiment that "these transcendental humors frighten me." They lead to trying to "escape from . . . man. That is madness: instead of changing into angels, they change into beasts. . . . We seek other conditions because we do not understand the use of our own."[8]

Wallace Stevens' lines echo Montaigne's words, although in another medium and a few centuries later:

> To say more than human things with human voice,
> That cannot be; to say human things with more
> Than human voice, that, also, cannot be;
> To speak humanly from the height or from the depth
> Of human things, that is acutest speech.[9]

2

Increasing Control

The preceding chapter was about an alternative to the unsubstantial dream of a moral order and to the disheartening view that the world is a senseless mélange of contingencies, chance, and change. The human condition allows us some control over how we live and we can rely on our system of values and practical reason to increase it. This chapter is the beginning of an account of what is actually involved in increasing control. In subsequent chapters I will deepen and expand it.

The possibility of increasing control is usually discussed in terms of the possibility of individual freedom, but there are good reasons for proceeding differently. One is that it is unclear what individual freedom is supposed to mean. A bewildering variety of interpretations have been proposed; among them are self-control, self-determination, self-direction, self-improvement, self-perfection, self-realization, autonomy, choice, strong evaluation, having alternate possibilities, acting on second-order volitions, not being hindered by coercion, interference, or obstacles, and so on and on.[1] Another reason is that the notion of increasing control can be made clear and the importance usually attributed to freedom can be captured in its terms. Lastly, the deterministic, libertarian, and compatibilist views in terms of which freedom is usually discussed are bogged down in perennial disputes, because what the parties to them seek cannot be found. I proceed, therefore, by proposing an alternative account of increasing control that avoids these fruitless disputes. It is a kind of compatibilism, but it differs from other kinds in an essential respect.

2.1. A Case in Point

Consider a man who finds it offensive if strangers or superficial acquaintances call him by his first name. He objects to the familiarity, the patronizing, the phony friendliness, and to the failure to recognize the difference between personal and impersonal relationships. As time goes on, he is more and more easily offended in this way. If circumstances make it prudent to bear it silently, he seethes, and it takes him a while to calm down. It so happens that he has to have an operation. He knows that in the hospital everyone from physicians to cleaners will address him in the offending manner. He also knows that having an operation is not the right time to fight battles, especially not with those on whom he relies for comfort and recovery. So he tells himself not be a fool, put up with it, swallow his pride, bear in mind that no one means to insult him, that people merely follow a custom, and that they are likely to treat him decently, given their faulty understanding of what that involves. He succeeds so well that by the time he leaves the hospital he does not even notice that he is bid good-bye as Adolf.

Adolf succeeds at increasing his control. He takes account of his emotions and actions; he believes that he has good reasons to refrain from acting on his emotions; guided by that belief, he decides against showing the resentment he feels; and his subsequent actions reflect his decision. In all of this, Adolf does what most of us do many times in the routine transactions of everyday life. And what we do in this way is just what I mean by increasing control. It would be absurd to deny that we and others often act in this way.

Adolf's increased control would be diminished, but not destroyed, if the reason he thinks he has for being offended is not the real reason. Perhaps he is offended because he hates sharing his first name with a monster. He does not really care about marking the difference between personal and impersonal relationships; he fears that he will be tarred by Hitler's evil deeds. Even if that were so, however, he would still have increased his control, because he decided not to allow his attitudes to influence his actions, and he succeeded. We may say, then, that increasing control requires us to reflect critically on our attitudes; to decide on that basis what we should do; and in appropriate circumstances do it. If our attitudes are mistaken, the extent of our control is diminished, but we have still increased it over what it would have been if we had not reflected at all, or if what we did was not based on reflection.

I assume, then, that increasing control is an undeniable, frequently occurring fact of life. Facts are one thing, however, and their significance is quite another. We need now to ask what the significance of increased control is. And as we ask it, we risk being drawn into the perennial disputes between libertarians, determinists, and compatibilists.

2.2. The Question of Significance

Libertarians consider the significance of increased control by beginning with common human experience and proceeding from there to the law-governed world. They go, as it were, from the inside to the outside. They argue that there are certain facts that any acceptable theory about human action must accept and explain. One of these facts is the virtually universal human experience that we can sometimes choose among alternative courses of action without being forced by physical or psychological necessity. Adolf did this and he was, on the occasion I have described, in control of his actions. The same is often true of most of us: what we do is sometimes up to us. Critical reflection may lead us to follow, revise, or abandon our attitudes, and then act accordingly. This libertarian view is backed by the experience all of us normally have when we act on the basis of critical reflection. Only very sophisticated theorists could deny that we do this.[2]

The significance of increased control may also be considered by beginning with the law-governed world and going on from there to our shared experience. This is how determinists proceed. Their view is that everything, including human beings and their actions, is part of the law-governed world and subject to its laws. Human actions are the effects of causes, their causes also have causes, and these and countless other causal chains form an unbroken continuity that spreads from the past that has no beginning to the future that has no end. The entities or processes that are the contents of these causal chains continually change. Galaxies and subatomic particles, living things and species, humanity and societies, come into being and cease to exist. All this is part of the indifferent, timeless causal order that permeates the scheme of things.

If we go from the outside in, the significance of increased control appears to be very different. Determinists grant that it often seems to us that critical reflection leads us to perform some action, but they think that this appearance is misleading. For critical reflection is also the effect of causes and the same is true of whatever it may lead us to do. It may seem that Adolf's actions were based on critical reflection, but in fact he was compelled by the strongest cause acting on him. His fear of being tarred by Hitler's monstrosity was weaker than his fear of alienating the staff of the hospital. Determinists claim that it is highly misleading to say that it was critical reflection that made one of Adolf's fears weaker than the other. His critical reflection was the effect of antecedent causes, and it registered, but did not alter, the causes that led to his actions. Adolf was merely the point at which a number of causes met. He did not originate these causes, he only witnessed them. He could observe what was going on in him, but could not change it. Determinism is backed by the immense weight of the scientific view of the world as a law-governed system of causes and effects and by the great implausibility of supposing that human actions are somehow exempt from the laws that govern everything else.[3]

Libertarians and determinists thus agree about the relevant facts, but disagree about their significance. Libertarians attribute special significance to critical reflection, because they think that our control over how we live and act depends on it. Determinists deny that critical reflection has greater significance than any other link in the endless, intersecting causal chains that lead to our actions. According to them, it is an illusion to believe that our actions are not the effects of causes. Whatever we do, including increasing our control, is the result of causes over which we have no control. If increased control is viewed from inside human experience, its significance appears to be great. If it is viewed from outside human experience, from the law-governed world, its significance seems negligible.

Libertarians and determinists have a deep disagreement, but they agree about the incompatibility of the conclusions they arrive at. If one is right, the other is wrong. They are, therefore, committed to incompatibilism. Incompatibilism, however, is rejected by compatibilists on the ground that the inside-out and the outside-in perspectives are compatible. Their key idea is that the significance determinists attribute to the causal chains that lead to actions and the significance libertarians attribute to critical reflection are compatible provided external and internal causes are distinguished. We lack control if our actions are the effects of causes external to us. But we can increase our control to the extent to which our actions are the effects of a particular kind of internal cause, namely, of critical reflection. When Adolf reflected on his attitudes critically, he was in control of the actions that followed. If he had reflected on them more critically, he might have found the real reason for his resentment, and then he would have increased further the control he already had.

Compatibilists, therefore, agree with determinists that critical reflection is a link in an endless chain of causes and effects. They also agree with libertarians that critical reflection is the key to increased control. According to them, there is a causal chain that leads to increasing our control, but it is a special causal chain, because by means of critical reflection we can alter it.[4]

The reconciliation proposed by compatibilists, however, is rejected by libertarians and determinists. They both deny that

internal causes have the significance compatibilists attribute to
them. They insist that internal causes have external causes, if the
external causes are present, internal causes will follow, and if external causes are absent, internal causes will not occur. If critical
reflection is the result of antecedent causes of whatever kind, then
it is an illusion to suppose that we control our actions through
it. Libertarians and determinists thus agree that compatibilism is
superficial, because it ignores that internal causes have external
causes. They also agree that only if critical reflection is somehow
outside the causal chain can we suppose that increased control
makes us masters of our actions. They disagree, because libertarians
assert and determinists deny that critical reflection can be outside
the causal chain.

Compatibilists, of course, attempt to defend their position.
Perhaps their strongest defense is to point out the implausibility of
both determinism and libertarianism. Determinists are committed
to holding that the ubiquitous conviction we all have, that at
least sometimes what we do is up to us, is always mistaken. We
are wrong to believe that we often weigh reasons and change
our minds because of them. No matter how things seem to
us, we never make genuine decisions, never weigh reasons, and
never change our minds. We simply act as causes dictate, and
the apparent difference between having and lacking control, or
having more or less control, is only the difference between the
causes that dictate our actions. Moreover, determinists not only
deny what we all know is true, they are also inconsistent, because
they simultaneously believe that all reasons are illusory and that
they have reasons for their own view and reasons against their
opponents' views. If determinism is right, no one could have a
reason for or against determinism, nor for or against any belief
anyone holds. There are only causes that compel us to have some
attitudes and reject others. This is why, according to compatibilists,
determinism is implausible and inconsistent.

Libertarians, in turn, have the impossible task of explaining how
anything that human beings do could be outside of the chain of

causes and effects that holds in the law-governed world. How could critical reflection and actions based on them not have antecedent causes? How could we have our attitudes if something did not cause us to have them rather than other attitudes? If attitudes have no causes, how could they occur? And if something inside or outside of us does not cause them, why would they be ours? What would be the point of giving reasons for our attitudes if the reasons do not cause us to hold our attitudes and prompt our actions? Compatibilists say that if libertarianism were correct, it would be impossible to explain how critical reflection and increased control are possible. But since the aim of libertarianism is to provide that explanation, the view dooms itself to failure.

Determinists and libertarians, of course, attempt, no less than compatibilists, to defend their own and to criticize their opponents' views. Their attempts have a familiar form. When defenders of the three positions argue constructively, they offer ever more fine-grained and analytically sophisticated accounts of their own views. Libertarians do this by elaborating what is involved in critical reflection; determinists by borrowing from science the most recent theories about the workings of the brain; and compatibilists by refining the distinction between external and internal causes. When they argue critically, they charge their opponents with missing the true significance of the facts. Libertarians stress the causal independence of critical reflection that, according to them, determinists and compatibilists miss. Determinists stress that human beings are subject to the laws of the law-governed world, and claim that their opponents fail to acknowledge the significance of that fact. Compatibilists stress the significance of internal causation, and accuse their opponents of overlooking it. Then the defenders attempt to respond by revising their positions just enough to show that their accounts can accommodate the significance of the facts that their critics charge them with missing. The critics deny that they have succeeded. And so their disputes go perennially on.[5]

This sketch of the disputes about the significance of increasing control will probably be familiar to anyone who has thought about the matter. The observation will also be familiar that the disputes have become extremely complex, because they are connected with a host of other disputes about causality, the relation between the mental and the physical, the nature of scientific laws, the distinction between causes and reasons, the logic of conditionals, the scope of science, the reliability of immediate experience, and so forth. All these disputes are interconnected, because the resolution of one presupposes the resolution of the others. The result is the proliferation of technical literature of great complexity in which arguments concerning ever more arcane points exfoliate and the prospect of answering the question that started it all recedes ever further. The big questions raise a multitude of small questions, and the answers to small questions depend on answers to many even smaller questions. The original question is left without a convincing answer, because the subject has become a multidimensional maze in which even intrepid explorers get lost.[6] This is my reason for trying a different approach.

The proposed approach is compatibilist, but it does not share the assumption of existing compatibilist approaches that there is a general answer to the question of what is involved in increasing control. Increasing control does depend on critical reflection, which is a kind of internal causation, but the critical reflection on which increasing control depends varies from person to person. I will, therefore, call this alternative compatibilist approach variable.

2.3. The Variable Approach

The variable approach, then, rejects the assumption that the question about the significance of increasing control can have the sort of general answer that libertarians, determinists, and compatibilists favoring a general approach seek. There cannot be a general answer to the question of what we can do to increase our control, because libertarians, determinists, and these compatibilists share the mistaken assumption that the account must apply to all or most cases in all or most circumstances. In their perennial disputes, they rightly criticize each others for failing to find such a general answer. If they stopped there, I would agree with them. But they go on, in their different ways, to seek an answer that is both general enough to fit all or most cases and escapes their opponents' criticisms. Individual variations, however, make such a solution impossible. And it is because libertarians, determinists, and other compatibilists seek an answer that cannot be found that their disputes have bogged down in endless reciprocal criticisms.

The question, however, has an answer. It depends on recognizing that what each of us can do to increase our control varies with our characters and circumstances. Once we recognize that, it becomes obvious why we should increase our control. And if that is obvious, then the significance of increasing control also becomes obvious. Let us begin, therefore, with the question of what we can individually do to increase our control.

We are part of the law-governed world and we are subject to its laws. We have no control over these laws and it is futile to try to seek exemption from them. We cannot increase our control in that way. But we can have some control over the conditions in which particular laws hold. These conditions are either external or internal to us. The variable approach to increasing our control is to try to change some of the internal conditions, namely, the psychological ones. Among them are the attitudes—composed of beliefs, emotions, and motives focusing on our desires and their satisfactions—that prompt our actions. We are alike in having such attitudes, but we are unalike in the particular attitudes we have and in the actions they prompt. Because we vary in these respects, what we can and what we should do to increase our control over these internal psychological conditions varies with persons and circumstances. The impossibility of a general answer to the question of what we can do to increase our control is a consequence of this variety.

Desire should be understood in the widest possible sense to include wishes, wants, needs, impulses, aspirations, efforts, inclinations, and indeed all spurs to action from the vaguest velleities to ruling passions. They may be serious or trivial, long-term or soon forgotten fleeting impulses. Adolf's desire was that strangers should not call him by his first name. Desires aim at satisfactions, which may be derived from pleasure, revenge, justice, recognition, wealth, a quick lunch, anonymity, or some combination of these and other forms satisfactions may take. Some desires are universally human, and, in normal circumstances, most of us want to satisfy them. Many others vary with persons and contexts, and so does seeking their satisfactions.

We all have beliefs and emotions about our desires, as well as motives that lead us to seek their satisfaction. The beliefs are about the identity and urgency of desires, about what would satisfy them, about the advisability and importance of satisfying them, about our possession of the needed capacities, about the context in which their satisfaction may be sought, and so forth. The emotions are hopes for satisfactions and fears of frustrations, the miseries of unfulfilled desires and the enjoyment derived from their satisfaction, the shame or guilt caused by having some desires, the confidence in or suspicion of our having or lacking needed capacities, and so on. And the motives lead us to do or to refrain from doing what the conjunction of desires, beliefs, and emotions prompts.

Our attitudes, then, are formed of desires, beliefs, emotions, and motives. It is a natural and unavoidable part of all human lives to have such attitudes. For we all seek satisfactions and our attitudes focus on getting them. The attitudes are the psychological conditions of our actions. The description I have so far given of them is a collection of truisms, and that is precisely its point. When our actions are prompted by our attitudes, we do what we want to do, and we have some control over our actions. We would lack such control if we were forced to act contrary to our attitudes. It is a plain and undeniable fact about us, however, that we sometimes do act on the basis of our attitudes, and then we do have some control.

This control, however, warrants no more than the unexciting claim that our attitudes sometimes give us reasons for what we do. But the reasons may not be good, because our attitudes may be mistaken. The beliefs involved in them may be false, the emotions may be much stronger or weaker than the desire or the satisfaction warrants. They may prompt us to try to satisfy irrational, imprudent, immoral, or inconsistent desires, or to pursue satisfactions that prevent us from pursuing far more important satisfactions, or they may lead us to misjudge our capacities or circumstances. Mistaken attitudes thus lead us to mistaken actions. But if having some control may lead us to make such mistakes, then what is the point of having it?

The answer that follows from the variable approach is that having some control is where we must start, but we can go on to increase it. And increased control will lead to better actions. What we look to the variable approach for is to tell us what we can do to increase the control we have. And, this is the crux of the version of compatibilism I am defending, what we can do is to correct our mistaken attitudes. This is the purpose of critical reflection. Critical reflection, however, must correct the attitudes with reference to some aim to which they are supposed to lead. This aim is well-being. We all have some conception of well-being, even if it is vague, inarticulate, unexamined, or deficient in some other way. I will assume for the moment that the conception of well-being to which we aim is not deficient. The reason, then, why we should increase the control we have is to act to satisfy or frustrate a desire, because doing so is more likely to contribute to our well-being than the alternatives.

If we can sometimes correct mistaken attitudes and thus increase our control in the way I have just described, then determinists are wrong to suppose that increasing control is an illusion. If the correction of mistaken attitudes is the effect of our critical reflection on them, then they have a cause, and libertarians are wrong to suppose that increasing control is somehow outside of the law-governed world. And if there is an endless variety of mistakes different individuals in different circumstances may make about their attitudes, then the general approaches of other compatibilists are wrong to suppose that increasing control has an identifiable internal cause that is present in all cases regardless of personal and circumstantial differences.

Determinists, libertarians, and these compatibilists share the mistaken assumption that the possibility of increasing control depends on some one thing that a successful account would have to identify. The search for that one thing is misguided, because increasing control depends on avoiding a wide variety of mistakes that may be involved in our attitudes, and these mistakes vary with persons and circumstances. That is why there cannot be a general answer that fits all cases of increased control. What we each need to do in order to correct our mistaken attitudes is to reflect critically on the beliefs, emotions, motives, and desires that jointly constitute these attitudes. But when we reflect on them critically, we are doing different things depending on what specific mistakes are involved in our specific beliefs, emotions, motives, and desires.

Having reflected critically and believing that we have corrected our specific mistakes, however, are not in themselves sufficient to warrant more than the conclusion that we appear to have increased our control. The appearance may be mistaken, because the corrected attitudes may prompt us to satisfy desires that are contrary to our well-being. Increasing control, therefore, depends also on critical reflection on the conception of well-being to which we appeal in correcting the beliefs, emotions, and motives that lead us to try to satisfy some desires rather than others. And this, in turn, depends on whether the satisfaction of those desires would actually promote our well-being. Real, as opposed to merely apparent, control, therefore, is to act on the basis of attitudes and conceptions of well-being that have passed the test of critical reflection. This is the beginning of the answer that follows from the variable approach to answering the question of what we can do to increase our control. It is only a beginning, however, because it does not specify what is involved in correcting our attitudes and conceptions of well-being by critical reflection. In the next two chapters I will try to specify it. However, even though the account of the variable approach is yet incomplete, the reason why we should increase our control follows from it. We should increase it, because it contributes to our well-being. And from that the significance of increasing control follows.

The human condition is that we are part of the law-governed world and subject to its laws. But since the world is indifferent to our well-being, we have created a system of values in terms of which we can define and pursue our well-being. We have no guarantee that our efforts will not be frustrated by various contingencies. We cannot escape them, but we can diminish our vulnerability to them by changing the internal, psychological conditions in which the laws hold. This, in turn, depends on correcting our attitudes whose constituents these conditions are. And we do that by critical reflection on our attitudes and conceptions of well-being (in ways I have yet to discuss). Critical reflection is thus the key to diminishing our vulnerability to contingencies, to making it more likely that our pursuit of well-being will be successful, to increasing our control over how we live, and to improving the human condition. The significance of increasing control is that it makes it possible for us to live by our values and attitudes in the midst of the indifferent law-governed world.

2.4. Objections Considered

This account of increasing control will be rejected by libertarians, determinists, and compatibilists who favor a general approach to answering the question of how we can increase our control. One of their objections is likely to be shared by all of them, and I will respond to it first. Their other objection reflects their differing theoretical commitments. The first objection is, then, that the variable approach is subject to all the disputes that it was supposed to avoid. Even if what is involved in critical reflection varies from person to person, questions remain. Is it the effect of causes or is it somehow outside of causal chains? If critical reflection is a species of internal causation, do internal causes not have external causes? Why is it not misleading to attribute greater importance to an internal cause than to any other link in the causal chain to which it belongs? These questions lead back to the endless arguments that the variable approach was meant to avoid. Is the variable approach, then, not a pointless exercise in begging the question?

My reply is that this objection rests on two mistaken assumptions. One is that increasing control through critical reflection consists in doing some one specific thing. What critical reflection actually consists in is the correction of mistaken attitudes. But since our attitudes may be mistaken in a great variety of ways, critical reflection on them consists in doing a great variety of different things. There are many reasons why we may hold false beliefs, have misdirected emotions, nurture misguided desires, or form the wrong motives. There is no one specific activity that is the key to the correction of mistaken attitudes. The correction requires finding out which of their many constituents hinder our well-being, and what we can do to put right what we got wrong. Reasonable answers, therefore, must be particular, concrete, and variable, because the mistakes we make vary with persons and circumstances. We cannot look to the theories of libertarians, determinists, and other compatibilists for such an answer, because their theories, by their very nature, are general and the answer we need is particular.

The second mistaken assumption on which this objection rests is that it treats the particular question of what particular persons in particular circumstances can do to increase their control as if it had a theoretical answer. But, as we have seen, it does not. The particular question can be answered without even considering the general theories of libertarians, determinists, and other compatibilists. This is just what Adolf did. Moreover, if the variable approach is right, no general theory could succeed, because increasing control requires doing particular things. Theoretical questions, therefore, do not just happen to be irrelevant to the variable approach; they can have no answer, because the theories that prompt the questions cannot possibly deliver the answers they were meant to give. There is no reason to struggle with questions that arise from impossible theories.

This first objection, then, collapses if the falsity of the assumptions on which it rests is recognized. But libertarians, determinists, and compatibilists who seek a general answer will not accept this. They will argue that the variable approach presupposes one or another of their general answers. If that were so, the variable approach could not disregard the theoretical questions raised by the general answer it presupposes. And this is the second objection to the variable approach. I will respond to it by rejecting first the claim that the variable approach presupposes determinism, next that it presupposes libertarianism, and lastly that it presupposes the general approach of compatibilism.

The variable approach seems to presuppose determinism, because it accepts that human actions are part of the law-governed world. It is a consequence of determinism, however, that the variable approach is mistaken in attributing special significance to increasing control through critical reflection. For increasing control does not depend merely on the individuals who are engaged in it but also on causes that enable individuals to increase their control. The attribution of special significance to increasing control is a mistake, because, it will be objected, it ignores that human beings could increase their control only if antecedent causes enable them to do so.

The variable approach, therefore, faces a dilemma. If it pre-supposes determinism, it cannot attribute special significance to increasing control. If it attributes special significance to increasing control, then it must reject determinism. Whichever alternative the variable approach favors, it cannot avoid facing the question of whether the theory it accepts or rejects is correct. And that question leads directly to the theoretical questions posed by the disputes between determinists, libertarians, and other compatibilists that the variable approach rejected as irrelevant.

My reply is that this is a false dilemma. For the special significance the variable approach attributes to increasing control is not the special significance that is inconsistent with determinism. The question of whether increasing control has special significance may be asked from the point of view of the law-governed world or from the human point of view. One crucial difference between these points of view is that the law-governed world is indifferent to human well-being, but the human point of view is essentially concerned with it. It is true that we would not be concerned with our well-being if we were not the kinds of beings we are, and we are what we are because we are the effects of antecedent causes. This, however, does not alter the fact that we are concerned with our well-being and the law-governed world is not. Consequently it does not follow from determinism that when the variable approach attributes special significance to increasing control, because our well-being depends on it, then it is making a mistake. The variable approach would be mistaken if it attributed special significance to increasing control from the point of view of the law-governed world, but that is not what the variable approach does: it attributes special significance to increasing control from the human point of view.

The variable approach, then, accepts that all human actions are the effects of causes and the causes also have causes, and so on. Whether or not this commits the variable approach to determinism is irrelevant to the question of whether we can increase our control. The variable approach, therefore, does not presuppose determinism. We can increase our control regardless of whether determinism is true or false. We know we can increase it, because, as Adolf's case shows, we do it routinely. The important question is what is involved in increasing it, and that is the question the variable approach asks and answers.

This brings us to the claim that if the variable approach does not presuppose determinism, then it must presuppose libertarianism. Libertarians argue that if the actions involved in increasing control were the effects of causes, then they would not be something we do, but something that happens to us. Prior causes rather than we would make them happen and that would show that we had no control over them. Increasing control, therefore, is possible only if the actions involved in it have no prior causes. Since the variable approach is committed to the possibility of increasing control, it must presuppose libertarianism. And then all the questions the variable approach was meant to avoid come flooding back.

My reply is that libertarians are mistaken in supposing that increasing control is possible only if the actions involved in it are not the effects of causes. They have causes, but the causes are internal rather than external. Their causes are the effects of something we do inside ourselves, rather than something that outside forces acting on us make happen. This something that we do is critical reflection on our attitudes. We tend to make mistakes about our attitudes, through critical reflection we try to correct our mistakes, and we thereby change the internal causes that lead to our actions. The more our actions are the effects of internal causes, the more we have increased our control over them. Increasing our control is not a matter of performing actions that have no causes but performing actions that are the effects of internal causes of this kind. Libertarians, therefore, are mistaken in supposing that the variable approach presupposes that increasing control depends on actions outside of causal chains.

It may now seem that the variable approach can avoid presupposing libertarianism only by presupposing determinism. For, it will be said, the internal causes to which increasing control is supposedly due have external causes. We can reflect critically only because we have the capacity to do so, and we have the capacity because of our genetic potentialities and their subsequent development, which, in turn, also have causes, and so on. And so we are back in deterministic causal chains.

This is partly true, partly false. We are back in causal chains, but the causal chains have been altered. What altered them is that the extent to which our actions are the effects of internal rather than external causes has shifted in favor of internal causes as a result of critical reflection. We increase our control by making our actions more and more the effects of our attitudes and less and less the effects of external forces acting on us independently of our attitudes. Adolf increased his control, because he decided not to allow his resentment to dictate his actions. If he had made the same decision because he had a gun pointed at him, he would not have increased his control. Increasing control, therefore, is possible even if we accept that our actions are the effects of causes. What matters for increasing control is that our actions should be the effects of internal, not external, causes.

It remains true that the further back we go in our lives, the more we find that our actions are the effects of external causes. In favorable circumstances, growing up involves acting more and more as our attitudes prompt us, and less and less as conditions external to us cause us to do. Our attitudes may be mistaken, of course. That is why we need to reflect on them critically. And the better we do that, the better are our chances that our actions will be instrumental to our well-being. I conclude, then, that since the variable approach accepts that our actions have causes, it does not presuppose libertarianism. And because it accepts that increasing control is made possible by actions that are the effects of internal causes, it does not presuppose the deterministic view of the illusoriness of increasing our control.

The last objection is that the variable approach presupposes the general approach of compatibilism, and I have added nothing to it. It may seem that the special importance I have attributed to internal causation is precisely what compatibilists claim. And my version of compatibilism also agrees with other versions about rejecting both determinism and libertarianism, because the first denies the undeniable fact that increasing our control has a special significance for our well-being and the second fails to deliver the explanation of its special significance that it set out to provide. Given their agreement on these crucial points, what is the difference between the general and variable compatibilist approaches?

To begin with, compatibilists following a general approach seek a general answer to a general question, whereas the variable approach seeks to answer a particular question, namely, what each one of us, given our different characters and circumstances, can do to increase our control. Both focus on the central importance of critical reflection to increasing our control, but they understand it very differently.

Those who follow a general approach understand critical reflection (they use different words to refer to the same activity) as an essential feature of our humanity. They say that "having second-order volitions . . . I regard as essential to being a person";[7] being "a free and responsible agent" requires that "he at all times knows what he is doing . . . and . . . acts with a definite and clearly formed intention";[8] "the web of [reactive] attitudes and feelings form an essential part of the moral life";[9] and the "capacity to evaluate desires . . . is an essential feature of the mode of agency we recognize as human";[10] Kant and his many followers see autonomy as the key to being a moral agent. They all think of what I am calling critical reflection as marking a threshold between being and not being a fully responsible agent. This commits them to thinking of critical reflection as one specific internal cause. If it is present, we are responsible agents, accountable for our actions, and appropriate recipients of praise and blame. If it is not present, we are missing an essential feature of humanity.

The variable approach rejects the view that critical reflection is an essential feature of humanity and the view that we are responsible agents only if our actions follow from critical reflection. Critical reflection is a matter of degree, depending on the extent to which our actions are the effects of internal rather than external causes. If our actions are largely the effects of external causes, we do not lose our humanity and do not cease to be responsible agents. Our humanity does not depend on the presence of this one kind of internal cause. It depends on the combined presence of a wide variety of conditions, such as having a human body, needing to satisfy certain physiological and psychological needs that are typical of our species, being able to reproduce our kind, having a certain DNA structure, using language, learning from the past, and planning for the future, and so forth. It is a simple and dangerous mistake to deny the humanity of those who have these characteristics, but do not reflect critically. Nor is critical reflection necessary for being a responsible agent who can be justifiably praised or blamed. For it is often, although not always, perfectly justified to hold people responsible and to praise or blame them for their unreflective, impulsive actions that benefit or harm others. (I will return to this in Chapter 7.)

The variable approach also rejects the general compatibilist approach according to which critical reflection consists in doing some one kind of thing. As I have stressed before, critical reflection involves the correction of our mistaken attitudes. Since the beliefs, emotions, motives, and desires that constitute attitudes vary from person to person, as do the mistakes we make about them, their correction involves a great variety of many different kinds of activities, not one specific kind.

I conclude that there is only superficial agreement between the general and variable compatibilist approaches to the significance of internal causation, increasing control, and critical reflection. As soon as we ask what specifically we have to do to increase our control and to reflect critically, the important differences between the two approaches emerge. Just as the variable approach does not presuppose either determinism or libertarianism, it does not presuppose a general compatibilist approach either. The variable approach is an alternative to them. It avoids the perennial disputes in which these other views are endlessly entangled and it actually says something helpful to those who try to make their lives better. It says: reflect critically on your attitudes, examine the beliefs, emotions, and motives that lead you to want to satisfy your desires, so that you will not act contrary to your well-being. The actual critical reflection, of course, we have to do for ourselves, but we can learn from the variable approach what it is that we have to do.

2.5. Loose Ends

Increasing control is centrally important for reducing our vulnerability to contingencies and improving the human condition. The key to increasing our control is critical reflection. It proceeds by correcting our natural inclinations to satisfy our desires. We begin with uncritical beliefs, emotions, and motives involved in these natural inclinations, but they are often mistaken and acting on them would make our lives worse. That is why we need to correct them. In the course of providing reasons for these claims, I have left several questions open and promised to answer them in subsequent chapters.

I close with reminders of what these questions are and an indication of where I will answer them. Chapter 3 is about the correction of mistaken attitudes and Chapter 4 about the correction of mistaken conceptions of well-being. Chapter 5 discusses what makes conceptions of well-being reasonable. Chapter 6 is about the secular problem of evil. Chapter 7 proposes an extension of the variable approach to the question of individual responsibility. Chapters after that discuss some of the social and personal implications that follow from the preceding discussion.

3

Correcting Attitudes

Chapter 2 was about the variable approach to increasing control. It concluded that increasing control depends on the correction of mistaken attitudes and conceptions of well-being by critical reflection, but I postponed detailed discussion of how critical reflection makes their correction possible. This chapter is a more detailed discussion of the correction of mistaken attitudes. The next one is about the correction of mistaken conceptions of well-being.

As we have seen, attitudes are composed of beliefs, emotions, and motives whose objects are our desires. Attitudes guide us to try to satisfy some of our desires and to refrain from trying to satisfy others. All the components of attitudes may be mistaken: beliefs may be false, emotions misdirected, motives inconsistent, and desires destructive, inconsistent, over- or under-valued. I will argue in this chapter that our attitudes are informed by values and the values we have accepted commit us to observe some limits. One main reason why beliefs, emotions, motives, and desires may be mistaken is that something has gone wrong with our commitments to values and limits. Correcting mistaken attitudes, then, depends, among other things, on correcting whatever has gone wrong with these commitments.

I will discuss values first, then limits, then commitments, and then critical reflection on the values and limits to which we have committed ourselves. In each case, I consider what can go wrong and how critical reflection might help us to correct it.

3.1. Values

Some of the important values in our society are aesthetic, economic, literary, moral, philosophical, political, religious, and scientific.
Values are the products of traditions. They are embedded in works
that have stood the test of time, became classic exemplifications
of real or imagined ways of living, acting, and perceiving the
world, and have continued to attract the admiration of those who
understood them. The beliefs, emotions, motives, and desires that
compose our attitudes are informed by such values. In trying to
increase our control over how we live and act, we endeavor
to conduct ourselves according to these values. We adapt them
to our character and context and by transforming ourselves and
our circumstances to conform more closely to them. These values jointly form an indispensable part of a society's system of
values.

It may seem odd that a secular view of the human condition
would include religious values among the important values of our
society. The oddity, however, disappears if we draw a distinction
between religion, as a way of life, and theology, as the theory that
aims to justify the assumptions on which the religious way of life
rests. The secular view is committed to rejecting theology, because
of its indefensible commitment to the existence of a supernatural
world. But there is no reason why a secular view could not
recognize that there are inspiring religious values and admirable
religious ways of life. It needs no theological commitment to
recognize that excessive pride, envy, rage, sloth, avarice, gluttony,
and lust may be incompatible with our well-being and love,
compassion, service to others, and other forms of *agape* are rightly
valued as essential to some conceptions of well-being.

My interest here, then, is in understanding mistakes about values
that allow and limits that disallow actions depending on whether
we think that they foster or hinder our well-being. And the
understanding is not general but personal: it is understanding *our*
mistakes affecting *our* well-being in order to correct them. The

obvious place to begin is with the values of the context in which we live, namely, our society. We derive from them a range of human and cultural values that are generally known and available as possibilities for those who live in it. The human values are assumed to be essential for the well-being of everyone in the society, while cultural values vary with individuals, circumstances, conceptions of well-being, and with the relative importance attributed to each value. In our society, some of the human values are nutrition, rest, and physical security; while cultural values range from important ones, like justice, rights, and responsibility, to less important ones, like dependability, self-reliance, and cheerfulness. This system of values continually changes, usually not by new values replacing old ones but by shifts in how existing values are interpreted and in what importance is attributed to them. Typically, shifts affecting human values are the slowest and cultural ones the fastest. The human and cultural values of a society provide some of the possibilities available to those who live in it. A society's system of values may be mistaken in several ways. It may be too narrow, exclude some reasonable human and cultural values, and thus impoverish well-being. Or it may be too wide and include values detrimental to well-being.

A society's system of values, however, may be mistaken even if it is free of the defects I have so far noted and even if there is nothing intrinsically wrong with its human or cultural values. Its mistake may be that the values are available only for a minority selected, for example, on the basis of religion, ethnicity, or wealth. For others, then, the values they need to realize for their well-being are unavailable, even though they have the required capacity and have not disqualified themselves by their conduct from the unobstructed pursuit of well-being, if only they would have the opportunity to do so. A society's system of values is mistaken if it undeservedly deprives some of its members of this opportunity.

I doubt that there has ever been a mistake-free system of values. But in some the mistakes are widespread and make even the pursuit, let alone the achievement, of well-being exceptionally difficult for many people. The reasonable attitude, then, is to try to reform the system, or, if possible, leave the society for a better one. In some other societies, the mistakes are confined to a few possibilities and they leave many conceptions of well-being unaffected. I am going to assume for the moment that, although our system of values is mistaken in numerous ways, it is not radically mistaken. In subsequent chapters I will give reasons for this assumption.

Our typical situation is, then, that we live in a society whose system of values is partly formed of human and cultural values. One significant feature of our system of values is that we find it simply given. We are born into it and grow up in it, and in the course of our upbringing we learn about its values, their interpretation, and their relative importance. We no more make a conscious commitment to it than we make one to locomotion, perception, or to sleeping and eating. These are just parts of our lives, some of the prevailing conditions of living, and normally we have no choice about them. We learn them as we learn our mother tongue. They are what they are, and they provide the possibilities they do. We start with and continue to be guided by them, at least during the early part of life.

Another significant feature of our system of values is that it provides many more values than we could pursue. There are many different values, many ways of earning a living, forming intimate relationships, using leisure, meeting difficulties, or valuing works of art, literature, morality, philosophy, politics, or religion; many different evaluative attitudes to money, illness, risk-taking, or death. With this richness and variety of available values comes the necessity of choice. We encounter the values as possibilities, and we must accept or reject them. Doing one or the other is unavoidable, because if we do nothing, we in fact choose to reject all of a range of available values. But the necessities of life force us to accept at least some of them, because most of us must earn a living in one way or another, relate somehow to family, friends, and sexual partners, find some way of facing adversity, and so forth.

We are, then, saddled with the necessity of making some choices, with the range of values among which we must choose, and with the inevitable consequence that by choosing one possibility we reject many others. We choose within these constraints, but we often choose without critical reflection. Most often we follow a familiar pattern. We practice our parents' religion; get married and have children just as everyone around us is doing; wear the same kinds of clothes, talk in the same way, drive the same cars, and watch the same television programs as everybody else does; acquire political preferences by repeating what we hear in the media, or from what our neighbors, friends, or colleagues tell us; eat the same kinds of food by and large the same time as others do; we shop in the same stores, choose among the same goods, and keep the same hours. All this is routine, everyday life in a particular society, and we make the choices it provides largely by default.

Life, however, is not always routine. There are emergencies, crises, unexpected opportunities, sudden passions, slowly growing dissatisfactions, sympathies and antipathies, social upheavals, serious disappointments, and they call for more than routine choices. We make them by asking what our attitudes are toward the range of available values and we act on what we find. These attitudes are complex mixtures, formed on the basis of limited experience, vague hopes and fears elicited by ill-understood possibilities, imagined pictures often derived from films or television of what it would be like to live according to some value or another, and weak desires that incline or disincline us toward some of the values.

The values of everyday life we are aware of form the possibilities we recognize. They are a subset of our society's possibilities, because they depend on our familiarity with the patterns surrounding us and on the attitudes we happen to have formed. The choices we make on this uncertain basis are not among human and cultural values in general, but among the much narrower range of values we recognize as possibilities we are aware of in our circumstances. We typically choose in the light of attitudes we take for granted, without the critical reflection that might lead us to revise them or our view of the range of values we recognize.

On the basis of these half-examined attitudes and assumed range of values, we find ourselves having a favorable attitude toward some of them. But since the beliefs, emotions, motives and desires that form our uncritical initial attitudes constantly change in the light of new impressions, new information, new circumstances, so do the values we recognize and accept. The resulting condition is one of permanent change, a restless quest for new values, and uncertain attitudes. This is one main reason why so many people in affluent circumstances are dissatisfied with their lives and try to alleviate their dissatisfaction through mindless entertainment, risible cults, drugs, feverish shopping, pornography, and false hopes and fears created by charismatic charlatans. For such people all values are fluid; their control over their lives is minimal, because all values seem arbitrary to them.

There are two main sources of the mistakes that lead to this widespread malaise. The first are false beliefs, misguided emotions, fantasies mistaken for actual possibilities, and vague desires artificially inflated into motives. Mistaken attitudes are formed out of such flawed components. The second involves getting wrong the range of available values. We get them wrong partly because our mistaken attitudes lead us to accept values we cannot realize, or ignore values whose realization would make our lives better. These mistakes are ours, not of our society's system of values. We make them because we lack understanding, love too much the comforts derived from familiar patterns, and we are reluctant to reflect critically on what others around us take for granted.

Let us suppose that the prevailing system of values is not radically defective and we have managed to avoid mistakes about the possibilities we recognize. We form our attitudes out of some of these recognized possibilities on the basis of critical reflection. We have, then, adopted them. They enable us to form priorities. We commit ourselves to living according to the universal and cultural values we have adopted. We know, then, how we want to live, we are committed to living that way, and our actions reflect our commitments. We know how to cope with the expected and unexpected situations in which we find ourselves, and how to make the choices they present. We are as much in control of how we live and act as possible, given our circumstances. We know that our control is imperfect, because the contingencies of life may interfere with it, but we also know that we have done what we could toward our well-being. We are, then, in possession of a great good: a conception of well-being that gives meaning and purpose to our lives.

3.2. Limits

The beliefs, emotions, motives, and desires that form our attitudes, and the attitudes that form our conceptions of well-being include not only what possibilities we value but also the limits we would not transgress. The values guide what we may do; the limits what we may not do. Both have varying strengths, depending on the importance of particular values and limits to our conception of well-being. The strongest limit is what I will call *the unthinkable*. The unthinkable is what we think and feel we cannot do, not even if it would be very important for the realization of some value that is crucial to our conception of well-being. We may even accept that doing it would be, all things considered, for the best, but we still cannot bring ourselves to do it. I find it surprising that the significance of this psychological phenomenon has not been generally recognized.[1]

Consider a young woman—I will call her Sarah—who is at the beginning of a promising career as a scientist. She is exceptionally talented and deeply involved in a medical research project that is likely to yield important and beneficial results. She is doing exactly what she had prepared herself to do throughout long years as an undergraduate and a doctoral student. She has found her conception of well-being and she is living a life that reflects it.

Sarah finds, however, that her aged and feeble parents can no longer look after themselves. They have to have a helper. The parents are poor and cannot afford to pay for it. The helpers provided by social services are incompetent and untrustworthy. Sarah's brothers and sisters have moved away, got married, have several children, and are struggling to make ends meet. Sarah cannot afford to pay for a helper either, because she lives on a research fellowship that barely covers her living expenses. She is single, lives close by, and realizes that if she does not look after her parents, no one will.

Her parents are poorly educated blue collar people. They raised their children as well as they could while working full-time at menial jobs. When the children were old enough, they too had to work to supplement their parents' meager wages. The family was not particularly affectionate, but they were fiercely loyal to each other. They stood together against the world, knowing that they had to help each other, because they could not count on anyone else. They were poor and struggling, but they struggled together. Sarah was the bright one of the family, and she alone had managed to escape the ranks of the working poor. Her loyalty to her family, however, is very strong and makes it unthinkable for her to ignore the need of her parents.

Sarah thus finds herself in a wrenching conflict between continuing the scientific career she values most in her life and her loyalty to her parents that sets a limit she feels she cannot transgress. She has to choose between continuing the life she has made for herself and giving it up in order to look after her parents. She loves her life, but she finds it unthinkable not to help her parents. She must choose and she knows that her choice will shape her future and her view of herself. She thinks hard about what to do.

Sarah thinks that an impersonal examination of her choice would conclude that she ought to continue with science. For, all things considered, that is likely to be the best for herself and for all those many people who are likely to benefit from the fruits of her research. Her parents will have a hard time without her, but they are old, feeble, and will not live long no matter what she does. But she cannot bring herself to view her choice impersonally. It is *her* loyalty and *her* parents that are involved and she finds it unthinkable to ignore them even if it would have the best consequences. She tells herself that if she chooses to look after her parents, she can still return to science later, and in the meantime perhaps she can keep up with the research literature. After much critical reflection she concludes that she must be loyal to her parents and interrupt her life in science. She cannot do what she regards as unthinkable, but she can postpone the pursuit of what she regards as most important for her well-being. She finds the limit set by the unthinkable stronger than the realization of the possibility she values most. She takes indefinite leave and looks after her parents.

Not everyone can have a conflict like Sarah's, because not everyone has as clear priorities as she, nor as clearly set limits whose violation would be unthinkable. Many people pursue many different values without regarding any one of them as the most important. And for many, nothing is unthinkable, if they believe that doing it would be, all things considered, for the best. Such people need not be opportunists. They may have many commitments, but they have not considered their relative importance. If their commitments conflict, they sometimes honor one, sometimes another. But there also are people, like Sarah, who pursue a value they prize above all others and who are bound by a limit set by what they find unthinkable. The two may conflict, and one or the other must prevail.

Sarah is not unique in resolving this conflict in favor of the limit. It was unthinkable for Antigone to leave her brother to rot, for Socrates to avoid death by fleeing Athens, for Thomas More to swear a false oath, for Luther to remain silent about the corruption of the Church, for Clarendon to acquiesce in regicide, for Lee to abandon Virginia, and for Captain Vere to let Billy Budd live. It was also unthinkable for many less famous people to compromise with the immoral regime in which they had to live. Such people arrive at a juncture in their lives where they feel compelled to take a stand, and to declare their allegiance or their opposition.

They cannot bring themselves to compromise, obfuscate, or remain silent. They take a stand knowing that they are jeopardizing the value whose pursuit gives meaning and purpose to their lives.

> For some people the day comes
> When they have to declare the great Yes
> Or the great No. It's clear at once who has the Yes
> Ready within him; and saying it
> He goes from honor to honor, strong in his conviction.
> He who refuses does not repent. Asked again,
> He'd still say no. Yet that no—the right no—
> Drags him down all his life.[2]

These are formative experiences with great personal significance. What that significance is emerges if we understand the force of the "cannot" when some cannot but say the great "Yes" to what they value most, or cannot but say the great "No" to doing what they regard as unthinkable. What happens when the great "Yes" and "No" conflict? Why is the "cannot" of the unthinkable stronger for those I named above than their highest value? Why can Sarah suspend her life in science, but not her loyalty?

3.3. Commitments

The "cannot" of the unthinkable is not like a logical or physical impossibility that explains why we cannot square the circle or fly by flapping our arms. It is not like a law that says we cannot vote unless we are citizens. Nor is it like lacking the necessary knowledge that explains why we cannot speak Sanskrit. Or like a locked door because of which we cannot enter a building. The "cannot" of the unthinkable expresses a psychological limit we find in ourselves. Others can do what we find we cannot, and perhaps we could also have done it before we found ourselves with the limit. I stress that we may *find* ourselves with it, because we may not be aware of it until we want to do something, but cannot make ourselves do it. We have the capacity to do it, but we cannot bring ourselves to act on it. What stops us is something that arrests our action. It is natural to say that it is our conscience. But conscience is just another word for the "cannot," not an explanation of it, and it is an explanation we need.

The explanation I propose is that what stops us is a commitment to a limit we will not violate. We normally have many different commitments of various strengths and to various limits, but some of our commitments are stronger than others. The strongest possible commitments are unconditional. The "cannot" of the unthinkable, the arresting limit of conscience, expresses an unconditional commitment.

Unconditional commitments are the most basic convictions we may have. They tell us what we must not do no matter what, what we regard as outrageous, horrible, beyond the pale, or, in religious language, as sacrilegious. They are fundamental to being ourselves. They are not universal, for people may be without unconditional commitments, and those who have them may be committed to very different limits. Nor are they categorical, for we may violate them. But if through fear, coercion, weakness, accident, or stupidity we do what we have unconditionally committed ourselves not to do, we inflict grave psychological damage on ourselves.

Antigone, Socrates, Thomas More, Luther, Clarendon, Lee, Captain Vere, and Sarah acted as they did, because they have honored their unconditional commitments, even though the cost of doing so was to act contrary to something they greatly valued. The limit set by their unconditional commitment was stronger than their commitment to any of their values. Their great "no" was stronger than even their greatest "yes." Many of us are made of softer stuff, but the violation of our unconditional commitment, if we have one, is no less damaging to us. We find ourselves at one of these pivotal junctures, do the unthinkable, because we are forced by torture or threats; or thoughtlessness or self-deception prevents us from realizing the significance of what we are doing; or we are cowardly, greedy, or vain and thus open to blackmail, bribery, or flattery; or we are in a terrible situation and all the alternatives are unthinkable. Whatever the cause, the effect of our realization that we have done what we have unconditionally committed ourselves not to do, what we regard as unthinkable is shattering. We cannot live with ourselves, because we have been false to our most basic conviction. We realize that we have been tried and found wanting, not by others but by ourselves. An abyss opens up at the center of our being and we face disintegration, madness, self-loathing, and we do not know how to go on, because the evaluative basis of our lives has fallen apart.[3]

Many people have no unconditional commitments, recognize no inviolable limits, and regard nothing as unthinkable if, all things considered, it would have the best consequences. Since accepting such a commitment renders us vulnerable to the sort of damage I have just described, we may well wonder why we should saddle ourselves with this burden. Who knows what circumstances may occur in the future, what emergencies or crises we may have to face? Why bind ourselves now to a limit that may prevent us from coping with unforeseeable future situations? If we do not take anything so terribly seriously, we are less open to lasting psychological injury. We should cultivate suppleness and thus become better able to withstand the inevitable buffeting we will suffer in navigating life's treacherous waters. I will try to show that this is an inadvisable stratagem by contrasting unconditional and conditional commitments.

Conditional commitments are to the various values of everyday life. They vary greatly in importance. More important ones guide our intimate relationships and the various forms our personal projects may take; the ways in which we raise our children, respond to friends, regard the work we do, follow where ambition takes us; how we cope with our fears; and how seriously we take our hopes. Such commitments can be changed, postponed, downgraded, or abandoned if we encounter good reasons against them. One crucial difference between conditional and unconditional commitments is that nothing we would recognize as a good reason could override the limits set by unconditional commitments, because our judgment of what reasons are admissible or inadmissible in these contexts derives from our unconditional commitments. They are the standards by which we judge the legitimacy of reasons and, short of abandoning the standard, we could recognize no reason in favor of violating the limit set by an unconditional commitment. But we may find that there are good reasons to revise or even to abandon our conditional commitments.

It is possible to get along in life by having only conditional commitments. Lucky circumstances, an easy-going temperament, much savvy, a great deal of flexibility, not being given to critical reflection or self-analysis, living in a well-ordered society, not suffering from injustice, having robust health, busy life, successful career, happy family, and many good friends may make it possible for a few exceptionally fortunate people not to have to ask themselves the kind of difficult questions that Sarah and others had to ask. For most of us, however, such questions do arise. Our circumstances make it hard or impossible to live according to all or most of our important conditional commitments, we waver in our allegiance to them, or we are attracted by ways of life that require different and incompatible conditional commitments.

The consequence of not having unconditional commitments is to be doomed to perpetual uncertainty about the identity and strength of the values and limits to which we should commit ourselves. This will seriously handicap us. It makes our inner life incoherent and filled with tension, because beliefs, emotions, motives, and desires will lead us in different directions, toward making and adhering to different commitments. Unconditional commitments can remove some of the uncertainty and provide a way of deciding what conditional commitments we can and cannot make.[4]

Our unconditional and conditional commitments form part of the structure of our conception of well-being. I say that this conception is structured to distinguish it from a conception of well-being we cannot lack. The latter is simply the satisfaction of our physical and psychological desires. Having such a conception is not an achievement. A structured conception of well-being, however, is an achievement. It involves the ranking of our commitments according to their importance and thereby enabling us to increase our control over how we live and act.

If we have succeeded in forming a structured conception of well-being, we know how to face adversity and resolve our conflicts with clarity and firmness. It defines where we stand. If we lack it, we lack the resolution that allows us to face the contingencies of life with a measure of equanimity. The psychological space left empty by the absence of a structured conception of well-being is filled with fantasy, anxiety, confused and floating hopes and fears, all of which tend to further weaken and misdirect our responses. Such a conception does not guarantee our well-being—nothing can do that—but it allows us to believe that if things go wrong, it is not because of our uncertainty or irresolution about how we want to live.

One consequence of this understanding of unconditional and conditional commitments is that it is a mistake to suppose that the motivational forces of the values we have accepted (to which we are conditionally committed) and the limits whose violation we find unthinkable (as a result of our unconditional commitment) are equally important.[5] It often happens that circumstances, prudence, limited energy, compassion, or a sense of duty leads us to postpone temporarily living and acting in ways we most value, and this may have no shattering effect on us. We can be genuine in prizing a value more than any other and yet postpone its pursuit for the sake of other people, or temporize about its pursuit because of illness, pressing obligations, or fatigue. But the unthinkable leaves no room for actions that violate the limit its sets. Its demands are specific, urgent, and uncompromising. The choice it imposes on us is always absolute: we either violate it or we do not.

The unthinkable, therefore, has greater significance in our inner lives than even what we value most. We may be able to provide reasonable explanation, excuse, or justification to ourselves if some of our actions are contrary to our highest value, but we cannot reasonably do this if we violate a limit we regard as unthinkable. For the unthinkable sets the limit that circumscribes the area of our life within which explanations, excuses, and justifications are possible, while outside of it anything goes. If we recognize this limit, we recognize the authority of our unconditional commitments. And if we violate it, we destroy or seriously damage our structured conception of well-being. But if we act contrary to our highest value, we merely pursue it less consistently than we might. Doing the unthinkable causes deep, often irreparable, damage to our sense of ourselves. Going against the highest value only weakens, perhaps temporarily, our conditional commitment to it. That is why the unthinkable indicates a more basic commitment than what we have to any value.

The explanation I propose, then, of what sets the limit that we "cannot" transgress, whose violation we find unthinkable, is an unconditional commitment we have made. Sarah's was loyalty to her family; Antigone's to honoring the dead as dictated by her religious tradition; Socrates' to justice as he understood it; Thomas More's to the priority of the demands of religion over politics; Luther's to a love of God uncorrupted by the worldly intrusion of the Church; Clarendon's to the rule of law; Lee's to the Southern sense of honor; and Captain Vere's to wartime naval law. All of them have gone against what they valued most, because they could have pursued it only by doing the unthinkable and violating the limit it set.

I have been stressing that the unthinkable rests on unconditional commitments, but I now must stress also that we can be mistaken when we regard an action as unthinkable, because we can be mistaken in our unconditional commitments. We may regard an action unthinkable, but we should not. This is not because we might not be genuinely convinced of the unconditional commitment that makes the action unthinkable. We may be really convinced, but ought not to be. Perhaps we have no good reason for it; or we have been indoctrinated; or we are influenced by unexamined emotions we have allowed to get out of hand; or we are mindlessly perpetuating an inherited prejudice; or we have a good reason for it, but there are even better reasons against it which we have not thought of or deliberately ignore; or we are overscrupulous, obsessed with rules we have made for ourselves, and exaggerate the importance of a minor violation; or we derive our reasons from a deeply flawed system of values that prevails in our context.

Consider again Sarah. We may think that she might have been mistaken in two kinds of ways. One is to grant that she was right to commit herself to the importance of loyalty in general, but disagree that its requirements are unconditional. Perhaps her parents forfeited their claim to Sarah's loyalty, because they were abusive, or because their imprudence was responsible for their poverty and for their children's miserable early life. Perhaps Sarah merely used loyalty as an excuse to quit science, because she doubted her talent. Or perhaps she decided in favor of her parents to prove her moral seriousness to her brothers and sisters who always suspected her of being too clever for her own good.

Another way we may think that Sarah was mistaken is that we may deny that loyalty is particularly important. We may think that the impersonal obligations of justice or the common good are far more important. Or we may think that Sarah was wrong not to use her talent to benefit many people rather than do loyal housework for her parents.

These doubts about Sarah's decision lead to the recognition that we may be mistaken not just about our unconditional commitments that make some actions unthinkable but about all our commitments, both to values and to limits. As a result, the attitudes out of which we form our conception of well-being may also be mistaken. Our commitments reflect our attitudes, and the attitudes may be mistaken, because the component beliefs are false, emotions misdirected, motives unexamined, and desires ill-advised. The correction of attitudes is necessary for avoiding such mistakes, the resulting faulty commitments, and ultimately the mistaken conceptions of well-being. In order to correct such mistakes, we need critical reflection that enables us to distinguish between good and bad reasons for accepting or rejecting values and limits.

3.4. Critical Reflection

The correction of our attitudes depends on critical reflection on what has gone wrong with them. Chapters 2, 3, and 4 are all concerned with how critical reflection can enable us to do this and thereby increase our control. But here I want to stress two characteristics of critical reflection.

One is that critical reflection is, by its very nature, backward-looking. The reason why a present attitude of ours needs correction is that something has gone wrong when we formed it in the past.[6] It may be thought, however, that backward-looking personal understanding can be, at best, only part of the understanding required for the correction of a mistaken attitude, because the object of the attitude is the realization of something that would enhance our future well-being. It may be supposed, therefore, that critical reflection must be at least partly forward-looking. And Aristotle's *Nicomachean Ethics* may be cited in support of this supposition.

According to Aristotle's famous opening remark in that work, "every art and every inquiry, and similarly every action and choice, is thought to aim at some good. . . . There is some end of the things we do, which we desire for its own sake (everything else being desired for the sake of this) . . . clearly this must be the good and the chief good. Will not the knowledge of it, then, have a great influence on life?"[7] This may be interpreted as claiming that critical reflection must involve forming a conception of well-being, and then trying to realize it. We are concerned with forming it, because we do not have it, so, it may be supposed, that its formation must lie in the future. Consequently critical reflection must be forward-looking.

This interpretation is shallow. It is true that the conception of well-being we seek is in the future. But our attitudes toward it have been formed in the past. We certainly care about our future, but how we envisage it and why some attitude we have toward it is mistaken must be understood by identifying the mistake we have made when we formed the attitude in the past. It is essential to the account of critical reflection I am formulating that it is backward-looking.[8]

The other feature of critical reflection I want to stress is that it is unavoidably personal, because the attitudes we aim to correct bear the imprint of our character and circumstances. The attitudes are composed of *our* beliefs, emotions, motives, and desires, the possibilities *we* have adopted, and the limits *we* regard as unconditional or conditional, and *our* pursuit of *our* well-being. We have direct access to these components, and the first step toward correcting mistaken attitudes is to identify the particular and concrete mistake we have made when we deliberately or by default committed ourselves to a mistaken component. Perhaps we were handicapped by wishful thinking, self-deception, fear, laziness, ignorance, dogmatism, prejudice, or by some other cognitive, emotive, or volitional failure. Whatever it was, the correction of a mistaken attitude requires us to do it for ourselves, because no one can do it for us. Critical reflection, therefore, cannot be general and impersonal. It is a personal, particular, and concrete task that is an essential part of increasing *our* control.

3.5. Corrected Attitudes

In this chapter I took another step toward enlarging the answer to Euripides' question. We do not have to choose between deceiving ourselves with the unsubstantial dream of a moral order that permeates the scheme of things and accepting that random careless chance and change alone control the world. Living according to our society's system of values is an alternative to these dispiriting options, because it provides us with values and limits that allow us to increase our control over how we live. Increasing control is our imperfect and fallible effort to pursue our well-being as much as the contingencies of chance and change allow.

Increasing control depends on correcting our mistaken efforts by critical reflection on the beliefs, emotions, motives, and desires that form the attitudes. But this is only the first step in critical reflection, because attitudes are directed toward the realization of values and conformity to limits to which we have committed ourselves, and these commitments may also be mistaken. The second step is to correct mistaken commitments to values and limits that are contrary to our well-being. Suppose we have succeeded in this as well. We have met, then, a necessary condition of having a conception of well-being to which we can appeal to guide how we live and act. The aim of this chapter has been to understand what we need to do to secure that necessary condition. To have done it is to have done a great deal, but not enough. For our mistake-free attitudes may be incompatible and then the resulting conception of well-being will be incoherent. In the next chapter I will discuss how further critical reflection can correct mistaken conceptions of well-being.

Two general comments will complete this chapter. First, I have relied on widely accepted, familiar facts of life whose denial is unreasonable. I attempted, then, to point out that the significance of these facts is that we have some control over the values and limits to which we have committed ourselves. It is a good reason for prizing our system of values if we can derive from it the values and limits we need for our well-being. There is no reason why they would require the existence of a moral order that permeates the scheme of things. Nor is there a reason why the contingencies of life would deprive us of the possibility of increasing control. We are certainly vulnerable to contingencies, but we are not doomed by them. And contingencies may also favor us. Living according to our system of values does not assure our well-being, but we can rely on critical reflection to make it more likely and to make us less vulnerable to contingencies.

The second general comment is that the pursuit of our well-being is a personal task that no general and impersonal theory can help us complete. For the task is to reflect critically on our attitudes and commitments, and correct the mistakes we are likely to make about them. But since attitudes, commitments, and mistakes vary with individuals and circumstances, the most we can reasonably expect from any theory is the trite observation that we ought to have reasonable attitudes and commitments. As soon as we ask what particular attitudes and commitments would be reasonable for us to have, we must leave behind general and impersonal considerations for the concreteness and particularity of a personal approach.

4

Aiming at Well-Being

My main concern is to explain and justify the secular view of the human condition. It is a preferable alternative to the unsubstantial dream of a moral order that permeates the scheme of things and to the defeatist assumption that through senseless chance and change contingencies rule the world. We *are* vulnerable to contingencies and we *do* lack sufficient control over how we live. But we can increase the control we have, and the more we succeed, the less vulnerable we become. The secular view is that increasing control is the key to our well-being. We increase it by critical reflection that aims to correct our mistaken attitudes and conceptions of well-being. In the last chapter, I argued that the correction of mistaken attitudes depend on making more realistic commitments to the values and limits derived from our society's system of values. This chapter is about the correction of mistaken conceptions of well-being.

A minimum condition of our well-being is the satisfaction of desires we share because of our nature. Our well-being, however, requires more than this minimum. We have many, much more complex, socially and individually variable desires, and we try to satisfy them by living according to our society's system of values. We construct our individual conceptions of well-being out of commitments to such values and out of our attitudes toward them. The attitudes, in turn, are composed of desires, beliefs, emotions, and motives that jointly prompt the actions by which we aim to realize the possibilities we value and observe the limits we accept, because, we assume, it would contribute to our well-being. Since our values, attitudes, commitments, and conceptions of well-being have an ineliminable individually variable component, there can be no general theory that would provide a blueprint for correcting the mistakes we might make. The approach to increasing control, therefore, must be practical, concrete, and particular.

4.1. Mistakes about Well-Being

I assume for the purposes of this chapter that both the attitudes that compose our conception of well-being and our society's system of values are free from mistakes. If so, then it is not obvious how a conception of well-being formed of these attitudes could be mistaken. What could go wrong if our desires, beliefs, emotions, motives, and values pass the test of critical reflection? A conception of well-being, after all, is our own, and if we are satisfied with it, who could gainsay us? It may seem to others that our conception is misguided, impoverished, vulgar, too intellectual or too emotional, foolishly risky, or just weird, but, provided we observe reasonable limits, we have the unimpeachable right to be the final judges of our own conception of well-being. This would have been disputed in past ages, and may still be by those who regard the judgments of some religious, ideological, psychological, or moral authority as overriding. Nevertheless, the right of individuals to judge their own conception of well-being has become a basic assumption of most people living in contemporary Western democracies. Others may think differently from us, we may listen to them if we respect their opinion, but in the end, it is up to us to judge whether or not our conception of well-being is mistaken—or so we assume.

There is a good reason, however, to question this basic assumption, even if we reject the judgments of external authorities. For our mistake-free attitudes may not cohere enough to form a structured conception of well-being. We may fail to see its incoherence, while others may see it, and they may be able to correct our faulty judgment. An example will make this possibility concrete.

Constant and Fecund are old friends. They grew up together, went to the same school, saw each other daily, still continue to meet and talk often, and confide in one another when some serious matter comes up in their lives. Constant did well enough at school, but Fecund did brilliantly. When Constant was learning a second language, Fecund was reading in his fourth. Constant was learning algebra, but Fecund, by special arrangement, was taking advanced college courses in mathematics. They played a lot of chess, but while Constant was looking at the board, Fecund played blindfolded and won without cheating. They took up orienteering and Fecund won all the competitions, not because he was fitter than others but because he had the map etched in his mind and, unlike others, did not have to slow down to consult it. When they discovered computer games, Constant played passionately for a while, but Fecund was writing software programs for games he had invented. Fecund excelled at everything he put his hand to and was always finding new interests and new challenges. He was not in the least conceited or proud of his accomplishments; he just took them for granted and matter-of-factly explored whatever his fertile mind and endless curiosity led him to discover.

Fecund graduated from university in record time, went to law school, and, after he passed the bar exam, joined a large law firm and specialized in tax law. He continued to play chess at the master's level; he became politically active and was passionately concerned with prison reform; he loved his wife and children and wanted to spend much time with them; he was writing a book tracing the effects of economic changes on the Roman Republic's legal system; and he stayed fit by playing a very good game of squash. His life, however, was not going well, because he was constantly frustrated by lack of time and energy to do as well as he wanted at his many activities. His law career suffered, his wife and children increasingly resented his frequent absences, he kept losing in chess, because he could not keep up with theoretical advances, work on his book got slower and slower, he did not have enough time to lobby effectively for prison reform, and he was gaining weight, because he could not play as much squash as he would have liked. He was often tired, short-tempered, worried about his family life, and chagrined by his lack of success.

Fecund had many talents, but he was not particularly reflective. If asked, he would have said that his conception of well-being was to succeed at his many pursuits. It had not occurred to him that his conception lacked structure, and that was the source of his frustrations. But it had occurred to Constant, and, after some hesitation, Constant had a serious talk with Fecund. He reminded Fecund that he was in his forties; that aging was inevitable and as his energy diminished so his frustrations will increase; that he treated all his commitments as if they were equally important, and he could not decide which one mattered more than the others when they came into conflict; that he could not possibly meet the demands of his many commitments; that he should find something to which he could unconditionally commit himself, hold his other commitments only conditionally, and rank them according to their importance as judged by his unconditional commitment; and that he should decrease his breadth for the sake of increasing his depth. Fecund listened carefully to his old friend, and said that he would think about it. And he did. Constant did not realize until later that he had precipitated a crisis in Fecund's life and set him off on a quest for understanding what he cared about most deeply.

Fecund thought that if he understood what that was, he could commit himself to it unconditionally, and order his other commitments accordingly. But knowing what he needed to understand did not give him the understanding. He asked himself what his deepest concern was, but the only answer he could honestly give himself was that it was sometimes one thing and sometimes another. He realized that he needed something more enduring, less fickle. This led him to look for an outside guide to understanding himself.

Fecund was raised in the lukewarm Christianity his family practiced, but after his talk with Constant he thought that he might take it seriously in the hope that it will give him the understanding he needed. He, then, resolved to try to make an unconditional commitment to living a Christian life and order his commitments accordingly. But after a while he found that he could not silence his doubts about the existence of God, the divinity of Jesus, and the possibility of immortality. He then gave up Christianity, and tried to make an unconditional commitment to Marxism, and began to reorder his other commitments. But when he realized that history did not go as Marxists said it should, he abandoned Marxism and committed himself to psychoanalysis in the hope that it will reveal to him what his unconditional commitment was. But that did not work either, and he turned to Buddhism, which was replaced by deep ecology, which he gave up for existentialism, which was followed by transcendental meditation, and, the last Constant heard, Fecund was thinking of chucking it all and becoming a monk.

As Constant watched Fecund zigzag through his life, he saw that Fecund always had a perfectly good reason both for his efforts to find an unconditional commitment and for discarding one candidate after another. Fecund was sincere in his search, but he did not succeed in finding something to which he was willing to commit himself more deeply than to anything else. Before his crisis, he had too many commitments. After it, he had fewer, but those few he changed as people who care about fashion change their clothes. First he cared too much about too many things, then he could not find anything to care about deeply enough. His life was a restless journey from one way station to the next. There was only the journey and never the arrival, because he lacked a destination. Whenever he got somewhere, he eventually found that it was not where he wanted to be. For some people, the journey itself may be satisfying, but Fecund was not one of them. He was driven by restlessness and his many great talents opened for him many more possibilities than most people have. But he found none of them satisfying enough to stay with it. He became frustrated with whatever he did. His attitudes were mistake-free, but they did not cohere into a structured conception of well-being whose achievement could have made him satisfied with his life.

4.2. Coherence

Reflection on Fecund's life allows us to form a better understanding of conceptions of well-being. To begin with, we have or should have an unimpeachable right to make what we can of our life, provided we stay within certain moral and legal limits. We also have the right to judge our conception of well-being, even if our judgment differs from those of religious, ideological, psychological, or moral authorities. But this does not mean that our judgments could not be mistaken, nor that others could not be better judges of our conception of well-being than we are. This is just what happened when Constant talked to Fecund about how he lived. Constant did not appeal to the authority of any person or doctrine. He judged Fecund's life from the point of view Fecund would have had if his critical reflection on his psychological and social conditions had been better. Constant's correction of Fecund's judgment was not objectionable meddling with his friend's private affairs. It aimed at what Fecund himself recognized as his own well-being. Nor did Constant impose his judgment of Fecund; he told Fecund what it was and let him do with it what he wanted. The essential point is that our right to judge our own life does not guarantee that the judgment will not be mistaken. And if it is mistaken, it may be corrected by others without violating any of our rights. Helping us do better what we want to do strengthens rather than weakens our right to do it.

Fecund's conception of well-being was incoherent as a result of his conflicting commitments. Understanding incoherence, therefore, requires understanding conflicts among commitments. We commit ourselves to some values we derive from our society's system of values. These values are possibilities we try to realize (they may also be limits but I will ignore them for the moment), because we believe that it would contribute to our well-being. They are the objects of our attitudes, and when the attitudes are lasting and favorable, we make a commitment to pursuing them.

Commitments thus connect our psychological condition, formed partly by our attitudes, to the prevailing values. Our attitudes are mistake-free if our desires conform to what we value; if our beliefs about them are true; if our emotions toward them are neither too strong nor too weak; and if our motives prompt us to act in conformity with our values. If our attitudes are mistake-free, then the source of conflicts among commitments is not intrinsic to the commitments, but the ways in which we hold the commitments. Our values are fine, but our valuing is not.

One way our valuing can go wrong is to have too few commitments. The result is an impoverished life, because we fail to recognize values whose realization would make our life much better. Many are the timid, imitative, unimaginative, or repressed people who keep treading in an inherited groove and mistake boredom for comfort. Another possibility is to have too many commitments. Given limited time and energy, we cannot honor all of them. The result is frustration, because our conception of well-being requires their realization, but our limitations doom us to failure. This is just what happened to Fecund. His commitments were incoherent.

It is important to realize, however, that commitments can be incoherent either simultaneously or successively. Before the crisis brought on by Constant, Fecund had too many simultaneous commitments. The trouble was not just the frustration caused by limitations of time and energy, but also that he could not decide the respective importance of his commitments, because all of them seemed to him equally important. He lacked priorities on the basis of which he could rank the commitments he had. After his crisis, Fecund realized that his frustrations resulted from the indiscriminate breadth of his commitments. He, then, searched for something to which he could commit himself unconditionally, so that he could distinguish between more and less important commitments, impose a structure on them, and resolve conflicts among them on that basis. Unfortunately, he failed in this as well, because his successive attempts to find something to which he could unconditionally commit himself were as conflict-ridden as his simultaneous conditional commitments used to be. As a result, he was frustrated no matter what he did. His successive commitments were incoherent, because, although he realized that his conception of well-being needed a structure and that he needed to commit himself unconditionally to something, eventually all the ones he tried to hold failed the test of his critical reflection. He looked for but could not find anything on the basis of which he could create the structure he realized he needed. Before his crisis, he had breadth, but no depth. After his crisis, he searched for depth, but could not find it.

Reflection on Fecund's incoherent conception of well-being allows us to understand that a coherent conception depends, in addition to mistake-free attitudes, on structuring our commitments in a way that enables us to resolve unavoidable conflicts among them. Such a structure would allow us to distinguish between unconditional and conditional commitments, and between our more and less important conditional commitments. We need now to ask how that structure may be found.

According to an influential contemporary answer, the structure is not found, but made and imposed on one's life. This basic idea is expressed in different ways. Harry Frankfurt regards as essential the control of our first-order desires for various satisfactions by subjecting them to evaluations that follow our second-order volition to satisfy only favorably evaluated desires and thus live the kind of life with which we could identify.[1] Stuart Hampshire's approach is to bring to consciousness our intentions and thereby formulate more and more clearly what we want to do and why, and then act accordingly.[2] Martha Nussbaum puts it in terms of constructing stories out of what she calls "narrative emotions."[3] Charles Taylor develops the notion of strong evaluation, which involves the articulation of our inchoate desires and permits living a full and responsible human life.[4] Richard Wollheim talks about the achievement of a mental connectedness that brings one's present dispositions and aspirations for the future under the influence of one's past through cleansing memory of defensive and self-aggrandizing falsifications.[5] But I will rely on Alasdair MacIntyre's terminology that involves the construction of a narrative of our life,[6] and in terms of which the answers of Frankfurt, Hampshire, Nussbaum, Taylor, and Wollheim could be expressed.

MacIntyre discusses "a concept of a self whose unity resides in the unity of a narrative which links birth to life to death as a narrative beginning to middle to end" (191). He says that "we all live out narratives and . . . we understand our lives in terms of the narratives" (197). And he claims that "the unity of a human life is the unity of a narrative quest. Quests sometimes fail, are frustrated, abandoned or dissipated into distractions; and human lives may in all these ways also fail. But the only criteria for success or failure in a human life as a whole are the criteria of success or failure in a narrated or a to-be-narrated quest" (203).

The answer, then, is that making and imposing a structure on our conception of well-being consists in forming a narrative in terms of which we explain to ourselves, and to others if need be, what we have done, are doing, and plan to do in the future. The narrative has two essential but inseparable components: the facts of our psychological and social conditions and their interpretation. Many of these facts are private; others can know them only if we tell them or if they infer them from what we do or do not do. Others are public, having to do with particular values we derive from our society's system of values and to which we commit ourselves. The interpretations ascribe greater or lesser significance, importance, meaningfulness to particular facts. A narrative, then, is a pattern that allows the systematic interpretation of our psychological and social conditions. MacIntyre would say that this is what Fecund lacked, and this was the source of his frustration. The narrative provides coherence by providing the means to distinguish between unconditional and conditional commitments, and between more and less important conditional commitments.

My own view is that it is clearly better to have succeeded in giving a narrative account of our psychological and social conditions than to have failed, or to have not even tried.[7] The narrative provides a needed framework in terms of which we can reflect critically on our attitudes, commitments, and values, and thereby try to make our conception of well-being coherent. Nevertheless, the coherence a narrative provides is not sufficient to give structure to our commitments. Narratives may be true or false, and the interpretations they contain may be far-fetched, fanciful, unreasonable, or untestable. If MacIntyre were right and our conception of well-being could be evaluated only in terms of criteria derived from a narrative, then the adequacy of the narrative could not be judged in terms of the life whose facts the narrative interprets. Narratives, then, would be self-authenticating and no narrative could be deemed better or worse than any other, just so long as it accounted for the relevant facts. We know, however, that this is not so, because we have good reason to reject, for instance, astrological, brainwashed, magical, and paranoid narratives. If MacIntyre were right, our rejection of such narratives, not the narratives themselves, would be unreasonable. And that, of course, is absurd.

4.3. Coherence is Not Enough

The basic assumption shared by Frankfurt, Hampshire, MacIntyre, Nussbaum, Taylor, and Wollheim is that our well-being depends on forming a coherent conception of well-being and using it to impose an order of priorities on our various commitments. They spell out the nature of coherence differently, but it makes little difference to the inadequacy of their shared assumption whether coherence is interpreted in terms of second-order volitions, conscious intentions, narratives, narrative emotions, strong evaluations, or mental connectedness. None of these attempts to impose a structure on our commitments is sufficient for a reasonable conception of well-being. Coherence is better than incoherence, but there are several reasons why coherence is not enough.

First, as we have seen in Fecund's case, he imposed numerous coherent narratives on his commitments: Christian, Marxist, psychoanalytic, Buddhist, ecological, existentialist, and he could have imposed many others. The essential point is that none of them satisfied him. He could not bring himself to believe and feel that any of them provided a realistic account of his psychological and social conditions. This shows that a reasonable narrative must do more than provide a language in terms of which we could identify and decide about the relative importance of our commitments. The narratives must fit our psychological and social conditions, and even the most coherent narrative may fail to do that. A coherent narrative is adequate only if it is true to what we most deeply care about in the context in which we live.

Defenders of the narrative approach will reply that we seek a narrative precisely because we are confused about our attitudes, commitments, and values, just as Fecund was. If the narrative does not ring true, the fault lies not with it but with our confusions. And, as it happens, every sufficiently sophisticated narrative has a built-in explanation of our failure to see the narrative as true to what our confusions disguise from us. Christians attribute it to our sinful state, Marxists to alienation, psychoanalysts to neurotic defense mechanisms, Buddhists to enslavement by desires, ecologists to anthropocentrism, existentialists to bad faith, and so forth. As MacIntyre has it: "the only criteria for success or failure in a human life as a whole are the criteria of success or failure in a narrated or a to-be-narrated quest" (203). Fecund's dissatisfaction with the narratives he tried and discarded was Fecund's fault, not the defect of discarded narratives.

If this defense of narratives were correct, then no sufficiently sophisticated narrative could be defective. But it is a matter of logical necessity, whose denial is absurd, that at least some narratives are defective, because they are contraries of other narratives, and contraries cannot be true together. The Christian narrative depends on the existence of a supernatural realm, which the Marxist narrative denies. The psychoanalytic narrative depends on the satisfaction of non-neurotic desires, while the Buddhist narrative rejects the satisfaction of all desires. The ecological narrative requires us to abandon anthropocentrism, whereas the existentialist one is basically committed to it. Since these narratives cannot be true together, there must be some external criterion that a defective narrative fails to meet. The obvious criterion is that the narrative fails to account for the facts it was meant to interpret. Such a fact, for instance, as Fecund's sense that none of the narratives he tried to impose on his commitments accounted for what concerned him most.

A second reason why a coherent narrative is insufficient for a reasonable conception of well-being is that it may reveal that what matters most to the person whose life is coherently narrated are incoherent commitments. Suppose that the truth about Fecund is that what he most cared about was to live a life in which he could freely explore whatever aroused his exceptional intellect and lively imagination. He had not realized at first that this will result in incoherent commitments and much frustration. But, after he listened to Constant and experimented with imposing order on his commitments, he understood that his life would not be worth living if he curtailed the free play of his intellect and imagination.

If, after he came to this understanding, he had constructed a narrative of his life, it would have recorded his incoherent explorations that had no purpose beyond the exploration itself. The narrative would have been coherent, because it would have accounted for the relevant facts, but it would have accounted for facts that did not cohere. What mattered most to Fecund was not to commit himself to possibilities whose realization would have contributed to his well-being but to explore many possibilities without dwelling on them long enough to make an unconditional commitment to any of them. He came to understand that living in this way was an obstacle to his well-being; nevertheless that is how he wanted to live. We can see, therefore, in yet another way that a coherent narrative is not sufficient for a reasonable conception of well-being. Moreover, there are criteria of success and failure that are independent of the narrative account that can be imposed on a life. A narrative that succeeds in being true to our psychological and social conditions need not indicate that the narrator is succeeding in pursuing well-being.

We now have two reasons against regarding coherence as the key to well-being: a coherent account may not be true to the psychological and social conditions on which our well-being partly depends and a coherent account that is true to them may reveal that our deepest concerns are detrimental to our well-being. These reasons point to a shared defect in the various coherentist accounts, regardless of whether they are expressed in a narrative or some other form. The defect is that they all assume that our psychological and social conditions are formed by the interpretations we impose on them. What is at fault in all this is the idea that our psychological and social conditions are one thing and their interpretations are another. The faulty assumption is that in trying to make sense of our psychological and social conditions it is open to us to impose on them whatever interpretation pleases us.

The third reason against regarding coherence as the key to well-being is that interpretations do not form our psychological and social conditions, because the relevant facts come bearing their own significance. Understanding their significance comes first, and finding an interpretation that fits their significance can come only second. Interpretations may be true or false depending on how faithful they are to the significance we believe and feel the facts of our psychological and social conditions have for us. These beliefs and emotions may be mistaken, of course, but if they have passed the test of critical reflection, we have good reason to accept them and to reject interpretations that are contrary to them. True interpretations are not imposed but found, and whether they have been found depends on whether they fit the significance critical reflection leads us to discern in the facts of our psychological and social condition. We are the ultimate judges of the adequacy of interpretations, and interpretations are not the ultimate judges of our sense of significance.

We must ask, however, what reason can be given in favor of this order of priorities and against the order favored by coherentist accounts. Why must the justification of significance we discern of the facts of our psychological and social conditions proceed from the inside, as I claim, rather than from the outside, as coherentist accounts claim? The reason is that there are some familiar facts of our psychological and social conditions that can be readily explained if we assign priority to our sense of significance, but the same facts become mysterious if we suppose that their significance derives from some interpretation we impose on them. The facts I have in mind are discoveries we often make about ourselves that surprise us and force us to revise how we understand ourselves. Such a discovery may be our adamant refusal to do something that on our existing view of our attitudes, commitments, and values we ought to be prepared to do, or the discovery of a surprising eagerness to do something that previously we would not have dreamt of doing. We discover that we have limits and values of which we have not been aware.

Fecund had supposed, as most of us do, that he had certain desires and his well-being consisted in satisfying them. But he discovered that he cared much more about exploring the intellectual and imaginative possibilities that occurred to his fertile mind than about well-being. Sarah, as we have seen in the last chapter, discovered that, although she was passionately dedicated to scientific research, she felt compelled to give it up to look after her parents. We are assailed by grief, surprised by joy, overpowered by indignation, lose interest, become resentful although we intend otherwise, cannot believe what the evidence clearly shows, remember what we have resolved to forget, opt for the lesser over the greater good, and so forth. Through such common experiences we discover what we find significant or that we no longer find significant what earlier mattered a great deal. These are truths about ourselves that are inconsistent with our previous attitudes, commitments, and values, but their significance is undeniable. Any reasonable interpretation of ourselves must do justice to the significance of these experiences.

Their significance is not an epiphenomenon of interpretations but a test of their adequacy.

Furthermore, not only are these significant experiences part of the psychological and social conditions to which interpretations must do justice but we also criticize interpretations on their basis. If we reject Christianity, because we cannot bring ourselves to believe in the virgin birth or in a providential order in which the horrors of Communism and Nazism have a place; if we reject Marxism, because we find its claim absurd that our sense of beauty is an expression of our economic interest; if we regard psychoanalysis incredible, because not even our most earnest soul-searching could reveal an incestuous or fratricidal desire; or if we are unable to take Buddhism seriously, because we think that a life freed of desires would not be worth living, we confirm my claim that interpretations depend on our sense of significance rather than vice versa. (I note in passing that this is not a reason for rejecting these world views but a reason for rejecting their interpretations of the relevant facts if they are contrary to our sense of significance that has been tested by critical reflection.)

I conclude that coherence is necessary, but not sufficient, for a reasonable conception of well-being. Coherence consists in a structured set of commitments, where unconditional commitments form the bases on which the relative importance of conditional commitments is evaluated. Such a coherent structure reflects the sense of significance we find in our attitudes, commitments, and values. But coherence is not enough for well-being, because we may be mistaken in our attitudes, commitments, and values, or we may be mistaken in the relative importance we suppose them to have.

4.4. Realism

Reasonable conceptions of well-being require, in addition to mistake-free attitudes and coherent commitments to values, that the structure of commitments be realistic. Realism goes beyond hierarchical order and consistency that make the structure of commitments coherent and consists in the congruence of the structure with something that is external to it and exists independently of any commitment we may make. What is this external and independent something? And what does congruence come to in this context?

The external and independent something is our society's system of values. We may commit ourselves to some of these values, because we believe that they would contribute to our well-being. Commitments, therefore, are *to* values that exist regardless of whether we have made a commitment to any of them. It is in this sense that a society's values are external to and independent of our commitments. I add as a reminder that I am assuming for the moment that the society's system of values is mistake-free, but, of course, it may not be. At least some of the prevailing values typically need corrections. I will discuss both their mistakes and corrections in the next chapter.

When we view our society's system of values from our individual perspectives, we see them as possibilities we may try to realize. In contemporary Western societies, the range of possibilities is exceptionally wide. The prevailing plurality of values in our context, therefore, is extensive indeed. Our typical situation is that we recognize only a much narrower range of values than what is in fact available. The reason for this is that our upbringing, store of information, imagination, curiosity, need for comfort and security prevent us from seeing values that are fact available to us. Our recognition of them may be quite superficial, amounting to little more than mere awareness of them as options. The options, however, may or may not be live ones, because we may lack a deeper understanding of what pursuing them might actually involve, how we would feel if we pursued them, whether we have the abilities needed for success, how pursuing them might change us, whether their realization would be satisfying, or, indeed, whether we want, or should want, to pursue them.

There is an even narrower range of values that we have not merely recognized, but took seriously enough to make our own. These are the values to which we have committed ourselves. In the best cases, our commitments are based on rigorous critical reflection. Most often, however, we commit ourselves simply by following a pattern familiar from our personal experience of people who actually lived by trying to realize some particular value.

The views we form of values are prone to error. We may misunderstand what the values are; we may think that something is a value, although it is excluded by some limit; we may think that there is a limit, when there is not; our view of the range of available values may be too narrow or too wide. One kind of realism we need for a reasonable conception of well-being is to correct the mistakes we tend to make about the available values. Their correction depends on critical reflection on our conception of well-being in order to make our commitments conform to the external and independent structure of values. We need realism to make our commitments fit the context in which we live.

There is, however, also another kind of realism we need. Our commitments have to fit not only our context but also our psychological condition: our sense of who we are and want to be, what we have or lack the ability to do, what matters to us deeply, lastingly, and what is merely a short-term enthusiasm or infatuation. This realism about ourselves, if we have it, largely guides our commitments to the available values. It allows us to make commitments that fit our understanding of psychological condition.

The key to the cultivation of this second kind of realism has been perceptively identified by Montaigne: "Things in themselves may have their own weights and measures and qualities; but once inside, within us, she [the soul] allots them their qualities as she sees fit. . . . Health, conscience, authority, knowledge, riches, beauty, and their opposites—all are stripped on entry and receive . . . new clothing. . . . Let us no longer make the external qualities of things our excuse; it is up to us to reckon them as we will. Our good and our ill depend on ourselves."[8] Montaigne adds "alone" to "depend on ourselves," and in this he is mistaken. For what we reckon depends on what we have to reckon with, how we reckon depends on the resources we can bring to it, and neither depends on ourselves alone. Both depend on our reckoning more or less realistically, and the more realistic we are, the more we avoid mistakes, increase our control, and the less we are at the mercy of contingency.

The understanding of realism we have reached so far requires that the structure of our commitments should conform to two external conditions that exist independently of our commitments: the social conditions formed of the system of values of our society and the psychological condition that includes our various attitudes formed by our desires, beliefs, emotions, and motives. Realistic commitments, then, connect our psychological condition, including our attitudes, to our social condition, including our society's system of values. The relative importance of our attitudes is reflected by the priorities we assign to our unconditional and various conditional commitments. Realism depends on how well we have conducted critical reflection on our psychological and social conditions. Realism and critical reflection are connected symbiotically: critical reflection aims at realism and realism is achieved by critical reflection.

There is, however, an additional requirement that realism must meet. The need for it becomes apparent if we recognize that the psychological and social conditions that our commitments aim to connect may be incongruous. If that happens, no matter how realistic we manage to be about each condition separately, our commitments will not succeed in finding a fit between them.

The congruence of our psychological and social conditions is a stricter requirement than compatibility. Conditions are compatible if they do not exclude one another. Our well-being, however, requires more. It requires that our commitments should be to values that are available in our context. A paradigm case of the failure to meet this requirement is Don Quixote's conception of well-being. The values of a chivalric life were coherent in the centuries preceding the Don's own, but they were anachronistic in his own time. In our context, incongruity is indicated by the experience of alienation. We feel estranged from our society if the values we prize are not available, and if we do not want to live by the available values.

This incongruity need not indicate that there is anything amiss either with the prevailing values, or with our conception of well-being. Our attitudes may be mistake-free, coherent, and realistic, given our psychological condition. And our society's system of values may also be mistake-free, neither promiscuously broad, nor impoverishingly narrow, and hospitable to a wide range of different conceptions of well-being—unfortunately, our own is not one of them. In some cases there may be another society in which we could feel at home and we could actually move there. Or we may just resign ourselves to doing as well as we can in our own society, even though well-being will elude us.

If, however, we are at a stage in life when we are deliberating about what conception of well-being we should form, or, if we have formed one, but left it sufficiently flexible to permit revision, then we will want our commitments to be to values that are available in our society. We will pursue our well-being by reciprocal adjustments between our attitudes and our society's system of values. Reasonable attitudes and commitments to values will not be unalterably rigid, and their flexibility will permit the reciprocal adjustments of our psychological and social conditions. The third requirement of realism will be met if such serendipity exists in our circumstances.

I conclude that a reasonable conception of well-being requires us to make commitments that connect our mistake-free, coherent, and realistic attitudes to some of the values available in our society and that we have committed ourselves to some of them on the basis of a realistic understanding both of them and of their suitability to our psychological condition. The key to forming mistake-free attitudes and well-ordered commitments is critical reflection. The more we succeed in making our conception of well-being reasonable, the more we increase our control over how we live, and the less we are vulnerable to contingency. Of course we cannot free ourselves from contingencies altogether. Much can still go wrong. But if anything does go wrong, we will have the satisfaction of knowing that it was not our fault.

4.5. Obstacles to Well-Being

Nietzsche memorably remarked that "there is no pre-established harmony between the furtherance of truth and the well-being of mankind."[9] I have been arguing that the furtherance of truth—which I called realism—is necessary for our well-being. Nietzsche does not deny this; he denies only the unsubstantial dream that knowing the truth guarantees well-being. He is right. For realism about our attitudes, commitments, and values may reveal that what we care about most is not well-being but the life-long exploration of imaginative or intellectual possibilities, as Fecund's case shows. Or realism may lead us to conclude that the achievement of well-being is not an unalloyed good, because its cost is the regret we inevitably feel for the many values we could have, but did not, try to realize. Or again realism may lead to the discovery that what we most want puts us at odds with our society's system of values. There is no pre-established harmony between our own well-being and our society's values either. In the next chapter, I will discuss this last possibility.

These possibilities, and there are others, show that, although well-being is undoubtedly good, it is neither unconditionally good, nor the only good that we may reasonably want to pursue. There are reasons against seeking our well-being, and not all of them are bad reasons. And there are reasons for living according to the values of our society, and not all of them are connected with our well-being. The requirements of our society's system of values and our well-being may conflict and there may be reasons for trying to resolve this conflict in favor of either.

5

Dimensions of Value

A reasonable conception of well-being requires mistake-free attitudes and well-ordered commitments to some values selected from our society's system of values. In the last two chapters, I considered what makes attitudes mistake-free and commitments well-ordered, but I simply assumed that our commitments are to values we value reasonably. I will argue in this chapter that what makes it reasonable to value them is that they are necessary for the well-being of individuals in a particular society at a particular time. I begin with a sketchy outline of the three dimensions of value. Each dimension provides some of the values on which our well-being depends, as well as the different reasons why we should value them. In subsequent chapters I will add breadth and depth to this outline by considering problems that arise within each dimension.

The central claims I defend in this chapter are as follows. First, there is an irreducible plurality of values that follow from the universal requirements of human well-being, from a shared cultural identity, and from individual conceptions of well-being. Second, no one value has permanently overriding importance in all reasonable conceptions of our well-being. We may commit ourselves unconditionally to some one value, but this is a fact about us, not about values. The plurality of values is one thing, the strength with which we are committed to particular values is quite another. Third, conflicts among values are unavoidable features of our system of values. And fourth, their conflicts can be reasonably resolved, even though there is no permanent non-arbitrary hierarchical order in which all reasonable conceptions of well-being must rank values.

Our system of values is three-dimensional both literally and metaphorically: it has a human, cultural, and personal dimension, each with its own values, and it is capacious enough to include a wide variety of evaluations. Human values are the same for all human beings; cultural values hold in a particular society at a particular time and may or may not hold in others; and personal values vary with individuals. The justification or the criticism of a society, then, depends on how well its conventions protect the human, cultural, and personal values on which our well-being depends.

5.1. The Human Dimension

This dimension of our system of values is concerned with the satisfaction of basic needs that are the same for all human beings. The most obvious ones are physiological needs (for nutrition, oxygen, protection from the elements, rest and motion, and so forth), psychological needs (for companionship, appreciation, the absence of terror and self-loathing, having a meaningful life, and the like), and social needs (for order and security, division of labor, protection against crime and illness, the coordination of individual activities, a life beyond mere subsistence, and so on).

The satisfaction of these basic physiological, psychological, and social needs is a condition of all reasonable conceptions of well-being. Their prolonged frustration damages everyone in normal circumstances. The specific satisfactions of specific basic needs constitute human values. Since all reasonable societies must aim to protect the conditions of well-being, each must have conventions that protect human values. These are *required conventions*, without which well-being is impossible. They are universal, because all human beings have basic needs they aim to satisfy, and they are impersonal, because they apply to all human beings equally. They set the standard by which actions and conventions are evaluated in the human dimension.

Consider the value of life as an illustration of how evaluation may proceed in the human dimension. All reasonable societies must protect human lives, so they must have a required convention prohibiting murder. But this leaves open when murder may be justified, how far its prohibition extends, what the status is of suicide, abortion, euthanasia, war, capital punishment, revenge, feuds, and the like, and what is recognized as an excuse. These are difficult questions that must be answered by all societies, and they may answer them differently. But they must all recognize that there is a difference between clear cases in which the required convention is unambiguously violated and unclear cases that stand in need of interpretation. In unclear cases, the application of required conventions is controversial. It may be unclear whether a homicide constitutes murder, but if it is motivated by fun, pleasure, or profit, then it is murder and any reasonable society will prohibit it. People, of course, may be unreasonable and act contrary to human values and required conventions. That, however, casts no more doubt on clear requirements of the human dimension than the actions of stupid or self-destructive people do on the clear requirements of health.

Reasonable people may agree that a murder has been committed and disagree whether it is justifiable or excusable. Such disagreements are not intractable. Those who attempt to justify or excuse the murder owe an explanation of why it is an exception. Good explanations excuse it on the ground that it was accidental or done in ignorance; or, if it was deliberate and informed, then justify it on the ground that the alternatives were worse. Killing in self-defense or war may be justified. Bad explanations will lack convincing excuses or justifications. There will also be explanations that are not clearly good or bad, because it is difficult to weigh the reasons adduced in support of them. But unclear cases do not call into question the requirement that all reasonable societies must meet: the protection of human values by required conventions.

Conformity to human values and required conventions is not an unconditional requirement. Required conventions may be justifiably violated in a particular case if the protection of human values in general warrants it. History is full of hard cases in which the protection of human values in general had made it reasonable and justified to do in a particular case what required conventions normally prohibit. We may conclude, therefore, that all reasonable societies must aim to protect human values and required conventions, and that both are derived from the satisfaction of basic needs being a necessary condition of human well-being. This is the primary concern of the human dimension. Evaluations in this context are reasonable if they further the well-being of people in a particular society, and unreasonable if they do not.

5.2. The Cultural Dimension

This dimension is concerned with protecting the *cultural values* of a society. There is a bewildering variety of cultural values within any society and their variety is further extended by the many different cultural values of different societies. I doubt that it is possible to provide anything approaching a complete or authoritative description of cultural values. Their number is countless, there are countless ways of classifying them, and they criss-cross, overlap, differ in scope, and presuppose one another. Describing the values of the cultural dimension requires some system of classification, but I acknowledge that what follows is merely one possibility among many. I propose, then, to distinguish between four types of cultural values likely to be found in a particular society: *interpretations* of human values; *forms* of expression and conduct; *institutions and practices within them*; and *modes of evaluation*.

I begin with the interpretation of human values. If we do not satisfy the basic need for food, we die. But there are many ways of satisfying it. In all societies, people reject some perfectly nutritious food, such as beef, pork, or insects, and often what is rejected in one is regarded as a delicacy in another. In all societies, there are close relationships that alleviate loneliness, provide mutual aid, respect, trust, satisfaction, and enable people to cope with adversities in their lives. Love, friendship, family, and sex exist everywhere, but there are great variations in whom and how it is thought proper to love, what friendship implies, who counts as a family member or as a proper sexual partner. Similarly, all societies must have ways of resolving conflicts, but some rely on the legal or political system, others on religious authorities or public assemblies, yet others on oracles, or bribery, or bargaining, or on some other method. Human values must be interpreted, but the interpretations vary with societies and times.

A second type of cultural value are forms of expression and conduct whose connection with human values is more remote. Among them are ways of making a living, practicing a profession, being a scholar, artist, teacher, or politician; raising children, expressing patriotism, participating in sports as a player or an observer, and pursuing hobbies; the various customs, rituals, and ceremonies that mark significant occasions, like birth, marriage, retirement, and death; conventions of flirtation, competition, clothing, and housing; the appropriate expression of gratitude, resentment, regret, contempt, and admiration; the accepted forms of politeness, tact, generosity, insult, making a promise, deferring to authority, and so on and on.

A third type of cultural value is provided by specific institutions and practices within them, such as commerce (retailers, consumers), communication (the media, Internet, email), defense (the military), education (schools, universities), finance (banks, insurance, the stock market), the law (courts, licensing agencies), law enforcement (police, customs, immigration), manufacture (industries, factories), medicine (hospitals, pharmacies), performing arts (museums, theaters, concerts, the opera), sports (tournaments, leagues, stadiums), transportation (travel, trucking, trains, airlines, highways), and no doubt many others.

The cultural values of all three types have the specific function of guiding the interactions of people living together in a society. They can do this well or badly, efficiently helping people to do what they want or need to do, or hindering them by silly restrictions or requirements that serve no useful purpose. One way of evaluating the first three types of cultural values, then, is on the basis of how efficiently they perform their function. Such practical evaluation is, of course, important, but it is not the only mode of evaluation. There are others, and this brings us to the last, but not the least important, type of cultural values.

This fourth type of cultural value includes a society's enduring modes of evaluation, such as the aesthetic, literary, moral, philosophical, political, and religious. Each mode has standards of evaluation and the standards are the most highly prized achievements that have acquired the status of classics. They may be works of non-verbal art (musical compositions, paintings, sculpture), written works (biography, drama, novels, philosophy, poetry), exemplary characters and their actions (great, wise, creative, just, kind, courageous men and women), political achievements (a legal system, a negotiated peace, a balance of powers), sacred books and saintly lives (canonical documents of various faiths, prophets). These classics are the touchstones of a society's evaluations of its forever changing values and limits. Interpretations, forms of expression and conduct, institutions and their practices are criticized or justified from aesthetic, literary, moral, philosophical, political, or religious points of view. Ultimately each aims at human well-being, but they are concerned with different aspects of it. And, of course, these modes of evaluation are not sharply distinguishable, because they overlap and because each mode can itself be evaluated from the point of view of the other modes.

These four types of cultural value are protected by *variable conventions*. They vary with societies and with changes within them. They are general but not universal, because they hold only in a society and may not hold in others. But when they hold, they apply to everyone in that society, so they are general. Some variable conventions are also impersonal, because they are supposed to protect cultural values for everyone equally, like law enforcement and public roads. Many others vary with individuals, because they protect cultural values attached to competitive or scarce positions, special training, or significant achievements. Part of the upbringing and socialization of people in a society consists in acquainting them with the prevailing cultural values and variable conventions. They jointly form their shared *cultural identity*, which is the general evaluative standard of the cultural dimension of a society's system of values.

People's cultural identity is formed by their shared recognition of the prevailing cultural values and variable conventions and by their shared sense of what kind of considerations are and are not relevant to the justification or criticism of values and conventions. Sharing cultural identity does not mean that its sharers agree about their evaluations of particular cultural values and conventions—far from it. What they agree about is their acknowledgment of one another as legitimate parties to their agreements or disagreements who are entitled to have a say in the matter, and who know or ought to know how disagreements should be approached. Cultural identity makes its sharers feel at home with one another, even if they disagree about their evaluations. They rely on one another to know what the available range possibilities is and the violation of what limits is beyond the pale. They treat each others as fellow participants in a shared form of life.

It would be a mistake to intellectualize cultural identity. Those who share it need not be aware of it, nor need they be reflective about the prevailing interpretations, forms of expression and conduct, institutions and their practices, and modes of evaluation. Sharing a cultural identity is like sharing one's mother tongue. Competent speakers simply use it, usually unreflectively, to communicate with others. They need not be grammarians, skilled writers, or eloquent orators. A shared cultural identity is usually analogously unreflective. The actions and evaluations it prompts often rest on the sharers' unconscious assumptions and sentiments colored by their emotions, prejudices, education, upbringing, and gut reactions. But their unexamined attitudes fall within the same range, recognize the same values, and they find one another's attitudes understandable, even if they deplore them.

As the satisfaction of basic needs is a condition of well-being and the standard of evaluation in the human dimension, so cultural identity is a condition of well-being and the standard of evaluation in the cultural dimension. And just as required conventions are conditional, because the protection of human values collectively may require the violation of a required convention in a particular case, so variable conventions are conditional, because the protection of cultural values collectively may require the violation of a variable convention in a particular case. But there is a difference. Well-being is possible only if the violations of required conventions are exceptional, but the violations of variable conventions are likely to be routine. The reason for this is that required conventions protect unchanging basic needs, whereas variable conventions protect cultural values that continually change in response to changing economic, technological, demographic, international, and other ambient conditions. These changes, however, do not make the protection of cultural identity less important than the satisfaction of basic needs. For cultural identity guides how people evaluate their possibilities and limits. Its guidance is as consistent with changes in particular constituents as the expressive capacity of one's language is with changes in usage. As speaking a language is to know how to say what one wants to say, so having a cultural identity is to know how to evaluate the prevailing possibilities and limits.

Part of what makes a society reasonable, therefore, is that it maintains the cultural identity of a people formed of changing cultural values and variable conventions. What matters, however, is the *having* of cultural identity, not any of the particular cultural values and variable conventions that temporarily constitute it. A reasonable society combines the maintenance of cultural identity with a great deal of flexibility that allows for changes in its constituents.

5.3. The Personal Dimension

The satisfaction of basic needs and the maintenance of cultural identity are necessary but not sufficient for well-being. They provide values we need. It is up to us, however, to make what we can of them by choosing and trying to realize some of them as part of our conception of well-being. This is the concern of the personal dimension of values. Forming a reasonable conception of well-being is only rarely a private activity that we can do by relying only on our own resources. Typically, we form such a conception out of values that have been judged admirable by the conventions of one of the modes of evaluation that partly constitute the prevailing cultural identity. These possibilities are exemplified by the classics, and we model our attitudes, commitments, and conceptions of well-being on them.

In the preceding three chapters I have endeavored to give an account of how we should go about doing it, but the account was incomplete, because I have left unspecified the nature and source of the available values and limits. I can now say that having a reasonable conception of well-being depends on increasing our control by forming mistake-free attitudes, well-ordered commitments, and making our conception of well-being more realistic. And the objects of our attitudes and commitments and the contents of our conception of well-being are the values and limits we derive from our cultural identity. We form our *personal values* out of these elements, which, in turn, provide the contents of our conceptions of well-being.

Conceptions of well-being, then, combine psychological and cultural elements. The psychological elements involve our efforts to correct our attitudes and to impose order on our commitments by deciding about their relative importance. If we succeed in ordering our commitments well, then we will unconditionally commit ourselves to the one we regard as most important for our well-being and conditionally commit ourselves to the rest.

Well-ordered commitments require us to be reflective about the relative strength of our commitments. The cultural elements of our conceptions of well-being are provided by the plurality of cultural values available in our society. Conceptions of well-being are thus formed by committing ourselves to some among the available cultural values and by deciding about the relative strength of these commitments on the basis of the importance we attribute to particular cultural values in our conceptions of well-being. There is no inconsistency, not even tension, between acknowledging the plurality of values and making an unconditional commitment to some particular value. I will return to this point (in 9.4.).

The standard of evaluation in the personal dimension, then, is our *conception of well-being*. Personal values and conceptions of well-being, of course, vary with individuals. This does not mean, however, that our personal values are reasonable if we happen to think that they are. They are reasonable if they are derived from mistake-free attitudes, well-ordered commitments, a realistic conception of well-being, and if the values and limits that form the content of our attitudes, commitments, and conception of well-being are informed by the admirable examples set by the classics.

According to this outline, then, the three dimensions of our society's system of values are human, cultural, and personal; each with values peculiar to itself; and each with a standard of evaluation, namely, the satisfaction of basic needs, the maintenance of cultural identity, and our conception of well-being. The aim shared by each dimension is individual well-being. Each dimension aims to protect a necessary condition of it. Meeting these conditions, however, still does not guarantee well-being, because the contingencies of life may prevent it. This outline, I stress again, is sketchy and incomplete. The rest of the book is concerned with making it less so.

5.4. Conflicts

An obvious feature of the human condition is that the values on which our well-being depends often conflict. Can these conflicts be reasonably resolved? I think they can be. I begin with conflicts between values of the same dimension. Suppose there is a conflict in the human dimension between the values of life and security. If security is threatened by determined foreign or domestic enemies, then its protection requires risking lives in its defense. The result is that either the value of life or the value of security will be compromised and defending one endangers the other. Or suppose that the conflict is in the cultural dimension between morally right and politically necessary policies. Opting for one will violate the other and a requirement of well-being will be damaged no matter what is done. Suppose last that the conflict is in the personal dimension between political activism and professional excellence both of which are part of one's conception of well-being. Given limited time and energy, pursuing one is incompatible with the pursuing of the other.

These are familiar conflicts in our society and we have found no generally accepted theory or principle to which we could appeal to tell us that one of the conflicting values is always and in all circumstances more important than the other. Which of the conflicting values would be reasonable to prefer depends on the circumstances. Whether security makes it reasonable to risk lives depends, among other things, on our judgment of how serious the threat is. Whether political necessity should override moral obligations requires estimating, for instance, how pressing is the necessity and how serious would the immorality be. And whether one's pursuit of professional excellence should be more or less important than one's political activism calls for weighing such matters as how excellent one could be and how effective would be one's political activism. There can be no authoritative theory or principle for guiding such judgments, because reasonable judgments differ from conflict to conflict. But that does not mean that there can be no reasonable judgments. It means that reasonable judgments must be particular and concrete, not general and abstract.

Each dimension of value has a standard to which we can appeal in struggling with the conflict. The standard will not tell us which of the conflicting values we should prefer, but it will tell us what sort of reasons we should seek in our particular circumstances whose respective weight would incline us to resolve the conflict one way or another. The human dimension's standard is the satisfaction of basic needs. Whether security or lives are more important in the situation I have described depends on which is more important for the satisfaction of the basic needs taken collectively. In the cultural dimension, the standard is the maintenance of cultural identity. We have to decide whether doing what is politically necessary is more important for maintaining our cultural identity than doing what is morally right. In the personal dimension, the standard is one's conception of well-being. The decision we have to make hinges on whether political activism is more important to our conception of well-being than professional excellence.

Making such decisions is always a matter of judgment. They involve assigning weight to reasons pointing in opposite directions, having detailed knowledge of the particular situation in which we have to make the decision, and applying complex standards to unclear cases on the basis of imperfect knowledge. Such judgments are fallible of course, but we have no alternative to trying to make them as reasonably as we can. It is not a mystery how we can do that. We can do it by increasing our control through critical reflection on our attitudes, commitments, and conception of well-being. And the object of critical reflection is to correct the mistakes we are all too likely to make in forming attitudes, making and ordering commitments, and constructing a conception of well-being.

I turn next to conflicts between the values of different dimensions. The requirements of basic needs, cultural identity, and individual conceptions of well-being often conflict, and the question is whether such conflicts can be reasonably resolved, given the three-dimensional account of values. The simplest approach to their resolution is unsatisfactory, but understanding the reason for it points to a better approach. The simple approach claims that human values are more important than cultural values, and cultural values are more important than personal values. This order of importance, according to the simple approach, reflects the fact that personal values presuppose cultural values, because they are derived from them, and cultural values presuppose human values, because they are necessary for staying alive so that we could value anything.

This approach is unsatisfactory, because, while it is true that personal values presuppose cultural values, which, in turn, presuppose human values, the presupposed values need not be more important than the presupposing ones. The values of the three dimensions are equally important for individual well-being. This becomes apparent if we recognize that well-being may be impossible even if our basic needs are satisfied and cultural identity is protected. For our well-being requires living in a way that reflects our moral, political, or religious commitments and attitudes that concern matters beyond our basic needs and cultural identity. Similarly, we may be miserable even if our basic needs are satisfied, if our shared cultural identity has been destroyed by invaders or adverse conditions. The simplest approach to resolving conflicts between the values of different dimensions is unsatisfactory, because it mistakenly regards the values of one dimension as always more important than the values of the others.

A better approach to conflict-resolution recognizes that there often are reasons for resolving conflicts between the values of different dimensions in favor of both of the conflicting values. Consider two examples. In the *Apocrypha* we read:

Eleazar, one of the scribes in high position, a man advanced in age and of noble presence, was being forced to open his mouth to eat swine's flesh. But he, welcoming death with honour rather than life with pollution, went up to the rack of his own accord, spitting out flesh, as men ought to go who have the courage to refuse things that it is not right to taste, even for the natural love of life.[1]

Eleazar's conflict was between the human value of life and personal value of his religion that formed an essential part of his conception of well-being. He resolved it by deciding that the personal value he attributed to his religious commitment was unconditional, whereas his commitment to the value of his life was conditional. He could make that decision, because he was reflective about the relative strength of his commitments.

The reason he might have given for his decision was that his life would not be worth living if it involved the violation of his unconditional religious commitment. And this is not such an *outré* thought, since most of us can envisage situations in which we would rather die than live on certain terms, even if the terms we might find unacceptable are likely to be quite different from Eleazar's. The reason against Eleazar's decision is that his belief that pork is harmful is false. The belief has long endured and its significance transcends questions of nutrition and spoiled food, but that does not make the belief less mistaken. Eleazar sacrificed his life in the service of an error, and that was a waste. There are, then, reasons on both sides. To decide between them we have to think further. We have to ask whether Eleazar's belief about pork was merely symbolic or whether he had supposed that the symbolism had a factual basis. If the first, we can see that he had a good reason to die, even if we do not share it. If the second, we will think that his reason was bad. The weight of reasons may fall either way depending on further reasons about the relative importance of facts and symbols in Eleazar's conception of well-being. If the symbols were more important, then the conflict could be reasonably resolved, but not in favor of the human value of life, as the simple approach to conflict-resolution supposes. There may be reasons, therefore, for regarding a personal value as more important in certain contexts than a conflicting human value.

The second example is a conflict Stuart Hampshire attributes to Flaubert:

Consider the romantic ideal of . . . [Flaubert] who, as an artist, neglects every duty and obligation which could stand in the way of the claims of his art upon him. He gives absolute priority to . . . imagination and to originality and to the invention of new forms of expression. . . . [He has] reasons, the result of long reflection . . . for this preferred way of life. . . . [He] will not dispute the established and essential virtues of moral character . . . but he will adapt and correct and restrict the ethical ideal to take account of . . . the peculiarities of his own temperament and emotional needs, as he believes them to be. He will find his justification in an argument that art has taken over some of the former functions of religion, and also that the distortions of modern life can only be rendered tolerable by aesthetic experience and the free exercise of imagination. . . . He argues that . . . he has to make a harsh choice and to discard some good things in order to realize others; a softer compromise would lead to an inferior achievement.[2]

Hampshire's Flaubert, then, faces a conflict between the personal value of a literary life that reflects his commitments and attitudes and the cultural identity he shared with others in his society. He resolved it in favor of his personal value, because his commitment to a literary life was unconditional and his commitment to other cultural values was conditional.

Once again, there are reasons both for and against Flaubert's resolution of his conflict. The reason against it is that Flaubert was mistaken in supposing that by opting for a literary life he had abandoned his cultural identity. He was right to think that his literary life was incompatible with the prevailing bourgeois hypocrisy and philistinism. But he was wrong to think that his education, eating and drinking habits, responses to the weather, attitude to illness, expectations about decent housing and what his money can buy, the way he dressed and moved, his sense of humor, and above all his language were not to a very large extent part of the cultural identity he mistakenly supposed himself to be rejecting. It is certainly possible to reject parts of one's cultural identity, but it normally involves appealing to other parts with which the rejected ones are thought to be inconsistent.

The main reason in favor of Flaubert's resolution of his conflict is that his commitments and attitudes were connected with literary life, which he regarded as essential to his conception of well-being and pursued in defiance of some of the bourgeois cultural values of the prevailing cultural identity. The main reason against Flaubert's resolution is that he got the relation between his literary life and cultural identity partly wrong. But this had little effect on his unconditional commitment to a literary life, which was essential to his conception of well-being.

These two examples illustrate what I think is the right approach to conflict-resolution. Its essential feature is that the reasonable resolution of conflicts among the values of different dimensions depends on adducing and weighing concrete and context-dependent reasons for or against particular resolutions. We find, once again, that there can be no blueprint, no a priori scheme, no overarching theory of conflict-resolution that could be appealed to, because by their very nature they abstract from the concrete and context-dependent considerations on which reasonable resolutions depend.

5.5. Right vs. Wrong Approaches to Conflict-Resolution

It may be objected that this approach to conflict-resolution is unsatisfactory. All that it seems able to do is to call for adducing and weighing reasons for or against particular resolutions without making clear which set of reasons is weightier. This objection is mistaken, but seeing why requires considering the wrong approach to conflict-resolution that the objection presupposes. What makes this approach wrong is that it regards one of the three dimensions of value as overriding and insists that its concerns are alone the reasonable requirements of well-being. The standards, conventions, and values of the other dimensions are, then, said to be reasonable only insofar as they conform to those of the favored dimension.

Absolutists think that cultural and personal values are reasonable only if they conform to the requirements of the human dimension. *Relativists* think that the cultural identity of a particular society determines what supposedly human and personal values are reasonable. *Individualists* think that human and cultural values are reasonable only and to the extent to which they contribute to one's well-being. Absolutists, relativists, and individualists each subordinate two essential dimensions of value by accepting only those segments of them that conform to the standard of the dimension they favor.

Individualists insist that the decisive voice in conflict-resolution is of the *I* who seeks well-being. Relativists claim that it is the voice of *us* who share a cultural identity from which we derive the significance of whatever we do. Absolutists are convinced that it is the voice of *everyone*, or rather would be if everyone were as reasonable as they are. Each hears the other voices, but only faintly, because each finds its own the loudest. What follows is cacophony in which conflict-resolutions proposed in one voice are challenged by those who speak with another voice. Absolutists, relativists, and individualists each mistake the dimension of value they favor for the whole system of values and they fail to see what they do as narrow and false.

Another reasons why these controversies are recalcitrant is that each party emphasizes the importance of some values that the others miss. Absolutists are right: there are human values without which well-being is impossible. But they are wrong to insist that reason requires that human values should always take precedence over cultural and personal values. It may be reasonable to prefer the personal value of a happy family life to the human value of going to Africa to save the lives of starving people, or to opt for the cultural value of saving great works art over risking the human value of lives that may be lost in the effort to save the works of art. It is a dogmatic prejudice to insist that reason always requires us to prefer human values if they conflict with social or personal values.

Relativists are right: cultural values are context-dependent requirements of well-being; protecting them depends on conventions that vary with cultural identities; and this makes cultural values and variable conventions important for well-being. But they are wrong to ignore that the satisfaction of basic needs is also a condition of well-being, and that such needs follow from human nature, not from the cultural identity of a particular society. They are also wrong to ignore that individual well-being depends on personal values that vary with individuals, and that the cultural identity of one's society may be an obstacle to one's well-being.

Individualists are also right: individual well-being has central importance. But they are wrong to ignore that individual well-being depends not just on personal values but also on human and cultural ones, even if individuals fail to recognize them and even if they find the limits human and cultural values set on their pursuit of well-being unacceptable.

The approach of absolutists, relativists, and individualists to conflict-resolution consists in appealing to the standard, conventions, and values of the dimension of value they favor. They all have reasons in favor of resolving conflicts in their own way. But all these reasons are flawed, because they are vitiated by a problem they can neither avoid nor satisfactorily resolve. The problem becomes apparent if we ask about the force of the "should" in the claims of absolutists, relativists, and individualists that conflicts among the values of different dimensions should be resolved in favor of their preferred dimension. According to absolutists, human values should override conflicting cultural and personal values, because these other values protect the satisfaction of basic needs without which well-being is impossible. Relativists insist that cultural values should override conflicting human and personal ones, because they are derived from cultural values. And individualists claim that personal values should override conflicting human and cultural values, because personal values are the ultimate reasons why anyone cares about anything.

None of these claims is obvious, to put it mildly. Why should reasonable people agree that one necessary condition of well-being is the standard of the acceptability of other equally necessary conditions of well-being? If absolutists, relativists, and individualists want to go beyond a question-begging claim that the dimension of value they favor is overriding, then they need to support their claim with reasons that do not assume the overridingness of the favored dimension. They have failed, however, to provide the required reasons. This has not been for lack of trying. It is likely, therefore, that the reasons cannot be found.

Consider absolutists first. Their view is that the reason for resolving conflicts in favor of human values follows from the very nature of morality and reason. Commitment to morality is commitment to a universal and impersonal principle that expresses the requirements of both morality and reason. If cultural and personal values conform to that principle, they are morally acceptable. If they violate the principle, they are immoral and unreasonable. This principle, according to Kant, perhaps the most influential absolutist, is "*the supreme principle of morality*" that provides "moral laws [that] hold for every rational being as such." It prescribes "an imperative which, without being based on, and conditioned by, any further purpose to be attained by a certain line of conduct, enjoins this conduct immediately. This imperative is *categorical* . . . the imperative of *morality*." There is "only a single categorical imperative and it is this: '*Act only on that maxim which you can at the same time will that it should become a universal law*'."[3]

According to Kant, morality requires us to act in the way we want everyone in that situation to act. The categorical imperative holds universally and equally for everyone. The implication is that since cultural and personal values are neither universal nor impersonal, it is unreasonable to favor them over human values if they come into conflict. The dogmatic proclamation of a principle, however, is not enough to make it reasonable to accept it. Why would it be reasonable to follow a principle that makes it our obligation to ignore both our cultural identity and our conception of well-being from which we derive the significance of whatever we do? Kant says that we should ignore them, because reason and morality require it. The obvious response is that there is something very wrong with Kant's conception of reason and morality. What is wrong is that they take no account of the plurality of values, of conflicts among values, and of the central importance of human well-being that any acceptable conception of reason and morality must recognize. This, I believe, was what motivated Nietzsche's response that we should seek a "new immoral or at least unmoralistic . . . anti-Kantian . . . 'categorical imperative' . . . which will articulate this *new demand*: we need a critique of moral values, the value of these values themselves must first be called in question."[4]

Kant had grossly inflated the importance of the human dimension of value in which moral considerations are indeed overriding. He unjustifiably denied the perfectly reasonable contributions of the cultural and personal dimensions to human well-being. And he arbitrarily reinterpreted the requirements of reason and morality to suit his mistaken views. Kant had thereby accomplished the remarkable feat of generating skepticism about what he was most concerned with placing beyond doubt. Reason requires us to acknowledge the importance of each dimension of value for human well-being.[5]

I turn next to the relativists' attempt to establish the supremacy of the cultural dimension in conflict-resolution. Their view is that what are thought to be human and personal values are in fact the cultural values of a society. There can be no genuine conflict between cultural and human or personal values, because all values are cultural, parts of the prevailing cultural identity of one's society. According to relativists, reasons for or against values must be internal to the cultural identity of those who hold the values. On this basis, they deny that the human or the personal dimension of value could provide a reason external to the prevailing cultural identity, because cultural identity is the standard that determines what counts as a reason. External reasons would have to be based on standards external to cultural identity, but, relativists say, we would never have a reason to accept such a standard.[6]

Relativists are right to stress that there are values that reflect nothing more than the prevailing cultural identity. But they are wrong to suppose that all values are like that. As we have seen, human values depend on basic physiological, psychological, and social needs that all human beings have and their satisfaction is a universal requirement of all human well-being, no matter how it is conceived. Cultural identity, of course, influences whether and how basic needs are satisfied in a particular context, but their satisfaction is necessary for human well-being independently of the prevailing cultural identity. The universal requirements of well-being, therefore, provide one type of reason external to cultural identity.

On the basis of such external reasons societies can be compared, criticized, or justified. A society whose standard of living is above the subsistence level is better than one whose standard of living is below it. One that prohibits child prostitution, the mutilation of criminals, or the torture of dissenters is better than another that allows such barbarities. There are, therefore, some external reasons, and cultural identity is not the bedrock on which all values must rest. Human values may conflict with cultural values and it is not a foregone conclusion that the cultural values should override the human ones. The relativist conflict-resolution, therefore, fails.

The same conclusion may be reached by noticing the not uncommon occurrence that individuals reject their cultural identity. Educated Westerners have become itinerant Buddhists monks; Indian peasants Cambridge dons; Dinka cowherds professional basketball players; socialites troglodytes; and many are the prophets and critics who stay at home to proclaim more effectively that their society's cultural identity is irredeemably corrupt. Not all such people were unreasonable and some of them have good reasons external to the prevailing cultural identity on the basis of which they come to reject it. One reason of this sort is that the prevailing cultural identity is impoverished and excludes conceptions of well-being that reflect many people's commitments and attitudes. The personal values of such people, then, conflict with their cultural values, and they may have a reason to resolve the conflict in favor of their personal values. We find, then, once again that relativists are mistaken in supposing that there are no reasons external to the prevailing cultural identity on which conflict-resolutions could be reasonably based.

This brings us to individualism, according to which all reasonable conflict-resolutions must appeal to personal reasons derived from the individual conceptions of well-being that is the standard of evaluation in the personal dimension.[7] Individualists need not deny that there are human and cultural values, required and variable conventions, basic needs and a shared cultural identity. What they must insist on is that individuals have reason to take them into consideration if, and only if, they contribute to their well-being. Individualists, therefore, resolve all conflicts between the values of the three dimensions in favor of the values of the personal dimension. This makes individualists similar to relativists, because both deny that there are any reasons external to the dimension of value to which they ascribe overriding importance; they differ only about the dimension they favor.

There is a sense in which the individualists' conflict-resolution is trivially true. If we are to resolve conflicts reasonably, *we* must recognize the reasons that count for or against the conflicting values, conventions, or standards. The question is what kinds of reasons we recognize as counting and how heavily do we deem them to count. Once this question is asked, the individualists' answer will be seen as false or unhelpful. False, if it leaves it simply up to us to decide what we count as reasons, since we often derive our reasons from mistaken attitudes, incoherent commitments, and unrealistic conceptions of well-being. This may happen, for instance, if we fail to count as reasons the satisfaction of our basic needs or of those we care about, or if we ignore our dependence on the prevailing cultural identity. Reasons can be given for criticizing such failures, and these reasons will be external to what we recognize as a reason.

If, however, the individualists' answer presupposes reasonable attitudes, commitments, and conception of well-being, then it will recognize the relevance of basic needs and cultural identity. In that case, however, conflicts among human, cultural, and personal values will recur within the personal dimension. Individualists, then, have not resolved the conflicts but merely reinterpreted them, and the need for a reasonable resolution will have been unmet. This time, however, it cannot be met by appealing to one's conception of well-being, because the conflicting components have all been acknowledged by individualists to be relevant to well-being. The conflict, then, will persist until reasons in addition to individual conceptions of well-being are adduced. If such reasons are found, the individualists' conflict-resolution fails, since it appeals to reasons other than individual conceptions of well-being. If they cannot be found, then the individualists' preferred conflict-resolution will be arbitrary.

I conclude that the absolutist, relativist, and individualist approaches to conflict-resolution fail. Each is vitiated by the narrow and false view of claiming overriding importance for one of the dimensions of value. Each is right to stress the importance the dimension it favors, but each is wrong to exaggerate its importance and denigrate the importance of the others. Their approaches rest on a shared mistaken assumption. In Isaiah Berlin's words, this assumption is "that all men have one true purpose . . . the ends of all rational beings must of necessity fit into a single universal, harmonious pattern . . . all conflict . . . is due solely to the clash of reason with the irrational or the insufficiently rational . . . that such clashes are, in principle, avoidable." I join Berlin in recognizing the long history and pervasive influence of this assumption, and yet holding that in accepting it "Socrates and the creators of the central Western tradition in ethics and politics who followed him have been mistaken for more than two millenia."[8]

The Socratic view mistakenly assumes that, if we have not erred in our thinking and considered all relevant facts, then reason will lead us to a universally and impersonally binding conclusion that establishes what we should believe and do. It is unreasonable to reject this conclusion, unless we have reason to think that we erred or have failed to consider all the relevant facts. But if we have no such reason, then we must either accept the conclusion and act on it, or stand convicted of irrationality.

The undoubted force and attraction of the Socratic view has been greatly strengthened by the spectacular successes of the physical and biological sciences when they employ reason thus understood to discover and explain the relevant aspects of the natural world. But the sciences do not exhaust our interest in the world. We are interested also in how we should live, given our understanding of the world. We all have some more or less articulate conception of well-being, and we want to live according to it to the extent to which circumstances allow. We are vitally interested in evaluating what we fallibly take to be the facts from the point of view of our well-being. Our system of values is an expression of this interest.

Part of the purpose of this chapter has been to show that, contrary to the Socratic view, there is no unitary point of view from which the facts could be evaluated, because our system of values has three dimensions and the evaluation of facts varies with their values, conventions, and standards. It may be the point of view of the personal, cultural, or human dimension of value. Since there is a great plurality of personal and cultural values out of which a great plurality of cultural identities and conceptions of well-being are continually formed, the cultural and personal dimensions of value vary with societies and individuals and do not form a unitary point of view. Moreover, the many different evaluations that follow from the different dimensions often conflict, and this makes the plurality of reasonable evaluations even greater and even less unitary. If we bear in mind this plurality, it becomes obvious that there can be no universally and impersonally binding answer to the question of what different people in different contexts should do to pursue their well-being.

When defenders of the Socratic view of reason behold what they see as the hopelessly messy plurality of points of view, conventions, values, conflicts, and standards within a society, they despair of reaching the kind of conclusions that the physical and biological sciences have succeeded in reaching. They are right to despair of that, but they are wrong to despair of the evaluative uses of reason. There are reasonable evaluations and conflicts among the values of different dimensions can be reasonably resolved, provided it is recognized that the evaluative uses of reason are very different from its scientific uses.

I have attempted to show that a society is reasonable if it enables those who live in it to form and to pursue their individual conceptions of well-being. This requires that the prevailing conventions should protect the human, cultural, and personal values we need for our well-being. And it requires also that there be a reasonable approach to the resolution of unavoidable conflicts between these values.

Our well-being depends, then, on the availability of a system of values that provides both the possibilities out of which we select some to form a reasonable conception of well-being and the limits within which we try to realize the selected possibilities. But, as I have argued in the preceding three chapters, it also depends on increasing our control by correcting our attitudes and commitments to these values and limits, and by forming realistic conceptions of well-being out of some of them.

All these activities can be done well or badly, better or worse. Doing them well, or at least better, depends on critical reflection. It guides us in making personal decisions about how, given our individual history, experiences, and circumstances, we should go about correcting our all too likely mistakes in forming a more reasonable conception of well-being, holding more coherent and realistic attitudes, and ordering better our commitments. Reasonable decisions about such matters are by their very nature particular and personal, and cannot be universal and impersonal. One consequence of the mistaken assumption that reasonable conflict-resolutions must be universal and impersonal is the widespread contemporary dissatisfaction with both reason and our society. I offer the three-dimensional view of value and the place of reason in it as a vastly preferable alternative to the loss of nerve that leads to this feckless dissatisfaction.

There is, however, a major problem that arises for each of these dimensions. For the human dimension, it is the prevalence of evil; for the cultural dimension, it is widespread disenchantment; and for the personal dimensions, it is pervasive boredom. In the next four chapters, I consider these problems and how we may reasonably cope with them.

6

The Human Dimension
and Evil

The last three chapters were about how we can make our lives better. I have argued that, although we cannot escape contingencies, we can increase our control, and thereby decrease our vulnerability to them. But increasing control, critical reflection, and reasonable conceptions of well-being belong to the bright side of the human condition, and it also has a dark side. It is an optimistic illusion to suppose that the possibility of human well-being has sufficient motivating force to lead us to try to realize it. The dark side of our condition reminds us that we also have contrary motives, that the values of the human dimension are routinely violated, and that evil is prevalent. A realistic view of the human condition is incompatible with optimistic illusions about our commitment to reason and well-being. Comforting as they are, these illusions ought to be abandoned, because they prevent us from facing the prevalence of evil. And unless we face it, we cannot do anything about it. This chapter is a secular attempt to face it; the next explores what we might do about it.

6.1. What is Evil?

Morality is the primary mode of evaluation in the human dimension, and evil is the most serious and succinct moral condemnation in English, much worse than moral badness. It involves depraved, malignant, monstrous actions that violate universal human values and required conventions in a way that breaches the bulwark between civilized life and barbarism. To discuss it, one must dwell on "a sense of . . . outrage, of horror, of baseness, of brutality, and, most important, a sense that a barrier, assumed to be firm . . . has been knocked over, and a feeling that, if this horrible, or outrageous, or squalid, or brutal, action is possible, then anything is possible and nothing is forbidden, and all restraints are threatened. . . . The fear that one may feel is a fear of human nature."[1] Facing evil makes us realize that if human beings can be that callous, cruel, fanatical, or ruthless, then there are no limits to man's inhumanity to man. An abyss opens up and a glimpse into it is horrifying. No wonder we are reluctant to face evil. But if we do not keep it at arm's length and think, feel, or imagine ourselves into the positions of the evildoers and their victims, we come to deeply disturbing malignant motives and immense suffering.

Clarity about evil calls for concrete examples. They are unfortunately readily available and familiar. The ones that follow involve murder, deliberate homicide committed, as the law says, with malice aforethought. It obviously deprives its victims of the human value of life and, in normal circumstances, violates a required convention that protects a necessary condition of well-being. The examples are from the last hundred years or so, but countless others could be drawn from other historical periods.

Between 1914 and 1918, the Turks massacred about a million and a half Armenians. In 1931, Stalin ordered the murder of prosperous peasants, called kulaks, and about two million of them were executed or deported to concentration camps where they died slowly as a result of forced labor in extreme cold and on starvation diet. During the great terror of 1937–38, two million more were murdered at Stalin's orders. In 1937–38, the Japanese murdered about half a million Chinese in Nanking. During World War II, about six million Jews, two million prisoners of war, and half a million gypsies, mental defectives, and homosexuals were murdered in Nazi Germany. After India's independence in 1947, over a million Muslims and Hindus were murdered in religious massacres. In the 1950–51 campaign against so-called counter-revolutionaries in Mao's China, about one million people were murdered, and the so-called Great Leap Forward of 1959–63 caused the death of an estimated sixteen to thirty million people from starvation. Pol Pot in Cambodia presided over the murder of about two million people. In 1992–95, about two hundred thousand Muslims were murdered in Bosnia by Serb nationalists. In 1994, almost one million people were murdered in Rwanda. To this list of mass murders many more could be added from Afghanistan, Argentina, Chile, the Congo, Iran, Iraq, Sudan, Uganda, and numerous other places. These examples, however, only illustrate, but do not define, what evil is.[2]

   The definition I propose focuses, in the first instance, on evil actions, and identifies five features that jointly make actions evil. First, the actions cause *grievous harm*. In the examples, the grievous harm is murder, but it may be dismemberment, torture, enslavement, blinding, and so forth. Second, the victims are *innocent*. They were not murdered because of something they have done, but because they were Armenians, kulaks, Chinese, Jews, gypsies, homosexuals, Muslims, Hindus, city dwellers, Tutsis, or just those who had the misfortune to be anathematized by some ideologically motivated fanatic. These victims have done nothing to deserve the grievous harm inflicted on them. What is done to them, there-fore, cannot be explained as punishment, revenge, or self-defense. Third, if the evil-doers are normally intelligent and not incapacitat-ed, for instance, by mental illness, drugs, or alcohol, then they must know that their actions cause grievous harm. Normally intelligent people may not know whether some actions, such as cosmetic surgery, running a marathon, or taking LSD, are harmful. But they cannot fail to know that murder, dismemberment, torture, enslavement, and blinding do cause grievous harm. If they know it and nevertheless do it, then their actions are *deliberate*. Fourth, the deliberate infliction of grievous harm on innocent victims may or may not reflect the evil-doers' ill will toward them. If it does, then their ill will, in turn, reflects their beliefs and emotions (a point to which I will return). For the moment, it will suffice to say only that if their deliberate infliction of grievous harm on innocent victims reflects their ill will, then the evil-doers' motives are *malevolent*. Cruelty, envy, fanaticism, hatred, jealousy, prejudice, rage, ruthlessness, or a combination of some of them are examples of malevolent motives. Fifth, actions that have the first four features may or may not be *morally unjustifiable*. It is hard to conceive how a malevolently motivated action that deliberately causes grievous harm to innocent victims could be morally justified. But let us suppose that there are some extreme situations in which such an action would help to avoid even more grievous harm. If, however, no moral justification is available, then the action is evil. Those who think that an action that has the four features is nevertheless morally justified must provide the justification, since there is an overwhelming presumption against its possibility.

An action is evil, then, if (1) it causes grievous harm to (2) innocent victims, and it is (3) deliberate, (4) malevolently motivated, and (5) morally unjustifiable. Actions that have these features may still be more or less evil, because they may differ in the quantity and quality of the harm they cause, and in the degree of deliberation and malevolence involved in them.

Evil actions are, by definition, morally unjustifiable, but they may be excusable if there are exempting or extenuating circumstances, such as irresistible coercion, great provocation, momentary insanity, or ignorance of relevant facts. The crucial difference between justified and excused actions is that justified actions are not evil, whereas excused actions are. Excused actions do not reflect adversely on their agents, because there are circumstances that acquit the agents or lessen their responsibility for doing them. Perhaps the most frequently proposed excuse is that the agents sincerely but mistakenly believe that their victims are guilty or that the grievous harm they cause is morally justified. If such beliefs were true, the actions would not be evil. But the beliefs are false, although the agents believe that they are true. Whether such beliefs qualify as excuses depends on how reasonable they are. If they are self-serving rationalizations, they fail as excuses. If others in the agents' position would also be likely to hold them, then they might serve as excuses. It must be remembered, however, that the excuse is sought for mass murder that includes children and obviously harmless adults. It is extremely unlikely that anyone could reasonably believe that such victims are guilty or that murdering them could be excused. If, nevertheless, a legitimate excuse is available, then the evil-doers' responsibility is lessened, although, of course, the actions remain evil. In this chapter, I consider only what makes actions, people, or social conditions evil and postpone discussion of responsibility until the next chapter.

We may say, then, that people are evil if their habitual actions are evil and there is no pattern of good actions that may counterbalance the evil ones. Social conditions are evil if they regularly lead people subject to them to do evil. The primary subjects of which evil can be predicated are actions; the secondary subjects are people; and tertiary subjects are social conditions. This is not merely a grammatical observation. It indicates the direction in which understanding evil must proceed. We must explain first what makes actions evil; then we can go on to ask why people do evil habitually; and lastly inquire why people create and maintain social conditions that lead to habitual evil-doing. Social conditions would not be evil if they were not created and maintained by evil people. And people would not be evil if their actions were not habitually evil.

Actions, people, and social conditions can be more or less evil, and evil actions may shade into morally bad actions, because the grievousness of the harm, the innocence of the victims, the malevolence of motivation, the deliberateness and moral justifiability of their performance are often matters of degree about which reasonable and morally committed people can disagree. Although there is often a clear difference between evil and bad actions, there are likely to be cases in which the difference becomes unclear. I do not think that this has a substantive bearing on the account I will provide. Given the mass murder of many millions, there can be no reasonable doubt that evil is prevalent. The question is why it is prevalent.

6.2. The Secular Problem of Evil

It is well known that there is a theological problem of evil. If God is perfect in goodness, knowledge, and power, then why has He created our world in which evil is prevalent? The favored answer, that evil is created by human beings, not by God, is unsatisfactory. God is said to have created human beings, as well as everything else, and if human beings cause evil, then God has created them in a way that they would cause it. Why would a perfect God create a very imperfect world? Christians, of course, have struggled with and proposed various solutions to this problem. My present concern, however, is not with their putative solutions but with pointing out the less well known fact that there is also a secular problem of evil that is surprisingly similar to the theological problem.

The secular problem arises in the following way. Normal human beings in normal circumstances prefer well-being to its opposite. Reason requires that we should do what we can to protect the conditions of well-being. Yet the prevalence of evil shows that we often violate these conditions. If we accept the optimistic view inspired by one version of the Enlightenment that human beings are basically reasonable and good, then how could evil be prevalent? The favored answer is that evil is prevalent, because human beings are corrupted by social conditions. But this is as unsatisfactory as the theological answer that attributes evil to human beings rather than to God. For just as a perfect God would not have created imperfect human beings, so reasonable and good human beings would not have created corrupting social conditions. Just as evil seems to be incompatible with the nature of God as conceived by many Christian theologians, so evil seems to be incompatible with human nature as conceived by many secular thinkers.

That many influential thinkers in the Enlightenment tradition do hold this view of human nature is borne out by what they say. Here is Rousseau: "Man is naturally good; I believe I have demonstrated it" and "the fundamental principle of all morality, about which I have reasoned in all my works . . . is that man is a naturally good creature, who loves justice and order; that there is no original perversity in the human heart."[3]

Kant says virtually the same: man is "*not basically* corrupt (even as regards his original predisposition to good), but rather . . . still capable of improvement" and "man (even the most wicked) does not, under any maxim whatsoever, repudiate the moral law. . . . The law, rather, forces itself upon him irresistibly by virtue of his moral predisposition."[4]

John Stuart Mill speaks of the "leading department of our nature . . . this powerful natural sentiment . . . the social feeling of mankind—the desire to be in unity with our fellow creatures, which is already a powerful principle in human nature, and happily one of those which tend to become stronger, even without inculcation."[5]

John Rawls, who acknowledges writing in the tradition of Rousseau and Kant, claims that "the capacity for moral person-ality . . . no race or recognized group of human beings . . . lacks" and that "moral personality is characterized by two capacities: one for a conception of good, the other for a sense of justice." A conception of the good gives "a moral person . . . a fundamental preference for . . . a mode of life that expresses his nature as a free and equal rational being." And "the sense of justice is continuous with the love of mankind." He claims that "men's propensity to injustice is not a permanent aspect of community life, it is greater or less depending in large part on social institutions."[6] And Philippa Foot treats "moral evil as 'a kind of natural defect'," claims that "acting morally is part of practical rationality," and that "no one can act with full practical rationality in pursuit of a bad end."[7]

It is not unfair, I think, to ascribe a secular faith to the numerous thinkers who hold that human beings are basically reasonable and good.[8] It is a faith, because no evidence is allowed to count against it. When human beings act reasonably and morally, it is counted as evidence that confirms the faith; when they act unreasonably and immorally, it is counted as evidence that they have been corrupted by social conditions, and that also confirms the faith. Defenders of the secular faith should pause to ask: how is it possible that supposedly reasonable and good human beings create and maintain social conditions that are contrary to the well-being of people in their own society? For these defenders of the secular faith, the problem of evil is as serious as it is for their Christian brethren.

Instead of facing the problem, however, they nurture a pleasing illusion and do not ask embarrassing questions about the prevalence of evil. They go to absurd lengths to find excuses for those who violate conditions of well-being. Rawls, for instance, says that "the effort a person is willing to make is influenced by his natural abilities and skills and the alternatives open to him. The better endowed are more likely, other things equal, to strive conscientiously, and there seems to be no way to discount for their greater good fortune." Efforts to contribute to rather than violate well-being, therefore, are "arbitrary from the moral point of view."[9] Enemies of well-being are just as reasonable and good as its friends. Only different social conditions lead them to act differently. Or, as Susan Wolf egregiously puts it, "being psychologically determined to perform good actions is compatible with deserving praise for them, but . . . being psychologically determined to perform bad actions is not compatible with blame."[10] But defenders of the secular faith do not ask the obvious question of why some social conditions are corrupting.

The secular view, however, can be held without this faith. There is another tradition whose defenders may or may not be secular thinkers, but they share realism about the prevalence of evil and unwillingness to accept optimistic illusions about human reason and goodness. Some who belong to this tradition are

Thucydides, Euripides, Machiavelli, Hobbes, Montaigne, Burke, James Fitzjames Stephen, and Freud. What follows in this chapter continues this realistic tradition. Realism, however, does not remove the need to explain why evil is prevalent. To be sure, human beings cause it. But why do they cause it?

6.3. Inadequate Explanations

I will consider four inadequate explanations. They attribute evil to natural causes, moral monsters, uncharacteristic actions, and corrupting social conditions. Each accounts for some cases of evil, but each fails to account for many others. In the next section, I will move toward a more general explanation. The first inadequate explanation is that evil has natural causes.[11] This may be interpreted as the claim that evil is the outcome of natural processes, not of human actions. The grievous harm that befalls innocent victims is the result of earthquakes, draught, tidal waves, and similar natural disasters, or of the non-culpable scarcity of food, money, knowledge, expertise, and other resources. These natural processes cause epidemics, poverty, starvation, and agony.

Such calamities undoubtedly cause much suffering to innocent victims, but they are not evil. For they are neither malevolently motivated nor deliberate. Of course, if the calamities were foreseeable and preventable, then the failure to avert them may be evil. In that case, however, what is evil are not the natural processes, as this explanation claims, but the actions or possibly the people who failed to avert them. And we still need an explanation of the failure to avert them. Furthermore, none of the murders I have listed can be blamed on natural disasters. They were caused by malevolently motivated deliberate human actions.

Natural processes, however, may be interpreted in a much wider sense to include psychological processes within human beings. To say that evil actions are the outcome of natural processes, then, becomes a truism that is no more informative than the banality that what will be will be or that everything has a cause. What we want from an explanation is to tell us why people act on malevolent rather than on benevolent motives, why they deliberately murder innocent victims, why they violate conditions of well-being. To say that they are led to do so by natural processes does not even begin to provide the needed explanation.

The second inadequate explanation attributes evil to moral monsters, among whom we may distinguish two classes. One contains those who do evil for its own sake. They deliberately and malevolently cause grievous harm to their innocent victims. They know what evil is, but they do not recognize that it limits what they may do. Their evil actions are not means but ends in themselves. They may be misanthropes, cynics, or sadists, who believe that everyone, or only those who belong to a particular group, are incorrigibly depraved; or they may be deep ecologists who think that human beings despoil the world, which would be a better place if the species became extinct; or they may believe that their victims are loathsome, because of some characteristic or belief shared by all members of the group to which they belong, as the Nazis believed of Jews and inquisitors of heretics; or they may be ruled by savage, primitive urges, as do the instigators of tribal murders in Africa and ethnic cleansers in Bosnia.

Another class of moral monsters do evil as a means to some end. They know quite well the requirements of morality, but they think that some other consideration is vastly more important. They talk about the teleological suspension of the ethical, where the *telos* may be religious, as do Muslims terrorists, Christian crusaders, or Hindu fanatics. Or the *telos* may be political, as it was for the Jacobins during the terror phase of the French Revolution, or for Lenin as he was consolidating Bolshevik rule in Russia. Or it may be sexual, as exemplified by the Marquis de Sade.

Moral monsters may be born as such, or they may be made. They may start out with dispositions for both good and evil actions, but become monstrous because they are brutalized by their experiences; or rewarded for evil actions; or embittered by disappointed expectations; or scorned, humiliated, or ridiculed time after time; or because they have accepted an evil creed. Regardless of what made them moral monsters, however, they are alike in wanting power in order to transform the world, or some segment of it, in accordance with their ghastly vision. They become mass murderers in order to destroy whoever stands in their way.

Moral monsters undoubtedly exist, and they account for some evil actions, but the vast majority of evil we are familiar with cannot be attributed to them. First of all, moral monsters are bound to be rare, because it is very difficult to be one. It requires great strength of character, self-reliance, and the capacity to live without love, friendship, and trust; the willingness to systematically squelch the little compassion or sympathy they may feel; and the capacity to sustain a perfervid, all-consuming misanthropy. Moral monsters, however, not only have to have these exceptional dispositions, they must also hide their true nature from others. If they did not, they would not be at large long enough in a civilized society to pursue their evil designs.

Secondly, the large-scale evil that led to the murder of tens of millions of people in the examples I have given would not have been possible without the cooperation of a large number of ordinary people. Perhaps Stalin, Hitler, Mao, and others were moral monsters, but they could not by themselves have arrested, transported, sorted, and guarded the innocent victims, organized the details of their murders, found and supplied the necessary resources, disguised from the rest of their society what was going on, pulled the triggers, and got rid of the corpses. Only a fraction of the evil that has been done to the multitude of innocent victims during the last century can be attributed to the actions of moral monsters. The rest had to be done by accomplices who lacked the strength, determination, and bitterness to become moral monsters. It needs to be explained why they did it.[12]

The third inadequate explanation is that evil actions are the uncharacteristic responses of normally reasonable and decent people to extreme situations, sudden emergencies, great provocations, or serious threats. In such cases, people are called upon to deal with predicaments that are far removed from the customary context of their life. It is hard to know what anyone, including oneself, might do when faced with unusual situations. This is partly why the many examples of the what-would-you-do-if sort, such as presented by the Milgram experiments, have an air of unreality. What people may or may not do in unusual situations is an unreliable indicator of what they may or may not do in the normal course of events.[13] Uncharacteristic actions, by their very nature, are rare, because most people most of the time act characteristically. Life would be in an intolerable state of permanent chaos if it were otherwise. Some evil actions are no doubt uncharacteristic, but the prevalence of evil must be explained by the characteristic actions of habitual evil-doers.

Cases in point are the mass murders committed by the moral monsters and their accomplices in the examples I have given. They were done over several years by the same cadre of murderers. They were the routine habitual patterns of action of the secret police, the concentration camp guards, the executioners, the military, and their vast supporting cast. They together made standard operating procedure the political, religious, ethnic, and tribal massacres, the death marches, and the starvation and forced labor of people suspected of being less than fully enthusiastic supporters of vicious regimes. An explanation of evil must account for the actions of ordinary people who become the accomplices of moral monsters, but who lack the monsters exceptional traits.

The fourth inadequate explanation proceeds from the optimistic secular faith I have discussed earlier. According to it, most evil actions are caused by corrupting social conditions, such as poverty, discrimination, persecution, and injustice. Evil actions are the enraged responses of basically reasonable and good people to being victimized by these conditions. Their actions are evil, but they reflect the social conditions that corrupted them, not their evil nature. The prevalence of evil, therefore, is not to be explained by the cruel, envious, fanatical, hateful, jealous, prejudice-ridden, or ruthless dispositions of murderers but by the social conditions that cause them to have these dispositions. The agents of evil actions are held to be as innocent as those on whom they vent their rage. Of the four defective explanations, this is the most widely held one and the least plausible. It is, in fact, obviously untenable, and cries out for explanation how normally intelligent people could take it seriously.

To begin with, there are ways and ways again to respond to corrupting social conditions. We may treat them as adversities and strive to overcome them; become politically active in order to reform them; decide to leave the society where the conditions hold for another we believe is better; resign ourselves to them and seek consolation in religion, family life, or solitude in nature; or become mass murderers. Since the possible responses are many, the response of mass murder cannot be explained merely in terms of corrupting social conditions. It must be explained why the response of moral monsters and their accomplices was mass murder, rather than any of the other possible responses. An adequate explanation, therefore, must take into account the psychological dispositions that inclined some people, but not others, to become mass murderers.

Next, suppose that rage at corrupting social conditions blinds evil-doers to possible responses other than violent ones. Why does the violence take the form of mass murder, rather than, say, the destruction of property, sabotage of public works, or wholesale theft? If the violence must take a murderous form, why is it directed indiscriminately at everyone, such as children, young men and women, and other victims, who cannot possibly be blamed for the social conditions? And if the violence is murderous and indiscriminate, why is it often combined with the humiliation, rape, torture, and mutilation of the victims? Once again, the malevolence of evil actions must be attributed to psychological causes, in addition to social ones.

Furthermore, many of the Nazi, Communist, religious, ethnic, and tribal mass murderers came from relatively prosperous families and were certainly not the victims of poverty, discrimination, persecution, or injustice. If anything, they belonged to a class whose members were exempt or actually benefited from the corrupting social conditions. Their evil actions, therefore, cannot be the result of corruption by social conditions.

Lastly, this often-repeated explanation simply takes for granted the existence of corrupting social conditions. But social conditions do not fall ready-made from the heavens. They are created and maintained by people. If they are corrupting, it is because those who created and maintain them are corrupt. It may be said that they were also corrupted by social conditions, but that merely postpones facing the question of why they created and maintained those corrupting social conditions? Sooner or later the evasion must stop, and reason compels the recognition that it is corrupting social conditions that must be explained by the psychological dispositions of people who create and maintain them, rather than the reverse, which is what this putative explanation attempts to do. Its basic defect is to explain the cause by its own effect: evil actions by corrupting social conditions, when, in fact, evil actions are not the effects but the causes of corrupting social conditions.

Why, then, do so many normally intelligent people accept this farrago of an explanation? Because they are unwilling to question their optimistic faith that human beings are basically reasonable and good. They refuse to face the prevalence of evil, because they would have to give up their comforting faith. But their faith is an enemy of well-being. It leads those who hold it to ignore the most serious threat to well-being: the psychological dispositions of human beings to inflict grievous harm on innocent victims, malevolently, deliberately, and without moral justification. The secular problem of evil is to explain why people act on these dispositions rather than on ones that protect the conditions on which well-being, including their own, depends.

6.4. Toward an Adequate Explanation

The prevalence of evil is a good reason for rejecting the secular faith that human beings are basically reasonable and good. But it is not even a bad reason for accepting the equally implausible view that human beings are basically unreasonable and evil. The facts point to the conclusion that human beings are basically ambivalent. Basic dispositions are mixed. Some incline us to act reasonably and morally, some to act unreasonably and immorally, and some have little to do with either reason or morality. The prevalence of evil shows that in some circumstances unreasonable and evil dispositions come to dominate contrary dispositions. To explain evil is to explain why and how this happens. The explanation must specify both the external circumstances and the internal dispositions that jointly motivate evil-doers to do evil. The explanation I propose proceeds in five steps.

The first step is to recognize that, unlike moral monsters, evil-doers typically do not see their actions as evil. In cases of mass murder, for instance, they may acknowledge that what they have done, and are doing over and over, is killing, but deny that it is evil. They deny that their victims are innocent, that their own motives are malevolent, and that the killings are morally unjustified. They may sincerely say to themselves, or to others if challenged, that their victims are dangerous enemies of their society, that their motive for killing them is the obligation to protect general well-being, and that the killings are morally justified, because the protection of well-being depends on the destruction of its enemies. Killing them is no different from killing in war or in self-defense. Evil-doers may readily grant, indeed might insist, that murder is evil, and indignantly deny that their killings are murders. Their denials are grotesquely mistaken, of course, because their victims *are* innocent, their motives *are* malevolent, and their actions *are* morally unjustifiable, but evil-doers may sincerely believe the opposite.

The ordinary people who became the accomplices of moral monsters may be Nazi or Communist party members, devout defenders of various true faiths, ardent nationalists, dedicated terrorists, or merciless revolutionaries, who may be genuinely convinced of the justice of their mass murders and the viciousness of their victims. If they have doubts about treating their imagined enemies in ways that are normally evil, they can appeal to like-minded political, religious, or historical authorities who reassure them that they are doing the right thing, and praise them for their selfless service to a fine ideal. We know from the testimony of mass murderers and from their histories and biographies that they see themselves as righteous champions of God, history, justice, racial purity, national glory, or whatever. They see evil all right, but ascribe it to their victims, not to themselves.

The second step of the explanation is to make clear that moral monsters and their accomplices see the evil they do very differently. Moral monsters see it as evil, and they do it either for its own sake or for the sake of something they regard as far more important than morality. Their accomplices do not believe that their actions are evil; they think that they are morally justified. In this, they are flagrantly, absurdly, obviously mistaken. Their mistakes are not ordinary errors we are all prone to make from time to time but perverse interpretations of plain facts that rest on no credible reason. They are akin to blaming mental illness on possession by the Devil, infertility on the evil eye, defeat in battle on misreading signs contained in the entrails of a freshly slaughtered chicken, or crop failures on not having sacrificed fat enough cattle to the god of plenty.

If we focus on the egregiously false beliefs of ordinary people who become accomplices to mass murders, we can only marvel at them. Communists say that their victims are plotting a counter-revolution to reverse the laws of history that move us toward a classless egalitarian society in which all manner of things will be well. Nazis claim that Jews are part of a conspiracy to rob the superior Aryan race of its right to dominate the world. Nationalists charge their supposed enemies, often an incompletely assimilated ethnic group in their society, of treacherously obstructing the nation's return to the past glory that rightfully belongs to it. Defenders of what they regard as the true religion condemn defenders of other religions for worshiping false gods, and hold that the true God demands ridding the world of them. Terrorists accuse arbitrarily selected targets of supporting a corrupt system that opposes the rule of those who know where goodness and truth lies.

These mass murderers appeal to ideals to justify the evil they do, but their ideals cannot withstand even superficial examination. Ineradicable differences in capacities, moral conduct, experiences, and reasoned judgment make an egalitarian society that ignores them blatantly unjust and detrimental to human well-being. Racial superiority is untenable, because of decisive historical and genetic evidence for the intermingling of races, because of normative biases involved in selecting for statistical comparisons supposedly important inherited racial characteristics, and because it is impossible to determine the relative importance of inheritance and environment for subsequent performance. The distinction between true and false religions simply ignores that all religions ultimately rest on faith, that all of them equally lack evidential basis, and that it is sacrilegious to suppose that God, if there were one, would demand mass murder. The terrorists' dream of rule by authorities with special access to goodness and truth ignores the overwhelming historical evidence of the incomparably greater suffering caused by such authorities than whatever it is the terrorists blame democratic regimes for causing.

The plots of which these mass murderers accuse their victims of hatching are, if possible, even less plausible than the ideals to which they appeal. Counter-revolution, worldwide Jewish conspiracy, worshiping false gods, and democratic conspiracies to perpetuate injustice are, one and all, absurd inventions used by evil-doers to justify mass murder. But even if their justifications were accepted, they would not explain why the victims of mass murders include children, barely intelligent adults, and the decrepit old who could not possibly be plotting anything. Evil-doers add to the false ideal and the absurd plot the grotesque claim that all their victims are essentially corrupted by an ineradicable component of their character—capitalist class consciousness, Jewish parentage, the values of a false religion, or Western attitudes—that makes them enemies regardless of what they actually do. That is why their victims cannot be innocent; why they have to be killed; why evil-doers can claim to act on motives that have the highest moral credentials; and why their mass murders are in fact the morally justified killings of the most dangerous enemies of human well-being.[14]

The third step is to explain how these grotesquely mistaken beliefs could be held by normally intelligent people who are the accomplices of moral monsters, and who believe themselves to be committed to morality. The explanation I propose is that they have been led to these beliefs by their acceptance of an ideology. I hasten to stress that I do not claim that all ideologies lead to mass murder or that all evil is ideological. I claim only that ideologies readily lend themselves to the justification of mass murder, and this makes them dangerous, regardless of whether they are secular or religious, political or moral, nationalistic or racial. The evidence for this is the historical record of the evil done in the name of Communism, Nazism, religion, nationalism, and terrorism.

The essential feature of ideologies is an evaluative attitude that combines a set of *beliefs* about the nature of the world, an *ideal* of how human life ought to be, an explanation of why there is a yawning *gap* between the ideal and the miserable actual conditions, and a *program* for closing the gap between how life ought to be and how it is. Ideologies are dangerous, because they tend to breed true believers with dogmatic attitudes who hold that theirs is the one and only ideal of how human beings ought to live. The ideal may be set down in a sacred text, exemplified in the life of an exceptional individual, dictated by the laws of history, sociology, or psychology, located in a past idyllic condition uncorrupted by civilization, or represented in a future Utopia of perfected human nature, and so on.

All ideologies hold that human well-being requires living in conformity to whatever the ideal happens to be. The failure to conform to it obstructs the pursuit of well-being, and reason and human well-being make it obligatory for ideologues to remove the obstruction from the way. This may be done by educating those who do not understand the ideal, or by preventing those who understand and reject the ideal from jeopardizing its pursuit. Mild coercion by education or forceful coercion by whatever means are necessary and natural concomitants of the pursuit of the ideal. According to ideologues, coercion for these reasons is not only justified but required by reason and morality, because human well-being depends on it.

The widespread appeal of ideologies is undeniable. They cut through the complexities, moral ambiguities, compromises, and malaise that beset so many people in modern life, and fill the gap left by the waning of traditional religious belief. They provide clarity about good and evil, and offer simple and consistent judgments to those who yearn for guidance about how they should live. Countless people survey their comfortable or miserable existence, the routines of everyday life, uninteresting or soul-destroying jobs, dispirited relationships with similarly disenchanted souls, and say to themselves, or perhaps to each other, that there must be more to life. Ideologies provide what they yearn for. By committing themselves to an ideology, people gain a sense of identity, acquire membership in a community of like-minded people, find an ideal they could follow, receive an explanation of why the existing conditions are wretched, and are told what needs to be done to improve them. One might be tempted to say that all this is to the good. But the temptation should be resisted, because ideologies encourage their accomplices to justify the evil they do.

The perniciousness of the justification the accomplices derive from ideologies becomes apparent if we do not allow abstractions to obscure the concreteness of what is going on in mass murders. On the one hand, there are the accomplices who time after time pull the triggers, hang, bury alive, bayonet, or burn hundreds of helpless victims, including children, old people, pregnant women. The immediate, undeniable experience of the accomplices is the face-to-face massacring of people who bleed, beg, pray, hold on to each other as they helplessly face imminent death. On the other hand, there is the grotesque story the accomplices tell themselves of why they are murdering these people. They reassure themselves with ideological catchphrases that they are working for the classless society, saving the world from a conspiracy, doing God's will, making the world just, and so forth. What could possess them to believe that these absurd abstractions, whose theoretical background they understand, at best, only faintly, could justify the suffering they cause and witness?

The answer, of course, is that the catchphrases are not the reasons for what they are doing. The accomplices use the ideological slogans to justify to themselves the horrendous actions that they know are normally evil. They can, then, say to themselves that their actions are justified, because they are saving the world from the enemies of human well-being. The ideologies whose slogans they parrot allow them to believe obvious falsehoods about their victims and thereby deceive themselves about the true nature of their actions. But what the accomplices care about is not human well-being but murdering their imagined enemies. They are not engaged in the ruthless pursuit of an ideological ideal. The ideal is only for show. That is why they can shrug off its utter implausibility. Their rhetoric of dedication to human well-being is phony, but the rhetoric excoriating imagined enemies is heartfelt. Why, then, do the accomplices join moral monsters in excoriating and murdering their imagined enemies? Why do they bother with the ideology and with swallowing a highly implausible case involving false ideals, ridiculous plots, and the ineradicably corrupt character traits of their imagined enemies? Why do they invent imagined enemies?

These questions lead to the final, fifth, step of my proposed explanation. I have stressed the importance of ideologies for the explanation of mass murders. Their importance, however, is not that they provide motives for the murders but that they direct and justify the evil actions prompted by motives evil-doers have independently of ideologies. These motives are the various forms of malevolence—cruelty, envy, fanaticism, hatred, jealousy, prejudice, rage, and ruthlessness—that are one of the defining characteristics of evil actions. In civilized societies and normal circumstances, most of us try not to act on such motives. We are constrained by moral limits, by commitment to the well-being of others, and by benevolent motives, which we have alongside malevolent ones. If these constraints are effective, they stop us from acting on malevolent motives, but they do not stop us from having them. They remain as possibilities, on which we may act, if we face serious hardships, provocations, or temptations.

We all have malevolent motives of various kinds and strength. If we did not have them, self-control, conscience, moral education, prudence, discipline, legal prohibitions, and law enforcement would be largely superfluous. But, of course, they are needed, as we all know directly from our own case, indirectly from the observation of our children and the testimonies of those close to us, and, a step further removed, from witnessing occasions on which people's self-control has slipped and their malevolence was momentarily revealed, as the venom may be in a clever witticism.

Malevolent motives clamor for expression when for good or bad reasons we become dissatisfied with our lives. Ideologies are dangerous, because they encourage the expression of malevolent motives by providing scapegoats—counter-revolutionaries, conspirators, idolaters, traitors, enemies of the good and the true—and justifying their persecution. Ideologies supply abstract claptrap whose slogans the accomplices can parrot to explain to themselves and others why they are right to vent their malevolence on their victims.

Ideologies provide tangible benefits for the accomplices: they make their evil actions acceptable; they legitimate the relief they feel when they express their malevolent motives; they transform their unsatisfying lives by providing them with activities said to be meaningful and important; they allow them to lay to rest their lingering doubts by camaraderie with fellow accomplices; and they receive authoritative praise for the evil they do. Accomplices shrug off the implausibility of the ideology, the absurdity of its ideal, the grotesque plots and character traits it attributes to the victims, because the benefit the ideology provides for them is a justification for venting their malevolence.

The foregoing are steps toward an explanation of evil, but they do not amount to a full explanation. I have discussed only mass murders committed by ordinary people who became accomplices of moral monsters. But there are many kinds of evil about which I have said nothing. I doubt that their explanation would be very different from that I have given of mass murder, but that, of course, needs to be shown. Nor have I claimed that this explanation of mass murder is the only one needed. Evil actions may be explained as the results of culpable negligence, or as the characteristic actions of moral monsters, or as uncharacteristic aberrations of ordinary people, or as responses to corrupting social conditions. I do think, however, that these explanations are inadequate, because they account only for a few evil actions, not for the prevalence of evil. The explanation I have given seems to me to go much further toward understanding why evil is prevalent than these other explanations do.

6.5. Evil and the Human Condition

The just-completed explanation of why many normally intelligent people, who are not moral monsters, become accomplices to mass murder has two essential components: one external, the other internal to these evil-doers. The internal explanation is their malevolent motivation. The external one is the ideology they opportunistically adopt to explain and justify the evil they do. Ideology enables them to express their malevolence and to disguise from themselves and others the true nature of their actions. They do evil, but they do not see it as evil.

Evil-doers often give reasons for their evil actions, and, as we have seen, reasons can be given to explain why they disguise from themselves their real reasons. Some of these reasons are rational-izations, but evil-doers may have reasons for their rationalizations as well, even if they are not aware of them. Evil-doing, therefore, serves a purpose. It need not be unreasonable, even though it is certainly immoral. The significance of the possibility of giv-ing reasons for evil-doing is considerable. It shows that a central assumption of Western moral thought is mistaken: the require-ments of reason and morality do not coincide. Immorality need not be unreasonable. The secular problem of evil is to cope with evil in light of the failure of this hoary assumption. Evil is an enemy of human well-being, but malevolent motives in combination with ideologies supply reasons for doing evil, just as benevolent motives in combination with moral commitments supply reasons for not doing evil. Our motives are divided, and we both seek and hinder our well-being. This gives rise to the secular problem of evil and forms part of the human condition.

The first requirement of responding to the secular problem of evil is to acknowledge its existence. A great obstacle to it is the optimistic faith of Rousseau, Kant, Mill, and their numerous followers. Their faith rests on the assumption that the requirements of reason and morality coincide. But the assumption is mistaken and their faith is just as unsubstantial a dream as the religious faith in the existence of a moral order that permeates the scheme of things. The assumption and the faith lead to their failure to face evil, and they ought to be abandoned. The second requirement is to hold evil-doers responsible for what they do, even if they do not believe that what they do is evil. I will discuss this in the next chapter. The third requirement is to weaken the reasons for doing evil and to strengthen attractive and morally acceptable alternatives to it. This will be one of the concerns of the chapters following the next. There is, however, as great an obstacle to meeting the second and third requirements as to meeting the first. If we are indeed divided in our motivation, then our efforts to cope with the secular problem of evil will be handicapped by the same problem with which we try to cope. The proposed treatment is infected with the disease it is meant to cure. This is also part of the human condition and a reason for abandoning the optimistic faith. It has been well said that out of the crooked timber of humanity nothing straight has ever come.

7

Responsibility for Evil

The conclusion reached in the last chapter was that there may be reasons for doing evil actions. The most obvious reasons are that evil-doers may believe that inflicting grievous harm on innocent victims, malevolently, deliberately, and without moral justification will be satisfying or will relieve the frustration of suppressing their malevolent motives. Since evil actions are contrary to morality, anyone committed to morality will be committed to respond to evil actions. Reasonable responses may aim to weaken reasons for doing evil. This is the topic of the present chapter. Or they may aim to strengthen reasons for alternatives to evil-doing. This is the subject of subsequent chapters.

The general approach to weakening reasons for evil-doing is to hold evil-doers responsible for the evil they do. This involves blaming them. But blame may range from the most severe punishment to regarding evil-doers as tainted, but excused. How severe should blame be depends on the availability and strength of excuses. Accordingly, responsibility for evil-doing may be full, if there is no excuse; mitigated, if there is some excuse; and non-existent, if the excuse is strong enough to exempt evil-doers from all blame. The strongest possible excuse is that the normally evil action was in a particular case the least morally unacceptable alternative. Such an excuse may shade into moral justification.

The discussion of responsibility that follows has three features that reflect the argument of the last chapter. First, it concentrates on evil actions, such as murder, dismemberment, torture, enslavement, or blinding, not on minor immoralities, like breaking a promise, telling a lie, or accepting a bribe, which normally do not cause grievous harm. Second, although responsibility is for evil actions, it is evil-doers who are held responsible, since they are the agents who performed evil actions. They are held responsible, however, for what they did, not for who they are. Evil actions normally reflect on their agents, so that evil is reflexive, but not all actions reflect on their agents, since actions may be coerced, uncharacteristic, done in ignorance, or in a fit of insanity. I will begin with the question of when an evil action reflects on its agent. Third, the discussion focuses on the responsibility of evil-doers for patterns of evil actions, rather than single ones. Such patterns are normally evidence that evil-doers possess some character trait, such as cruelty, ruthlessness, or fanaticism, that regularly prompts them to act cruelly, ruthlessly, or fanatically and cause grievous harm to innocent people. Single evil actions may be excused on various grounds, but habitual patterns of them are far less likely to be excusable in this way. And, as we have seen, the prevalence of evil is due to habitual patterns of evil-doing, not to the much rarer uncharacteristic evil actions of normally decent people.

7.1. The Reflexivity of Evil

When do patterns of evil actions reflect on their agents? The received view is that only if their actions are done *freely*, that is, uncoerced by either external force or threat, or by internal compulsion; if they *know* both what they are doing and what the relevant circumstances are; and if they *understand* the moral significance of their actions. I will call such actions *intentional*, but nothing depends on this label; they might be called autonomous, or reasonable, or informed, or self-conscious, or freely willed, and so forth. The salient point is that the actions reflect on their agents only if the actions are the direct consequences of the agents' psychological states that are uncoerced, self-aware, and factually and morally informed. If evil actions follow from such a psychological state, then the agents are rightly blamed and held responsible for performing them. A concise statement of the received view, then, is that agents are responsible for their intentionally evil actions and they are not responsible for their unintentionally evil actions. I will argue that the received view is indefensible and one of the major obstacles to responding to evil reasonably. First, however, I want to document that the view is actually held. Here are some illustrative examples from well-known works.

According to Stuart Hampshire, "a man becomes more and more a free and responsible agent the more he at all times knows what he is doing, in every sense of this phrase, and the more he acts with a definite and clearly formed intention."[1] Harry Frankfurt says that the conditions of moral responsibility are "that a person has done what he wanted to do, that he did it because he wanted to do it, and that the will by which he was moved was his will because it was the will he wanted."[2] H. L. A. Hart writes that "all civilized penal systems make liability to punishment . . . depend not merely on the fact that the person . . . has done the outward act of a crime, but on his having done it in a certain frame of mind or will. These mental or intellectual elements are various . . . but the most prominent . . . and in many ways the most important is a man's intention. . . . Intention . . . is usually . . . *sufficient* . . . for conviction of a man who has killed another. Intention . . . is also generally *necessary* for serious crime."[3] Thomas Hill defends the Kantian view that "in trying to decide whether one should do something, it is extremely important to determine what one's intentions and policies would be in doing it. These, together with one's underlying motive for having those intentions and policies, are what determine the kind of moral worth one's actions will have."[4] Robert Kane reports that "most of us naturally assume that freedom and responsibility . . . require that if we acted voluntarily, intentionally, and rationally, we could have done otherwise voluntarily, intentionally, and rationally." And he adds that " 'voluntarily' means here 'in accordance with one's will'; 'intentionally' means 'knowingly' and 'on purpose';

and 'rationally' means 'having good reasons and acting for those reasons'."[5]

Bearing in mind the received view, let us now consider the well-documented and extreme case of Franz Stangl's pattern of mass murders.[6] The Nazis had two kinds of concentration camps: one for forced labor on starvation diet, the other for extermination. There was a slim chance for survival in the former, but virtually none in the latter. The most conservative estimate is that about two million people were murdered in the extermination camps and about eighty survived. Treblinka was one of the four extermination camps, and the estimate is that 900,000 people were murdered in it between 1942 and 1943, when it was closed down. During this time, Stangl was the commanding SS officer in charge of the camp. He set up the system and supervised its efficient functioning. Each morning trains transporting about 5,000 men, women, and children arrived and were unloaded. By the end of the day all were gassed, their corpses incinerated, and the gas chambers and crematoria readied for the next day. Stangl was decorated and promoted for being the best of all camp commanders.

After the war Stangl fled from Germany and eventually settled in Brazil. In 1968, he was arrested by the Brazilian police, extradited to what was then West Germany, tried and convicted, and received the most severe available penalty: life imprisonment. During the trial he admitted the facts. After the trial, while in prison, he agreed to be interviewed at length by a journalist, Gitta Sereny. She spoke German as a native, was a widely respected authority on the horrors of Nazi Germany, and the author of a classic work, *Into that Darkness*,[7] based on her tape-recorded interviews with Stangl. She was passionately concerned with understanding Stangl's character, motivation, and feelings about what he had done. Stangl agreed to the interviews, during which only the two of them were present. Sereny made it her business to find out all she could about Stangl's past, career in the SS, the workings of Treblinka, and Stangl's life between the camp closing and his arrest. Sereny believed Stangl when he told her that the interviews were the first occasions on which he felt free to talk about what had happened. I strongly recommend this book to anyone who has doubts about there being a secular problem of evil.

Let us now consider Stangl's responsibility. If this man was not responsible for the mass murders in Treblinka, it is hard to see how anyone could ever be held responsible for anything. But Stangl denied his responsibility. We need to understand how Stangl thought about this and whether there was more to his thinking than a craven attempt to obfuscate his guilt. Sereny asks Stangl, "You . . . had acknowledged . . . that what was being committed was a crime. How could you, in all conscience . . . take any part in this crime?" Stangl's badly expressed or translated reply is, "It was a matter of survival—always survival. What I had to do . . . was to limit my actions to what I—in my conscience—could answer for. At police training school they taught us . . . that the definition of a crime must meet four requirements: there has to be a subject, and object, and action, and intent. If any of these four elements are missing, then we are not dealing with a punishable offence. . . . The 'subject' was the government, the 'object' the Jews, and the 'action' gassing. . . . I could tell myself that for me the fourth element, 'intent' . . . was missing" (164). Stangl thus claimed that since he did not intend his actions—which even he conceded were evil—they did not reflect on him and did not make him an evil person. He claimed that he did not act freely, that he was coerced into doing what he did, because his own and his family's survival was at stake, and no alternatives were left open for him.

Sereny pressed Stangl by citing several cases of people in the SS and among concentration camp guards who had opted out without anything happening to them. Stangl said in response, "it wasn't a question of 'getting out': if it had only been as simple as that! . . . We heard every day of this one and that one being arrested, sent to concentration camp, shot. . . . What it had already become . . . was a question of survival" (35). And he explained, "Don't you see? He [his superior] had me just where he wanted me. . . . Can you imagine what would have happened to me . . . under these circumstances? No, he had me flat: I was a prisoner" (134). "It was a matter of survival—always survival" (164). "My conscience is clear about what I did . . . I have never intentionally hurt anyone" (364).

Assume that Stangl sincerely held these obviously false beliefs. Perhaps he held them, because he succeeded in deceiving himself, or because he was cowardly and more easily threatened than courageous people, or because there was some other psychological explanation of how he managed to convince himself of patent falsehoods. It does not matter what the explanation was. What matters is that if he held the false beliefs sincerely, then he did not act freely in murdering 900,000 people; he was coerced by whatever the correct explanation would reveal about his psychological state. If he felt coerced by what he sincerely believed were serious threats, then, since the absence of coercion is necessary for intention, he was right to say that he did not intentionally murder 900,000 men, women, and children. Given the received view that responsibility depends on intention, the absurdity follows that Stangl was not responsible for what he did. What this shows, however, is not that Stangl should not be held responsible but that the received view is badly mistaken in holding that intention is necessary for responsibility.

The same absurdity follows from another line of thought. Sereny asked Stangl, "What was the worst place in the camp for you?" Stangl said, "The undressing barracks . . . I avoided it from my innermost being; I couldn't confront them; I could not lie to them; I avoided at any price talking to those who were about to die: I could not stand it" (203). He agreed with Sereny that he "had acknowledged . . . that what was being committed here [at Treblinka] was a crime" (163). How could he have done what he wanted to avoid at any price, from his innermost being? The answer is that he erected a protective shield between his actions and himself. This enabled him to prevent the knowledge of the nature of his actions from affecting his motivation for performing the actions. He acknowledged that his actions were evil, but he denied that they reflected on him and made him an evil person. The key was to desensitize himself to the horror that he had a major share in causing. He did this by teaching himself not to think of those he murdered as human. This was not a difficult task, because it followed from the Nazi ideology to which he was committed and whose propaganda apparatus relentlessly delivered the same message.

He said about this desensitization that "it started the day I first saw the *Totenlager* [the death camp] in Treblinka. I remember . . . the pits full of blue-black corpses. It had nothing to do with humanity—it couldn't have; it was a mass—a mass of rotting flesh . . . that started me thinking of them as cargo" (201). Sereny asked, "There were many children, did they ever make you think of your children, of how you would feel in the position of those parents?" and Stangl replied, "No, I can't say I ever thought that way. You see I rarely saw them as individuals. It was always a huge mass. I sometimes stood on the wall and saw them in the tube [the path to the gas chamber]. But—how can I explain it—they were naked, packed together, running, being driven by whips like . . . " and Sereny says, "the sentence trailed off" (201). Something Stangl said, however, makes obvious how the sentence should be completed. "When I was on a trip once, years later in Brazil, my train stopped next to a slaughterhouse. The cattle in the pens, hearing the noise of the train, trotted up to the fence and stared at the train. They were very close to my window, one crowding the other, looking at me through that fence. I thought then . . . that's just how the people looked, trustingly. . . . Those big eyes . . . which looked at me . . . not knowing that in no time at all they'd all be dead. . . . Cargo. . . . They were cargo" (201).

On one level, Stangl knew perfectly well that he was engaged in mass murder. He taught himself, however, to disregard his knowledge by refusing to see his victims as human and by desensitizing himself to the grievous harm he inflicted on innocent people deliberately, malevolently, and without moral justification. He accomplished this psychological feat with the aid of the Nazi ideology that denied the humanity of those it was dedicated to exterminating. Thus Stangl could habitually do horrendous evil, because he did not see what he was doing as evil. He could sincerely say, or it could be truly said of him, that he did not know what he was doing and did not understand the moral significance of his actions. But he lacked the knowledge and the understanding, because he contrived to dismiss them from his consciousness. According to the received view, this made his evil-doing unintentional, and hence he ought not to be blamed for the murder of 900,000 people.

As Bernard Williams writes, "blame rests, in part, on a fiction; the idea that ethical reasons, in particular the special kind of ethical reasons that are obligations, must, really, be available to the blamed agent. . . . *He ought to have done it*, as moral blame uses that phrase, implies *there was a reason for him to do it*, and this certainly intends more than the thought that we had a reason to want him to do it. It hopes to say, rather, that he had a reason to do it. But this may well be untrue: it was not in fact a reason for him. . . . Under this fiction, a continuous attempt is made to recruit people into a deliberative community that shares ethical reasons."[8] Since Stangl had no reason to refrain from mass murder, blaming him for the murder of 900,000 innocent people is a fiction.

What must be said about this absurdity is, first, that Stangl ought to have had the reason he contrived to lack by hiding from himself his knowledge and understanding. He ought to have known and understood what he was doing. That he made himself lack the knowledge and the understanding of the true nature of his actions does not excuse his evil-doing, as the received view absurdly claims, but makes him more blameworthy and more responsible for them. And what must also be said is, second, that blaming him is not an attempt to recruit him into a deliberative community that shares ethical reasons but to hold him responsible for the mass murder of innocent people regardless of what reasons he had or lacked for it.

What could lead so many thoughtful people to accept the received view? The answer is neatly encapsulated in the following two passages. Gary Watson discusses Robert Harris, a particularly cruel multiple murderer, and he says, "The fact that [Harris's] . . . cruelty is an intelligible response to his circumstances gives a foothold not only for sympathy, but for the thought that if *I* had been in such circumstances, I might have become as vile. . . . This thought induces not only an ontological shudder, but a sense of equality with the other: I too am a potential sinner."[9] In a remarkably similar passage, Susan Wolf writes of a thief: "He ought not to be blamed for committing his crime, for, from his point of view, one cannot reasonably expect him to see anything wrong with his action. We may suppose that in his childhood he was given no love—he was beaten by his father, neglected by his mother. . . . In light of this, it seems that this man shouldn't be blamed for an action we know to be wrong. For if we had his childhood, we would not have known either. . . . It is because he couldn't have had reason that this agent should not be blamed."[10]

Watson and Wolf oddly find the thought persuasive that if they had these people's background, they too might have done what they did. But neither says why that fact, if it is a fact, would have the slightest effect on the moral status of the actions they describe. If they had done what these people did, then they too should be blamed and held responsible. If they had been Nazis, they too might have been mass murderers. But does that make mass murder any the less evil? The received view is widely held by people whose misguided sympathy leads them to agonize over the evil-doers and forget about victims to whom the evil was done. They should be more tough-minded and less tender-hearted, especially since the reasonable response to evil depends on it.

7.2. Intention and Responsibility

The rejection of the received view does not commit one to the equally mistaken view that intention is irrelevant to responsibility. Habitual patterns of evil actions are often intentional, and then the evil-doers' responsibility for them is greater. My claim is that they may be responsible even if their habitual patterns of evil actions are not intentional. The crucial question is why evil-doers lack the freedom, knowledge, or understanding that would make their actions intentional. It is one thing if they are insane or have subnormal intelligence. It is quite another if they cannot now act freely, because they are overpowered by compulsions they have allowed in the past to come to rule them; or if they lack knowledge through self-imposed ignorance; or if they are without understanding as a result of blinding themselves to moral considerations. Evil-doers may be responsible precisely because they lack the freedom, knowledge, or understanding they ought to have. Stangl could—perhaps—sincerely claim that his mass murders were unintentional, but he nevertheless remains responsible, because he ought to have had the freedom, knowledge, and understanding that would have made his evil actions intentional. This is one crucial consideration the received view misses.

Another consideration it misses is that what makes intentions morally relevant is that they tend to prompt actions and if the intentions are malevolent, then the actions they prompt deliberately cause morally unjustified grievous harm to innocent people. If intentions did not prompt actions, then their moral significance would be comparable to the moral significance of dreams. Bad dreams are not morally blameworthy. Yet, when defenders of the received view come to the evaluation of actions, they focus on the intention of the agents rather than on the consequences of their actions. The point, of course, is not that only consequences matter and intentions do not, but that intentions matter because of their consequences for the people who are affected by the actions that follow from them. The salient point about Stangl's mass murders is not whether he intended them, but the immense amount suffering he caused to innocent people. And the same goes, of course, for Williams' claim that blaming evil-doers is based on a fiction if they do not have a reason to refrain from doing evil, for Watson's agonizing about Harris, and for Wolf's desperate efforts to make excuses for the thief. The received view concentrates on evil-doers at the expense of the evil they do. Its blinkers are self-imposed.

The received view also misses the systematic indeterminacy of intentions. People can usually be described as intending an action under one description, but not under another. A homicide may be intended, but the murder that it constitutes may not be intended if the killer believes that it is justified self-defense. Stangl's actions were described by him as intentionally doing what was necessary for his survival, but he repudiated their description as intentional mass murders. What is and what is not intended, therefore, is usually an open question that may be asked and answered from several different points of view. Consequently the same action may reasonably said to be both intentional and unintentional. To make intentions the pivot on which responsibility turns makes the ascription of responsibility an endlessly contestable matter. And, then, evil-doers, like Stangl, could reasonably excuse their evil actions and claim that they should not be held responsible for them.

An additional problem for the received view is the great difficulty of determining whether an evil-doer has acted intentionally. Intention depends on the absence of both external coercion and internal compulsion, on adequate knowledge of one's motives and of the facts relevant to one's circumstances, and on sufficient understanding of the moral significance of one's action. But it is extremely hard even for the agents, let alone for others who try to determine the agents' intention, to judge how strong external and internal influences have to be to qualify as coercive or compelling; or what knowledge is adequate of their motives or of the relevant facts; or what constitutes sufficient depth and breadth of moral understanding. The result is that even if the received view were acceptable, it would be virtually impossible to apply it.

A reasonable account of responsibility for evil actions must avoid these pitfalls. It should regard the evil done as of primary importance and the intentions of the evil-doer as secondary. It should concentrate on what happens to the victims, rather than agonize about the psychological state of the evil-doers. The force of these "shoulds" derives from the nature of human well-being, whose basic requirements the evil actions of evil-doers violate. The intentions of evil-doers have only secondary moral importance, because they derive from the evil to which they lead. A minimum condition of a reasonable account of responsibility is that it should provide a standard about whose application reasonable people could agree. The received view fails to do so. I will now propose such a standard.

7.3. The Standard

The standard is that people should be held responsible for the readily foreseeable consequences of their actions. To be held responsible is to be liable to moral blame, which ranges from mild disapproval to generally felt outrage that unites people in a society by their reactions to the deliberate, malevolent, and morally unjustified grievous harm inflicted on innocent victims. Blame expresses an attitude and a judgment that follows from it. The attitude is a response to a violated expectation and the judgment is directed against those whose actions violate the expectation. Since the actions are evil, the blame for them should be severe. If this seems harsh, the concrete details of evil actions should be remembered. They involve the murder of innocent people, including the helpless old and bewildered children, not the failure to return a book to the library.

The expectation whose violation provokes blame is that people in a society will respect each other's physical security. This, of course, is not the only expectation that people living together have of each other, but it is perhaps the basic, or one of the basic ones. It is an essential part of morality, politics, and the law to assure that this expectation is generally met. Occasional violations of it do not endanger the society itself, but if the violations are frequent, the society cannot long sustain the voluntary membership of those who live in it. People can be forced to live in the society by terror and propaganda, as numerous dictatorships have done, yet fear and insecurity will spread, and elementary prudence will compel people to choose between actively or passively opposing the unacceptable status quo, siding with the violators by becoming at least their tacit accomplices, and leaving the society if they can. Whatever they choose, it will worsen the already wretched state of their society.

Evil actions violate this expectation and spread insecurity. Their direct consequences are the grievous harms inflicted on innocent victims, but they also have the indirect consequences of showing contempt for the expectation that sustains the society and lays claim to the allegiance of those living in it. Evil actions thus undermine the foundation on which the society rests. It is natural, therefore, that they should be severely blamed. If they are not, something is amiss with those who fail to react in this way. The blame, of course, attaches to the evil-doers who performed the actions, but it need not take the form of punishing them. It may consist in holding them up as examples to avoid; expressing public or private detestation of them; expelling them from the society; teaching children not to be like them; motivating various forms of refusal to associate with them; preventing them from getting into influential positions; and generally regarding them as undesirable presences in a society toward whose moral, political, and legal expectations they have shown contempt.

Holding evil-doers responsible is thus to hold them liable to such blame. The attitude expressed by the blame is not a moralistic urge to vent indignation but a desire to protect the physical security of those living together in a society and to deter potential evil-doers who might threaten it. The attitude combines feelings and beliefs, facts and values, expectations and judgments. As all attitudes, it can go wrong, and it has gone terribly wrong on numerous occasions as a result of misdirected feelings, mistaken beliefs, misperceived facts, false values, wrong expectations, and baseless judgments. But a society cannot protect the well-being of people living in it without such an attitude. The fundamental interest of everyone dictates maintaining the attitude and preventing it from going wrong.

Responsibility thus consists in holding evil-doers liable to blame. It has been rightly called a "reactive" attitude,[11] because it is a reaction to actions that violate the expectation that people in a society will respect each other's physical security. Responsibility can be internalized, but this is not the reason for holding people responsible. The reason is that they have violated a basic requirement of their victims' well-being. If, however, responsibility is internalized, then evil-doers are not only held liable to blame by others, they feel it themselves, and would feel it even if their actions escaped detection and they were not blamed for them by others. Regret, shame, guilt, and remorse are some of the feelings through which internalized responsibility may manifest itself.

Responsibility has to be taught and learned. It is an attitude acquired from the outside. People can direct it toward themselves only because they have learned to share the attitude that others direct toward evil-doers. It is essential to this account of responsibility that people have it, because they are held to it, not because they feel it, since they would be rightly held to it even if they did not feel it. It is good to feel it, but evil-doers are not exempt from responsibility if they do not feel it. On the contrary, it makes them liable to even more severe blame, because if they do not feel responsible for their evil actions, they are more likely to repeat them.

An account of responsibility as liability to blame must explain how the distinction between justified and unjustified ascription of it should be drawn. Responsibility is not for all evil actions. People who are insane or have subnormal intelligence are not responsible for their evil actions and should not be blamed for them. The justification for holding evil-doers responsible, therefore, must depend not only on their evil actions but also on some component of their psychological state that the insane and the subnormally intelligent lack. This component is being able to foresee the readily foreseeable consequences of their own actions. It is like intention in being a psychological state, but it is unlike it in being very much simpler and more easily ascertainable. Judging whether or not an action was intentional involves complex and difficult decisions about the strength of external coercion and internal compulsions, the adequacy of the agents' knowledge of themselves and their circumstances, and the depth of understanding they possess and need to possess of the moral significance of their actions.

The ability to foresee the readily foreseeable consequences of one's actions, however, is one that the vast majority of adults possesses and constantly uses. It is like the ability to speak one's mother tongue, imagine possible state of affairs, or recognize familiar faces one has not seen for a while. The ability to do such things can be taken for granted and it requires no special explanation. What needs to be explained is if someone lacks it. Since actions and consequences are incalculably various, it is impossible to say in advance what actions and consequences are or ought to be readily foreseeable. But it is not hard to convey the basic idea: pushing someone off a tower, burning someone's hand, keeping people awake for 72 hours, driving a car into a crowd, dropping a large rock on someone's head normally have consequences that anyone acquainted with the facts could readily foresee. It would be absurd to claim that the immediate consequences of such actions were uncertain or difficult to foresee. Of course, what holds normally does not hold necessarily. There may be unusual circumstances, technological manipulations, or interferences with perception or judgment that invalidate ordinary expectations. But if there are no unusual circumstances and those considering taking such actions are not handicapped, then the immediate consequences of the actions will be readily foreseeable by them.

The test of what consequences are readily foreseeable is to ask whether others in the agents' situation would readily foresee them. What is readily foreseeable for an agent is what would be readily foreseeable in normal circumstances by any unhandicapped agent. This test is not foolproof, because appearances could deceive. If some situation is supposed to be deceptive, then those who suspect deception owe an explanation of why the facts are contrary to appearances. Normally, the immediate consequences of evil actions are readily foreseeable. There can be no reasonable doubt that murder, torture, enslavement, dismemberment, or blinding constitute readily foreseeable grievous harm. Evil-doers are normally readily able to foresee that, so they are normally in the psychological state necessary for holding them responsible. That is why it is normally justified to blame evil-doers for their evil actions, as it is justified to blame Stangl for the mass murders he committed.

This must be qualified, however, because, although evil-doers may normally be able to foresee the consequences of their evil actions, it may happen that in the circumstances preceding their actions they have not been able to do so. Competent speakers may become speechless, normally imaginative people may be prevented by a psychological block from imagining some possibility, and evil-doers may be generally able to foresee what actions would cause grievous harm and yet be prevented from foreseeing it in a particular situation. Blind rage, much stress, great provocation, panic, drugs, alcohol, or sleeplessness may prevent them from foreseeing what they could normally foresee. This was certainly not true of Stangl. But it may be true in some cases, and then the evil-doers may be excused for their evil actions. The account of responsibility, therefore, is not complete until more is said about what is and what is not a justified excuse.

7.4. Excuses

There are three types of cases in which people should be excused for performing normally evil actions: they may be exempt from responsibility altogether; or, although their actions would be normally evil, in the circumstances in which they perform them, they are morally justified; or, their responsibility for their evil actions is mitigated.

People should be exempted from responsibility if they are unable to foresee the readily foreseeable consequences of their actions. The most obvious examples are those who are insane or have subnormal intelligence. Children are more complicated, because as they mature they gradually develop the ability. Their exemption from responsibility, then, is temporary and partial, depending on the stage of their maturity. More complicated still are cases in which people have the ability, but are unable to use it in some situation. Their responsibility then hinges on whether their temporary inability is their fault. Shock, deprivation, and stress may render most people unable to foresee much of anything, but if they have not brought it upon themselves, they should not be held responsible for their inability. If, however, they know, or should know, that alcohol, or a drug, or some experience they seek will deprive them of the use of their ability, yet they get drunk, take the drug, get into the situation, and temporarily lose their ability, then they should be held responsible for their resulting evil actions, because they have made themselves unable to use their ability. Inability exempts only those who did not bring it upon themselves.

The second type of case holds when people perform a pattern of normally evil actions, but in a particular situation the normally evil actions are morally justified, and thus not evil. In such cases, what is needed is an explanation, not an excuse, because the agents have done nothing for which they should be excused. The situations in point are those in which exceptional circumstances demand that normally evil actions be regularly done in order to prevent far greater evil from being done. These are heartbreaking experiences in which morally committed people regularly violate their commitments.[12]

It was the official Nazi policy to demand that leaders of Jewish communities in German-occupied territories during World War II draw up successive lists of Jews to be sent to concentration camps. The leaders knew that those on the list were to be murdered immediately, as in Treblinka, or more slowly by forced labor under below subsistence conditions. The majority of leaders, their knowledge notwithstanding, met the demands, because they hoped

RESPONSIBILITY FOR EVIL 155

that they might slow down the process, bargain for lives, or just temporize until the war already lost by the Nazis would come to an end. They accepted the terrible responsibility and sent thousands to their deaths, believing that any alternative would hasten the process and result in many more deaths. For this reason they collaborated with the Nazis and became accessories to mass murder. There are serious doubts about the success of their delaying tactics and the absence of alternatives, but let us suppose that these doubts are misplaced and the judgment of the collaborating leaders was right, that they in fact saved many lives that otherwise would have been lost. The patterns of their normally evil actions were then morally justified. They deserve praise, not blame, for taking upon themselves the horrible burden of making the choices involved in drawing up the lists.

Cases of this sort are rare, but they exist. They show that the expectation of people living together in a society about the protection of physical security is not unconditional. Its protection in general may require the violation of physical security in particular cases. Such cases may not just be ones in which evil-doers respond to the violation of their own physical security but also cases in which the victims are innocent. These are terrible cases. Denying their existence, however, is to fail to recognize just how heavy is the burden of responsibility. Human well-being may require that evil be done, if there is no other way of avoiding even worse evil.

The third type of case arises, because there are degrees of responsibility and excuses may mitigate the responsibility of agents for their patterns of evil actions. I will proceed by discussing cases of full responsibility first, and, then, going on to cases of mitigated responsibility in which the conditions of full responsibility are not met, but a degree of responsibility nevertheless remains. The conditions of full responsibility depend on the consequences and contexts of evil actions and on the characters and motives of evil-doers. The consequences have to do with the grievous harm caused by an evil-doer's actions. If the harm is grievous, as it is in murder, torture, dismemberment, enslavement, or blinding, then its immediate consequence is readily foreseeable. One condition of full responsibility, then, is that the grievous harm was readily foreseeable by the evil-doer.

The contexts involve the particular circumstances of the evil-doers' actions and the general state of their society. It is impossible to enumerate all these conditions, because they vary with time, place, individuals, and societies. I will focus instead on a particular and a general condition, each normally central to holding people responsible. The particular condition has to do with the interactions between evil-doers and victims. It is one thing if the evil-doers' actions are overreactions to the provocations, challenges, or threats by their victims. It is quite another if their victims have done nothing to which the evil-doers could reasonably react. It may also be that, although the victims have done nothing that would call for a reaction, the evil-doers falsely believe that the victims have done something. The question in that case is how good were the evil-doers' reasons for their false beliefs. One condition of full responsibility is that the victims have done nothing, the evil-doers' reasons for believing otherwise were bad, and their evil actions were not reactions to the victims.

The general condition concerns the system of values prevailing in the context of the evil-doers' actions. The simplest case is when the values protect the physical security of people and the evil-doers' actions violate the generally recognized expectation. Then their evil actions meet another condition of full responsibility. In more complicated cases, the prevailing system of values is defective, because it fails to extend the protection of physical security to everyone and the evil-doers' actions conform to the defective system of values. Their actions, then, are still evil, although they have some reasons for believing that they are not. In such cases, it needs to be determined once again how good the evil-doers' reasons are.

It is very unlikely, however, that anyone would have good reasons of this sort. For, on the one hand, the evil-doers have before them the suffering and mangled bodies of their victims. On the other hand, they have a system of values at least nominally committed to the protection of everyone's security, while inconsistently making an exception of some group of people. The exception requires justification. The usual ones either demonize the victims or deny their full humanity. Ideologies typically lead to the first alternative, colonizing and slave-holding societies tend to lead to the second. We have seen in the last chapter how untenable are ideological justifications. The denial of the victims' full humanity is just as untenable, because they look, act, bleed, and suffer just like other humans. It further weakens the evil-doers' reasons that it is virtually impossible for anyone in contemporary societies to be ignorant of alternative systems of values in which those victimized by the evil-doers' defective values are not demonized or dehumanized but treated the same way as others.

The position of evil-doers in contexts where the prevailing system of values is defective, then, is as follows. They have to weigh the readily foreseeable consequences of their evil actions and their immediate experience of their victims' suffering against the bad reasons that follow from the prevailing values. If they act on the bad reasons, they are rightly held responsible, although their responsibility is mitigated. How mitigated it should be depends on just how defective the prevailing system of values is, how bad their reasons are, how far are they able to question the prevailing values, how much they know of alternative values, and so forth. Their responsibility is full if they lack even bad reasons for their evil actions.

Another condition of full responsibility follows from the connection between the characters of evil-doers and their actions. I am assuming that their actions are evil and form a pattern. The question is whether the pattern reflects the evil-doer's character. Patterns of actions usually do that, but there may be exceptions. People may find themselves in circumstances where they have no reasonable alternative to becoming evil-doers, because their survival is at stake or they have to protect those they love. This was, as we have seen, what Stangl falsely claimed for himself. Such circumstances require the radical alteration of the characteristic patterns of their actions. As Hume put it on behalf of those in these circumstances, "I shou'd be the cully of my integrity, if I alone shou'd impose on myself a severe restraint amidst the licentiousness of others."[13] People, then, may perform patterns of evil actions and yet the patterns reflect the circumstances they face rather than their characters. A good reason for thinking that this is the case is that if the circumstances change, they revert to their usual morally acceptable patterns of actions. Their responsibility for their patterns of evil actions is, then, mitigated. If, however, their evil actions form characteristic patterns, if they are not responses to circumstances in which evil-doing is forced on them, then another condition of their full responsibility is met.

This brings us to motives. People usually have many motives, and they may or may not act on any of them. Motives may prompt actions, because they are stronger than other motives, or because the agents have endorsed them after critical reflection, while they have decided to suppress competing motives. People may or may not be aware of their motives, and they may or may not identify with or approve of the motives of which they are aware. Motives are important for human well-being, but only because they may lead to action. If it were not for their connection with actions, motives in themselves, like fantasies, would be neither good nor bad. If we call motives that reliably lead to good actions virtuous and those that reliably prompt bad actions vicious, then a further condition of full responsibility is met by evil-doers whose vicious motives lead them to perform patterns of evil actions.

Motives and actions, however, may miscarry. Evil actions may be prompted by virtuous, neutral, or indeterminate motives. People may believe that they are acting virtuously, although they are acting viciously. They may decide on the basis of critical reflection to endorse one of their vicious motives, do the actions it prompts, but the actions may accidentally fail to be evil, because the gun misfired or the bomb did not explode. In such cases, their responsibility is mitigated.

It is now possible to sum up the conditions of full responsibility. Evil-doers should be held fully responsible for their patterns of evil actions if they are able to foresee the readily foreseeable grievous harm that results from their actions; if their victims have not provoked their actions; if their actions violate the requirement that prevails in their society and protects the physical security of its members; if their actions reflect their characters; and if the actions are viciously motivated. All these conditions were met by Stangl's patterns of mass murders, so he should be held fully responsible for them.

If any one of the conditions of full responsibility is not met, the evil-doers' responsibility is mitigated. Mitigated responsibility ranges from severe blame that falls only marginally short of full responsibility to mild blame barely distinguishable from exempting or justifying the actions. The recognition that some evil-doers should be held only to mitigated responsibility does not mean that they are not liable to blame. It means only that the blame should not be as severe as it might be. Just how severe it should be must be judged individually case by case.

The ascription of responsibility should proceed on the assumption that normally evil-doers should be held fully responsible for their patterns of evil actions. If it is claimed that they should be excused, then reasons must be given to support the claim. These reasons may be that they should be totally exempt from responsibility, because they lack the ability to foresee the readily foreseeable consequences of their actions; or that their actions are morally justified, because they were the only ways in which much greater evil could be prevented; or that their responsibility was mitigated by legitimate excuses.

The reason for holding evil-doers responsible and liable to blame is that they violated the physical security of their innocent victims and grievously harmed them. Human well-being depends on not allowing this to happen. The ascription of responsibility expresses an attitude formed of the expectation that people living together in a society will conform to this basic moral requirement. It also expresses the moral judgment that those who fail to meet this expectation should be blamed for it. This attitude is not one of gratuitous moralizing, but a necessary condition of individual well-being. And that is the reason for it. This completes my account of responsibility.

7.5. Weakening the Reasons for Evil-Doing

Chapters 6 and 7 were concerned with evil-doers, evil actions, and the reasonable responses to them. I have argued that evil actions are prevalent and this forces us to realize that human nature is a complex mixture of dispositions that foster and those that hinder our well-being. These dispositions prompt both good and evil actions. Our well-being requires the suppression of evil actions, and one of the central aims of morality is to pursue this necessary end. We may have reasons to act both morally and immorally, and both reasons derive from our mixed nature. We have to acknowledge that both good and evil actions may yield satisfactions that our dispositions lead us to regard as desirable. If a society's system of values is in good order, it strengthens the reasons for good actions and weakens the reasons for evil ones. The first is the bright side of a system of values, the second is its dark side. The bright side and the reasons for good actions are generally recognized, but there is a widespread and dangerous tendency to ignore the dark side and the reasons for evil actions. I stressed in opposition to this tendency that there is a secular problem of evil and that it is perilous to ignore it. For the refusal to face its implications makes us unable to cope with evil. The source of this refusal is a misguided optimistic faith in the basic goodness of human nature. Evil appears to the faithful as regrettable interference with our natural bent. Instead of blaming evil actions on those who do them, they are blamed on the corrupting influence of bad social conditions. But social conditions can only be bad if they are created and sustained by people who are acting on their malevolent dispositions. The optimistic faith blinds those who accept it to malevolent dispositions that are also parts of our nature. This is why the faithful invent absurd excuses to mitigate the responsibility of evil-doers for the evil they do, why they focus on the minute examination of the evil-doers' psychological states rather than on the great suffering of their grievously harmed innocent victims, why they are blind to the fact that evil actions are as natural expressions of basic malevolent dispositions as good actions are of basic benevolent ones, why they suppose that the requirements of morality and reason are bound to coincide, and why they deny that there may be reasons for evil actions.

Reasons for evil-doing originate in malevolent dispositions, but they are greatly strengthened by religious and secular ideologies that frequently lead to horrendous large-scale evil, as their history so amply shows. Ideologies lead their followers to divide humanity into the good who accept their dogmas, and the evil who reject them. By demonizing some group, ideologies count on, encourage, and justify the expression of their followers' malevolent dispositions through evil actions directed against their designated enemies. The prevalence of evil is largely the result of the indefensible tendency of ideologies to encourage those who are duped by them to violate basic requirements of human well-being.

In these two chapters I have stressed the dark side of our system of values and the need to acknowledge that there is a secular problem of evil. I have argued that the reasonable response to it is to hold evil-doers responsible for the evil they do and thereby weaken their reasons for evil actions that hinder our well-being. I will now go on to argue that, although this is necessary, it is not sufficient, because we need also to strengthen the reasons for good actions that foster our well-being. This will allow me, with relief, to return to the bright side of our system of values, a subject considerably more cheery than evil and responsibility for it.

8

The Cultural Dimension and Disenchantment

At the end of the last chapter I concluded that, although there are reasons against evil actions, given the ambivalence of human nature, these reasons, by themselves, are not strong enough to make evil less prevalent, unless they are strengthened by reasons for actions that aim at well-being. In this chapter I begin and in subsequent chapters will continue to show that the secular view of the human condition can supply additional reasons.

One of the objections to the secular view is that it cannot provide what is needed. Reasons for pursuing well-being must have a motivational source, but secular conceptions of well-being are said to be much too impoverished, insipid, and dull to inspire the active pursuit of well-being when critical reflection brings us to acknowledge the contingencies of life, the ambivalence of our nature, and the tedium that follows once our basic needs are satisfied. In the apt translation of Max Weber's observation, the secular view of the human condition leads to disenchantment.[1] One of the attractions of religious or secular ideologies, and of the evil actions they so often prompt, is that they inspire their followers and fill their disenchanted lives with activities claimed—speciously—to be valuable.

I acknowledge, indeed insist on, both the prevalence of evil and disenchantment in contemporary affluent Western societies. But I deny that the secular view is responsible for them. I think that they plague us precisely because of the widespread failure to take advantage of the great plurality of values that the secular view makes available. These values are to be found in the cultural dimension of our system of values. In Chapter 5 I have described four types of cultural value: interpretations of universal values, forms of expression and conduct, institutions and practices within them, and modes of evaluation. A full treatment would require a long book about each type of value, but this is not one of those books. I will consider only modes of evaluation in this chapter. I will argue that the values they provide are more than sufficient to lay to rest the objection that the secular view lacks attractive alternatives to evil-doing and leads to disenchantment with the human condition.

8.1. Disenchantment

Of the numerous religiously-oriented critics who have argued that the secular view leads to disenchantment, I will consider one, who can be taken to speak for the others.[2] Leszek Kolakowski says that "the question arises . . . whether society can survive and provide a tolerable life for its members if the feeling for the sacred, and, indeed, the phenomenon of the sacred itself vanish entirely" (68). He says that "the dissolution of the sacred . . . threatens culture and heralds, in my view, its degeneration if not its suicide," for "one of the functions of the sacred in our society was to lend . . . significance . . . to all the basic divisions of human life and all the main areas of human activity. Birth and death, marriage and the sexes, disparities of age and generation, work and art, war and peace, crime and punishment, vocations and professions—all these things had a sacred aspect. . . . The sacred . . . confer[red] on them a specific value. . . . [and] added the weight of the ineffable, as it were, to every given form of social life" (69–70). Part of the function of the sacred was "making fast the fundamental distinctions of culture by endowing them with an additional sense that may be drawn only from the authority of tradition. . . . With the disappearance of the sacred . . . arises one of the most dangerous illusions of our civilization—the illusion that there are no limits to the changes human life can undergo, that society is 'in principle' an endlessly flexible thing, and that to deny this flexibility and this perfectability [sic] is to deny man's total autonomy and thus to deny man himself. Not only is this illusion demented, but it sows disastrous despair. The omnipresent Nietzschean or Sartrian [sic] chimera which proclaims that man can liberate himself . . . of tradition and of all pre-existing sense . . . leaves us suspended in darkness. And in this darkness, where all things equally good, all things are equally indifferent. . . . To be totally free . . . of all pressure from tradition, is to situate oneself in a void and thus, quite simply, to disintegrate. And sense can come only from the sacred. . . . To reject the sacred is to reject . . . the idea of evil, for the sacred reveals itself through sin, imperfection, and evil, and evil, in turn, can be identified only through the sacred. To say that evil is contingent is to say that there is no evil. The bottom line, as it were, . . . is the sanctioning of force and violence and thereby, finally, of despotism and the destruction of culture" (72–3).

The reasonable secular response to these impassioned *obiter dicta* is mixed. It is certainly important to preserve our cultural identity, because we derive most of our values from it. It is also true that the attempt to free ourselves from cultural traditions undermines values. And, as I have argued in the last two chapters, it would indeed be disastrous for human well-being to refuse to face evil. Nevertheless, if the sacred is understood in a religious sense, as Kolakowski clearly understands it, then it is a bad mistake to suppose that abandoning it has the dire consequence of committing cultural hara-kiri.

If by the "sacred" is meant whatever provides the deepest source of value and sets limits whose violation causes irreparable damage to our well-being, then the sacred is the unthinkable. I have argued (in 3.2.–3) that our well-being depends on regarding some actions as unthinkable. If the sacred is understood in this way, it has no essential connection with religious belief. A reasonable secular view would not only recognize, but insist on, the great importance of holding that there are some limits that ought not be violated, and whose violation is what I have described in the last two chapters as evil. Kolakowski, however, understands the sacred as having an essential connection with religious belief and impossible without it. He insists that unless the unthinkable is derived from a supernatural God-given moral order that permeates reality, it cannot be sustained. In this, however, he is doubly mistaken.

First, there is no such thing as the religious understanding of the sacred. There are many different religious understandings of it and they have led to bitter disagreements about what is sacred. These disagreements are responsible for the horrors of religious wars and persecutions of infidels and heretics. Overwhelming historical evidence testifies to the enormous amount of evil caused by crusaders, holy warriors, inquisitors, witch hunters, and sundry defenders of one faith or another, precisely in the name of the sacred. It is a gross mistake to suppose that a secular understanding of the unthinkable is any more likely to lead to evil than a religious understanding of it as supernaturally ordered. To be sure, secular ideologies are also responsible for horrendous evil, but not because they are secular, but because they are ideologies.

Second, Kolakowski's view—that we must either derive value from the religious sense of the sacred or embrace Nietzschean relativism and the disenchantment that comes with it—is unacceptably crude. It is as crude as the much-criticized positivist view (castigated, among many others, by Kolakowski in *The Alienation of Reason*) that we must either derive value from verifiable propositions or regard them as unreasonable appeals to emotions. The sources of values are far more various than religious or positivistic simple-mindedness allows.

Kolakowski is right to insist on the importance of religion and positivists are right to do the same for science, but both are wrong to fail to see that neither religion nor science is the sole source of value. Values may also be derived from aesthetic, literary, moral, philosophical, and political modes of evaluation. These modes of evaluation are essential parts of our cultural identity, and they are not destroyed if we reject the supremacy of the religious evaluations over them. We do not need to derive from a supernatural moral order the importance we attribute to "birth and death, marriage and sexes, disparities of age and generation, work and art, war and peace, crime and punishment" (69). We may continue to believe, as we in fact do, that these stages in life's way are redolent with non-religious values.

Thucydides and Aristotle, Epicureans and Skeptics, Euripides and Shakespeare, Hume and Gibbon, Mill and Tocqueville, Diderot and Jefferson, Balzac and George Eliot, Voltaire and Freud, and countless other atheists, agnostics, and religious skeptics were not doomed to disenchantment by their doubts about a supernatural moral order or by their lack of a religious sense of the sacred. They derived the values of their rich lives and works from other sources. Kolakowski and other critics of the secular view are mistaken in supposing that we must choose between religious values and relativism. To insist that there are sources of value other than religion is not to cast doubt on religion, but to refuse to regard it as the sole source of value.

8.2. Modes of Evaluation

We may begin with the useful distinction between first- and second-order activities as it bears on modes of evaluation. Among the relevant first-order activities are the creation of non-verbal works of art, of music, painting, and sculpture; literary compositions of poems, novels, plays, and biographies; conscientious moral actions, like keeping promises, being kind, and doing one's duty; the philosophical examination of basic axiological, epistemological, and ontological assumptions; political involvement in legislation, conflict-resolution, and the regulation of commerce; and the practice of religion through prayer, charity, and worship.

To each of these first-order activities corresponds a second-order activity that is concerned with the evaluation of the first-order activity. Modes of evaluation are these second-order activities. Their evaluations may be internal or external to the first-order activities. Internal evaluations have to do with the justification or criticism of the results, manner, and direction of first-order activities. Such criticisms and justifications are often indistinguishable from the first-order activities themselves, because they are done by artists, writers, moral agents, philosophers, politicians, or religious people of their own and their fellow participants' activities and their results. Internal evaluation is a part of all intelligent activities. It is how participants monitor what they and others are doing. It is an indispensable means of criticism, correction, improvement, and the acknowledgment of achievement.

External evaluations are usually quite distinct from engagement in first-order activities. Art and literary critics, as well as moralists, are identifiable as external evaluators, but there is no comparably convenient label for the external evaluators of philosophy, politics, and religion. I will refer to all external evaluators jointly as *critics*, although it is important to remember that their evaluations may also be favorable. The task of critics is complex. It includes, first, the evaluation of specific works of art, literature, or philosophy; or of the moral status of individuals and their actions; or of the merits or demerits of particular political systems, institutions, or practices; or of the inspiration, consolation, or salvation that may be provided by religious liturgy, ceremonies, or other forms of worship. The task of critics also includes, second, an overview of how well or badly the first-order activity is going. The evaluation of the overall health, so to speak, of art, literature, morality, philosophy, politics, and religion. And it includes as well, third, a general reflection on the larger significance of the first-order activity in relation to other first-order activities, to the culture as a whole, and to the betterment of the human condition. It is the second and third critical tasks that are my main concerns in trying to show that the secular view can avoid disenchantment and provide attractive alternatives to evil-doing.

The first-order activities corresponding to modes of evaluation provide a wide variety of benefits. Works of non-verbal art may delight, elicit emotions, challenge customary ways of looking at the world, decorate, take us out of ourselves, and enrich us by being beautiful objects we can behold. Literature may entertain, provoke, enlarge the language, expand our imagination, acquaint us with unfamiliar ways of life, show us heroes and villains, and enable us to understand better our own and others' motivation. Moral examples may shame, inspire, or teach us, may make us question or reject them, may show us what true virtue is, or why vice is bad, or they may make us formulate the reasons why we dislike or distrust them. Philosophical writings may call our basic assumptions into question, help us form a systematic view of the world, make us distrust dogmatism, and teach us to discipline our speculations by reasons. Political systems or institutions may help strangers live peacefully together, coordinate interests, and provide rules that enable us to live with minimum interference from others. And religious practices may teach us optimism, consolation if misfortune befalls us, hope for the future, and fellowship with others who share our faith.

These and other benefits of first-order activities are generally available in our culture. Our recognition and enjoyment of them is part of our cultural identity, but this must be qualified in two important ways. First, "our cultural identity" can be interpreted in two senses. In a collective sense, cultural identity is the possession of all at least moderately intelligent and educated people in a society, and the benefits derivable from it are available to them. In a personal sense, however, sharing cultural identity does not mean that we take advantage of all that it offers. We can share a cultural identity and lack an aesthetic sense, not read literature, be averse to philosophical reflection, ignore politics, or participate in no religious activity. It is more difficult to be altogether without moral sensibility, but not even that would exclude the sharing of a cultural identity. What would disqualify us from sharing it is if we were indifferent to all such evaluative considerations. We would then lack a central part of the evaluative dimension of life. We might still care about the human values that allow us to satisfy our basic needs, otherwise, however, we would live as disenfranchised strangers in our society. We would be to values, as the color blind are to colors. It may be thought that we could still have personal values, but it is hard to see what they could be. They may be derived from the efficient performance of whatever activities we fancy, but activities normally have a purpose, and they are worth performing efficiently only if we find the purpose they serve valuable from some point of view. What could that point of view be if it is not aesthetic, literary, moral, philosophical, political, or religious?

The second qualification is that sharing our cultural identity in a personal sense allows for a wide range of responses to cultural values. The simplest one is the unreflective enjoyment of a piece of music or a poem, unanalyzed admiration of an incisive philosophical question or of an ingenious political compromise, or being uplifted, we know not why, by a moral ideal or a religious ceremony. More reflective responses involve giving reasons for them, and the more concerned we are with giving reasons, the closer we come to responding as critics do. But, of course, there are many degrees of reflectiveness before we reach the level of the disciplined evaluations of critics.

The reason for stressing this point is to avoid two ways of misunderstanding what I have been saying. One is to over-intellectualize it and suppose that we can share a cultural identity only if we become thoughtful critics immersed in the traditions and practices of a first-order activity. The other is to suppose that all evaluations prompted by a shared cultural identity are equally good. How good evaluations are depends on how good the reasons are that have been or could be given for or against them. And how good the reasons are depends on how well those who give them understand the first-order activities from which the reasons are derived. The enjoyment and appreciation of the benefits derivable from first-order activities, however, do not depend on reasons for or against them. Reasons may enhance or diminish our enjoyment and appreciation, but the responses come first and the reasons can only follow. Reasons may improve our responses, but cannot prompt them. Our responses are prompted by the direct experience of the products of first-order activities. We respond to them first innocently and then with various degrees of reflectiveness. It is a matter of logic, not of cultural identity, that the objects of reflection necessarily precede reflection on them.

Cultural identity in a collective sense, then, is partly formed of the shared modes of evaluation, and, in a personal sense, it provides the possibilities some of which form the content of our conceptions of well-being. It would be a misunderstanding of the connection between evaluations and well-being to suppose that it holds between means and an end; between activities we perform in order to achieve a state and a state in which we comfortably rest. We do not think of our admiration of a musical performance, a poem, a courageous act of integrity, depth of understanding, an act of justice, or of unswerving compassion for human misery as means to anything. We value them in themselves, for what they are, and we value them regardless of the incalculable consequences they may have. Nor is our well-being a state that allows us, once we have reached it, to regress into inactivity. Well-being consists in doing well what critical reflection leads us to want to do most. It involves activity, even when it is derived from the passive appreciation of the achievements of others, because the appreciation is still something we do. Commitment to at least some modes of evaluation, therefore, is part of reasonable conceptions of well-being. Shared modes of evaluation are not tools we may use and lay aside after they have served their purpose but essential components of the activities that constitute our well-being.

As we have seen, each mode of evaluation provides a great variety of benefits, but most important for our well-being are the significant and lasting achievements that have become classics. They enlarge human possibilities by showing us ways of living, seeing, and acting that stand as enduring models of how we ourselves might live, see, and act. These achievements are the *exemplars* in our cultural identity, and what follows are some illustrations of them drawn from each mode of evaluation.

8.3. Exemplars

Consider Gustave Caillebotte's painting of his brother in his garden.[3] He sits on a chair reading a book, under an orange tree, his back is turned toward us, the sun gently suffuses the picture outside of the cool shade of the dark green leaves of two trees. A few feet away there is a woman, probably young, perhaps the sitting man's wife or daughter, also reading. And a little further on, in the sun, a dog is napping with his nose resting on his paws. There is an atmosphere of calm, quiet enjoyment, evoking wonderful summer days when undisturbed by the world, unworried by disasters, we reflect in tranquility. We are shown a possibility of what life may be like. It is not intrusive or didactic; it hints at no ominous revelation just around the corner; there is no enigma; and no attempt to unsettle our ordinary perception of the world. It is not sentimental, because it falsifies nothing by phony or overwrought emotions. We know it is true, because we know, although tend to forget, that rarely, all too rarely, life could be like that at least for some of us some of the time. It helps us remember what we might hope to have in the future or what a few fortunate ones among us have had in the past. It strengthens us when we face evil, war, disease, poverty, stupidity—when the news of the world is brought home to us.

Think next of Melville's Captain Vere, an intelligent, reflective, conscientious commander of a ship in time of war who found it his duty to sentence to death Billy Budd, the sailor.[4] An evil officer of the ship falsely accused Billy of instigating mutiny. Billy's instinctive response to encountering evil for the time in his simple life was dictated by his outraged innocence and frustrating inarticulateness. He struck and, because he was exceptionally strong, killed the officer. Vere understood Billy's frustration and reaction, knew that the accusation was false, but Billy killed an officer of the ship in time of war, and the penalty the naval code prescribes for that is death. Vere did what he had to do, and then lived with it. As we reflect on Vere's predicament, we see that public and private responsibilities may create wrenching conflicts; that there are predicaments in which whatever we do, we violate something we deeply care about; and even if we do what we think we should, what we would do again if we had to, we will be assailed by guilt, shame, and regret. We see that we may have to face tragic conflicts no matter how well we reflect and how good our will is. And we come to understand better, more deeply, with greater sympathy those, like Vere, who had to make such decisions. We may learn from serious literature that there are limits to how much we can accomplish by reason and prudence.

Lamoignon de Malesherbes, a French aristocrat, Tocqueville's much-admired grandfather, was a remarkable moral exemplar.[5] He witnessed the corruption and the abuse of power countenanced by the particularly stupid monarchy of Louis XVI in the years immediately preceding the French Revolution of 1789. He was influenced by and in contact with the *philosophes*, he was a patron of Rousseau, and he was also a royalist of impeccable credentials and close adviser of the King. He did all he could to criticize the prevailing political system and to suggest far-reaching reforms from the inside. But his advice was not heeded and he became increasingly unpopular with the King and with his other advisers. It is impossible to say whether the Revolution, the Terror, the untold misery, and the loss of many tens of thousands of lives would have been avoided if Malesherbes' advice had been accepted. The chances are, however, that the ensuing events would have been less violent. Be that as it may, Malesherbes foresaw the approaching calamity, warned against it, and proposed numerous measures to ameliorate its causes. He failed. When he realized that he had become totally ineffective, he retreated to his estate and resumed his full and interesting private life.

The Revolution came, of course, and the King was tried for his life. The monarchy was eventually replaced by terror and many people lived in constant and justified fear for their and their family's lives. Malesherbes was among them. When the King was put on trial and no one was willing to defend him, Malesherbes volunteered. He knew that the verdict was foreordained and he was putting himself in greater danger than he already faced. He nevertheless mounted a vigorous defense of the stupid, hapless, doomed King, who spurned his advice that might have averted the disaster that followed. Malesherbes thought that it was his duty to remind his countrymen of law and humanity when they ran amok in orgiastic anarchy. The King was convicted and executed, and soon thereafter the same fate befell Malesherbes, even though he was known to have advocated many of the reforms the revolutionaries wanted.

Reflecting on his life, we see what it is to have integrity and honor, to stand up for decency in a world gone mad, to recognize that with the privileges of high position come responsibilities that ought to be discharged even, and especially, when it is costly. The world would be a better place if politicians, lawyers, academics, generals, and intellectuals followed Malesherbes' example, rather than expediently and cravenly succumb to threats and bribery in order to hang on to their privileges.

Not all philosophers would agree that there is a philosophical mode of evaluation. They would say that the aim of philosophy is to understand the scheme of things, and that is what it is regardless of how we evaluate it. This is a recognizable, but much too austere view that ignores a substantial, perhaps the greater, part of the history of philosophy whose concern was with how we should live. And that, of course, is an evaluative question to which many evaluative philosophical answers have been given. One philosopher who did not ignore this aspect of the subject was David Hume. He lived and acted as many of the great philosophers have done: his thoughts informed his life. He never forgot his own injunction, "Be a philosopher; but amidst all your philosophy, be still a man."[6] Throughout life he was guided by the realization that "Good and ill are universally intermingled and confounded. . . . Nothing is pure and entirely of a piece. All advantages are attended with disadvantages." The best we can do is maintain a "steady virtue, which either preserves us from disastrous, melancholy accidents, or teaches us to bear them" and if we succeed, enjoy the greatest benefit of all, a "calm sunshine of the mind."[7] It was with calm sunshine of the mind that he faced what he knew was his imminent death at the age of 65 from chronic ulcerative colitis.

In a religious age and in a Scotland of perfervid religiosity, he was a lifelong skeptic. The ever-obstreperous Boswell visited the dying Hume mainly to find out how the philosopher viewed then death and immortality. Hume said to him that "he never entertained any belief in Religion since he began to read Locke and Clarke." Boswell asked him if it was not possible that there might be a future state. Hume answered: "it was possible that a piece of coal put upon the fire would not burn; and added that it was a most unreasonable fancy that we should exist for ever." And Boswell concludes, "The truth is that Mr. Hume's pleasantry was such that there was no solemnity in the scene; and Death for the time did not seem dismal." Hume writes in one of his last letters, "I see Death approach gradually, without any Anxiety or Regret," and he says to a friend almost at the end, "I have done every thing of consequence which I ever meant to do, and I could at no time expect to leave my relations and friends in a better situation than that in which I am now likely to leave them: I therefore have all reason to die contented."[8] Not many of us could say the same, but we can all aspire to the contentment this great philosophical exemplar had achieved.

It happens sometimes that a politician rises to a momentous occasion and becomes an admirable exemplar whose actions secure some of the possibilities we have learned to value from the political mode of evaluation. One such occasion was the beginning of World War II, when France was about to capitulate to the German invaders, the British Army faced annihilation at Dunkirk, and five men of the War Cabinet in London had to decide whether Britain should fight on alone or hope for the best from a negotiated peace with Hitler. The five were Churchill, who just became Prime Minister, Chamberlain, the previous Prime Minister, Halifax, the Foreign Secretary, Atlee, the leader of the Labour Party, and Greenwood, his deputy. They deliberated for three days in May 1940.[9] They had to decide between waging a war against heavy odds or negotiating a humiliating peace. They had no illusions about Hitler and knew that the fate of Europe depended on the decision they had to make. They were all committed to the best interest of Britain, but they disagreed about what that was. They all loved their country, all were steeped in its history and traditions, and all cared deeply about the welfare of their fellow citizens. They were experienced men of affairs, used to making decisions based on imperfect knowledge, in rapidly changing circumstances, about complex matters, as the march of events forced them to judge the relative importance of conflicting considerations. But never before had they been faced with such a momentous decision when so much depended on making the right one.

Churchill was for fighting on, Chamberlain and Halifax favored a negotiated peace, and Atlee and Greenwood were undecided. Churchill eventually succeeded in convincing first Atlee and Greenwood, then Chamberlain, and last Halifax that he was right about the forces of evil Hitler represented and unleashed about the grit and willingness of the British people to fight on even at the cost of great hardship, about Britain's chances of holding out until America would enter the war and change the odds, and about his own capacity to lead and inspire the country at this pivotal juncture in its long history. On all these points his judgment was right and the others' in various degrees wrong. As he said, "I felt . . . that all my past life had been but a preparation for this hour and for this trial."[10] Sometimes politicians face adversity and succeed, as Churchill has, because their judgments are good, their will strong, and they are convinced of the righteousness of their cause. They become exemplars, and we call them statesmen.

I come last to religious exemplars, and I take them from everyday life where we can often encounter them, even if we do not realize that we have done so. I have in mind people who are described as born again. They reach a point where they find the way they have been living corrupt, depressing, or conflict-ridden, and they can no longer accept it. Then they have a religious experience, or meet an inspiring religious person, or stumble into a church and their lives are transformed. They find an ideal, when they had none before, and it inspires and motivates them to make a new beginning, to break with their unsatisfactory mode of existence, and be guided by the new-found ideal. They feel as if they had been born again, and that it might be possible to regain their lost childlike purity and innocence. This is the sort of experience that transformed Saul into Paul on the road to Tarsus, made the Apostles leave everything behind and follow Jesus, changed a socialite into St. Francis, and led many lost souls to Pentecostal churches. For such people, religion becomes a way of life, and just as some people lose their faith, so they find it. Finding it need have nothing to do with theological speculation, doctrinal issues, proofs for the existence of God, or indeed with reason. It has to do with a transforming experience that gives to the lives of those who have had it the meaning and purpose they lacked before, even if they did not realize it. There is no reason why defenders of the secular view could not accept the importance of such transformations. It is only the theology that often goes with them that they reject.

These are among the experiences that religious critics, such as Cottingham, Graham, James, Kolakowski, and Taylor among others, have in mind when they talk about the disenchantment that follows from the secular view.[11] But we can now see how wrong these critics are. They are wrong to suppose that disenchantment must be a consequence of the secular view and that it can be overcome only by turning to religion. Many disenchanted people are religious believers who have found their faith unbelievable. Many atheists and agnostics live full, satisfying, and meaningful lives. And the disenchantment of both religious and secular people can be overcome by drawing on the resources of the aesthetic, literary, moral, philosophical, and political modes of evaluation and on the inspiration provided by the exemplars I have described and by dozens of others that could be culled from each of the first-order activities. There are many admirable works of non-verbal art, literary creations, morally excellent characters and actions, inspiring philosophical lives, and statesman-like political achievements that enlarge the possibilities of our lives. Many religious critics of the secular view are well-educated, civilized people who know and appreciate as well as anyone the riches of the cultural dimension of our system of values. How, then, can they fail to see that our lives can be enchanted by the exemplars regardless of whether we have or lack religious commitments? The answer is that they are misled by a misguided quest for an overriding mode of evaluation.

8.4. The Quest for an Overriding Mode of Evaluation

Modes of evaluation are general evaluative perspectives. Their objects are produced by the first-order activities on which modes of evaluation depend. It is very hard and probably unjustifiably meddlesome to try to set reasonable limits to what qualifies as a non-verbal work of art, a literary creation, a matter of moral concern, a subject for philosophical examination, a political issue, or as having religious significance. To proceed otherwise is an unwise attempt to curtail the creative imagination of artists and writers, to attend to the promptings of conscience only in familiar cases, to prohibit philosophers from questioning certain assumptions, to take a narrow view of how the public interest may be served, or to dictate the direction in which faith might take religious believers. All this is anathema to liberty, one of the most basic values of our cultural identity. But if we do not set limits on what may come within the purview of modes of evaluation, then we must recognize that among the objects of each evaluative perspective are the first-order activities and the evaluations of the other modes. Moral questions may be raised about works of art and literature, religious practices may become matters of philosophical or political concern, and so forth. As we know, these are not just theoretical possibilities, but live issues in the culture of our society. And herein lies the origin of the misguided quest for an overriding mode of evaluation.

The evaluations by modes of evaluations of other modes of evaluation are not merely different: they are incompatible. For each mode of evaluation has its own standards and values, and when a mode is evaluated by another mode, it is done in terms of the standards and values of the evaluating mode, which are other than the standards and values of the evaluated mode. The unavoidable consequence is that the evaluations of the evaluating mode will be inconsistent with evaluations of the evaluated mode. When works of non-verbal art or literature are evaluated from a moral perspective, their aesthetic or literary value becomes, at best, secondary and the primary concern is with their moral praise or blameworthiness. When religious practices are evaluated from a philosophical or political perspective, it becomes a secondary question how important they are to the religious way of life of the faithful, and the primary question is whether the assumptions on which they rest are epistemologically or ontologically justifiable, or whether the practices serve or hinder the public interest.

The evaluations of first-order activities that follow from the standards and values of one mode are necessarily incompatible with the evaluations of the same first-order activities that follow from other modes. This could not be otherwise, since the standards and values of different modes are different. If they were not, the modes would not be different. The result is that when critics working in different modes view each other's evaluations of the same object, they inevitably and rightly conclude that the other critics mis-estimate the true significance of the object that is being evaluated. The critics charge one another with regarding as primary a feature of the object that is, at best, secondary, and with assigning, at best, secondary importance to the object's primary feature. This is felt to be an intolerable state of affairs, an offense to reason, and the high road to relativism. Is there a way out of it?

One possibility is to attempt to defuse the conflict by pointing out that the scope of modes of evaluation is only general, not all-inclusive. Although nothing can in principle be excluded as an object of aesthetic, literary, moral, philosophical, political, or religious evaluation, in actual practice there are many objects, experiences, character traits, and actions that are evaluatively indifferent. There are countless preferences, personal habits, hobbies, casual encounters with others, ways of relaxing, forms of entertainment, small talk, and so forth that ordinarily carry no evaluative weight, even if they may come to do so in unusual situations. It may also be, therefore, that modes of evaluation need not conflict, because what has evaluative significance from the perspective of one mode is indifferent from the perspective of another.

This is clearly a possibility, but it does not change the fact that good works of art may be morally offensive, philosophical arguments of great depth may have politically unacceptable implications, important literary creations may be sacrilegious, and so forth. Not all evaluations need to conflict with other evaluations, but some of them do conflict, as we know from the familiar tensions within our cultural identity.

The most widely sought remedy is to claim that reason requires that one mode of evaluation should take precedence over the other modes when they come into conflict. And so the quest for an overriding mode of evaluation gets under way. It is felt to be an urgent quest, because the alternative to finding the overriding mode is thought to be relativism. Kolakowski and others think that the overriding mode is religious; Kant that it is moral; Marxists and Rawlsians that it is political; Plato and Hegel that it is philosophical; many post-Kantian German romantics that it is aesthetic; and new critics, such as Wimsatt and Nuttall, that it is literary. Others appeal to science, history, or psychology to avoid this supposedly intolerable state of affairs.

There are at least two, to my mind fatal, objections to accepting that one mode of evaluation should override the evaluations of other modes when they come into conflict. The first objection is identical to the one I have made in Chapter 5 against the attempt to resolve conflicts among the human, cultural, and personal dimensions of our system of values always in favor of any one of these dimensions. The objection hinges of the force of the "should" in the claim that one mode of evaluation should always override conflicting ones. If the "should" follows from the standards and values of the supposedly overriding mode of evaluation, then appeal to them simply begs the question. This becomes obvious if it is realized that this kind of overridingness can be claimed with exactly equal plausibility on behalf of each mode of evaluation. If overridingness depends on the standards and values of a particular mode of evaluation, then of course the evaluations of that mode should override the evaluations of any of the conflicting modes.

If, however, the "should" does not presuppose the standards and values of one mode of evaluation, then from where does it get its force? Why should the "should" be heeded? It is no use saying that it is the should of reason, unless it is explained why reason requires that one mode of evaluation should always override the others if they conflict. The usual answer is that reason requires it, because the alternative is relativism. But what reason can at most be said to require is that one or another mode of evaluation should be overriding in a particular case, not that the particular one favored should be overriding always, in all cases. Furthermore, the usual answer contains its own refutation. For it says that unless one mode of evaluation always overrides all the others, relativism follows. But relativism obviously does not follow, because it could be avoided by assigning overriding status to different modes of evaluation in different cases. There is no reason to assume that conflicts among evaluations could be resolved only if it were shown that one of aesthetic, literary, moral, philosophical, political, or religious evaluation is always more important than the others. All attempts to justify this assumption arbitrarily presuppose what they are meant to show.

The second objection is that by assigning overriding importance to one of the modes of evaluation the conflict is not resolved, but falsified. When there is a genuine conflict, say between the religious and the moral modes of evaluation, then the same person or action is evaluated in incompatible ways from the religious and the moral perspectives. Cases in point are Abraham's willingness to sacrifice Isaac at God's behest and Job's acceptance of the calamities to which, he believed, God had subjected him. From a religious perspective, Abraham's and Job's willingness were exemplary. From a moral perspective, Abraham's willingness to murder his son was deplorable and Job's acceptance of the gross injustice heaped on him showed a craven lack of self-respect.

If such conflicts are resolved by claiming, say, that the religious mode of evaluation is overriding, then the moral mode of evaluation becomes acceptable only insofar as it conforms to the standards and values of the religious mode. Defenders of the overridingness of the religious mode will say that what morality requires is to conform to the will of God. Both Abraham and Job did that, so they did nothing morally blameworthy. They have done precisely what morality required them to do. But looking at the matter in this way has the fatal consequence of denying that there could be a conflict between religious and moral evaluations. And if there could not be a conflict, then there could not be a reason for regarding the religious mode of evaluation as overriding, since there could be nothing to override.

This "solution" of the conflict consists in denying that there is a conflict. That farrago of a solution, however, is available to the defenders of the overridingness of all the modes of evaluation. They could dogmatically insist that the conflict is merely apparent, because the mode of evaluation from which the apparently conflicting evaluation follows actually conforms, or should conform if it were reasonable, to the standards and values of the mode they are defending. In this spirit, politicians could say that what morality requires is whatever serves the public interest; writers could say, as Faulkner has done, that "the 'Ode on a Grecian Urn' is worth any number of old ladies"; philosophers, like Plato, could advocate the expulsion of poets, because they deny what he took to be the truths of philosophy; ideologues, like Zhdanov, could require artists to toe the party line; and moralists could condemn writings that use the masculine pronoun in a grammatically correct gender neutral sense. These arbitrary claims are dogmatic assertions that a favored mode of evaluation should take precedence over the others. They offend against both reason and a decent respect for the preferences of others.

But if the occurrence of conflicts among evaluations cannot be reasonably denied, if the conflicts cannot be reasonably resolved by claiming that the evaluations of one mode should always override the conflicting evaluations of other modes, and if practical exigencies make it necessary to resolve the conflicts one way or another, then how do we avoid the arbitrariness of conflict-resolutions and the resulting breakdown of reason that, according to relativists, is the truth about the human condition?

8.5. Modus Vivendi

The key to avoiding the alleged breakdown of reason is to reject an assumption on which both the case for overridingness and relativism rest. I have been inveighing against this assumption throughout the book, and I do so once more. The assumption is that the requirements of reason are universal and impersonal. This is true of the theoretical use of reason that aims at true beliefs, but it is false of the practical use of reason that aims at successful action. If a belief is true, it is true universally and impersonally. If it is true that cancer is caused by viruses, it is true regardless of what anyone believes or how the belief affects our well-being. Whether a belief is true depends on the facts. Whether an action is successful depends on what success consists in. But that, in turn, depends on whether the action conforms to the particular and variable requirements of a society's cultural identity and the agent's conception of well-being. If we go beyond the human dimension of our system of values, we find that cultural identities and conceptions of well-being vary with societies and individuals. The cultural and personal dimensions of our system of values allow many different and reasonable conceptions of well-being formed out of our many different attitudes and commitments whose objects are the many different possibilities we try to realize. Given a society's cultural identity and an individual's particular conception of well-being, there will be a reasonable resolution of a conflict between the evaluations of different modes, but the resolution will be particular and personal, not universal and impersonal. The resolution will not depend on there being a mode of evaluation whose evaluations always override the evaluations of other modes, but on which evaluation is more important in that context as judged by the prevailing cultural identity and the conception of well-being of the person who faces the conflict.

Whether that conception of well-being is reasonable depends on whether it is formed out of mistake-free attitudes, well-ordered commitments, and whether it conforms to the prevailing cultural identity. And whether the prevailing cultural identity is reasonable depends on whether its interpretations of human values, forms of expression and conduct, institutions and practices, and modes of evaluation provide a sufficiently wide range of possibilities and set no more than necessary limits on their pursuit, given the prevailing climatic, demographic, economic, historical, and technological conditions of a particular society at a particular time. To seek universal and impersonal conflict-resolutions under such circumstances is to seek an impossibility. The unavoidable failure to find it signifies a mistaken view of reason, rather than its breakdown. Practical reason is not theoretical reason; its requirements are not universal and impersonal; and what is practically reasonable for particular persons to do is likely to be different from what is practically reasonable for other persons to do, especially when what is at stake are conflicts between evaluations on which their well-being depends. It is as unreasonable to expect practical reason to conform to the standards of theoretical reason as it is to expect theoretical reason to conform to the standards of practical reason.

This is not because either lacks standards, but because they have different standards. Why, then, are they both species of reason? Because both the true beliefs arrived at by theoretical reason and the successful actions to which practical reason leads are the best ways we have found for improving the human condition.

I claimed at the beginning of this chapter that the secular view has the resources to avoid disenchantment and to provide attractive alternatives to evil-doing. I hope that the argument has made both claims obvious enough so that I can state them very briefly. The needed resources are provided by modes of evaluation and their corresponding first-order activities. Non-verbal art, literature, morality, philosophy, politics, and religion provide the valued possibilities by which we can live interesting, enriching, and fulfilling lives. The exemplars I have briefly described and the dozens of others that could be added are concrete illustrations and inspirations of what we can do to make our lives better. If the contingencies of life permit it, we can avoid disenchantment by drawing on the ample resources of the cultural dimension of our system of values. If we do so, we will not be tempted by ideologies that appeal to the dark side of our ambivalent nature and we will have attractive alternatives to evil-doing. The strongest reason against doing evil is provided by the combination of these alternatives, the reliable enforcement of required conventions that prohibit the violation of basic requirements of human well-being, and by holding people responsible for the readily foreseeable consequences of their actions.

9

The Personal Dimension and Boredom

We have seen in the last chapter that our various modes of evaluation provide admirable religious and non-religious exemplars. We are, therefore, not doomed to disenchantment if we do not regard religious evaluation as overriding. Yet disenchantment is a widespread social phenomenon. Its cause may be a weakening commitment to religion, but, I will argue, there are other ways of avoiding it than by strengthening religious commitments. Disenchantment is prevalent, because there is a gap between the possibilities of well-being we have reason to value and our active pursuit of them. Something within us stands in the way, so the obstacle is psychological. When many of us are hindered by the same obstacle, it becomes a social phenomenon, much as it is a social phenomenon when many of us are attracted by the same possibility. The obstacle in question is boredom. Disenchantment is a social phenomenon, because boredom is widespread.

There cannot be many things about which Russell and Heidegger agree, but boredom is one of them. Russell says that "boredom as a factor in human behavior has received, in my opinion, far less attention than it deserves. It has been, I believe, one of the great motive powers throughout the historical epoch, and it is so at present day more than ever."[1] Heidegger says the same, even if with the aid of a surfeit of mixed metaphors, "this profound boredom, drifting hither and thither in the abysses of existence like a mute fog, drowns all things, all men and oneself among them. . . . All things, and we with them, sink into a kind of indifference. . . . There is nothing to hold onto."[2] The psychologist Karl Scheibe writes that "boredom . . . is the paramount motivational issue of our times."[3] According to the sociologist O. E. Klapp, "a strange cloud hangs over modern life . . . now it is thicker than ever. It embarrasses claims that the quality of life is getting better. . . . Like smog, it spreads to all sorts of places it is not supposed to be. . . . The most common name for this cloud is boredom."[4] The literary historian Reinhard Kuhn observes that "in the twentieth century ennui is not one theme among others; it is the dominant theme."[5] And Jacques Barzun describes our condition at the end of his monumental cultural history that "after a time, estimated over a century, the western mind was set upon by a blight: it was boredom."[6]

9.1. Boredom

We are all bored sometimes, because we all have to put up with boring experiences. Long flights, waiting in reception rooms, monotonous chores, the often-heard stories of a relative, most political speeches, social realist novels, and the loving descriptions of their ailments by casual acquaintances are boring. They are irritating nuisance, but not threatening. Episodic boredom is not a momentous experience. Boredom, however, may be chronic, serious, and threatening. Its cause, then, is an attitude, rather than the object of the attitude. When the attitude is dominant, everything is boring, even objects that others find very interesting. As William James describes the experience, "from the bottom of every fountain of pleasure . . . something bitter rises up: a touch of nausea, a falling dead of delight, a whiff of melancholy . . . bring[ing] a feeling coming from a deeper region and often hav[ing] an appalling convincingness. The buzz of life ceases at their touch as a piano-string stops sounding when the damper falls upon it." And he adds a few pages later, "the lustre and enchantment may be rubbed off from the goods of nature . . . there is a pitch of unhappiness so great that the goods of nature may be entirely forgotten, and all sentiment of their existence vanish from the mental field."[7] This is what I will be calling boredom in what follows.

In the Catholic tradition, boredom was called *acedia* and condemned as one of the cardinal sins. "*Acedia* (or accidie) is a word derived from Greek . . . signifying lack of interest . . . a condition of the soul characterized by torpor, dryness, and indifference culminating in disgust. . . . Unlike the other capital sins, acedia may bring about a crisis in which man becomes aware of his actual condition. . . . The dangers inherent in this state of affairs are immense, for it can lead to the greatest of evils. . . . Acedia is especially pernicious because it opens the way for all other vices. . . . Its victim . . . [is] alienated from his fellow men, feels himself misunderstood. He holds his peers and superiors in contempt and considers himself as being better than they."[8]

Boredom is a state of mind in which we have nothing to live for. Everything seems pointless and indifferent; nothing seems to matter. Facts are acknowledged, but none has more significance than any other. The distinction between important and unimportant matters disappears. We remember our earlier beliefs, emotions, motives, and commitments, but they no longer carry conviction. All our evaluations appear arbitrary, because the ground has disappeared from under them. Others who are not similarly afflicted seem naïve and childlike, because they have not looked into the abyss which we face without the possibility of relief. The threat is the dissolution of the evaluative dimension of our life. If we do not believe that anything matters, if all facts appear to lack significance, then our emotional reactions deaden and we have no reason left to make an effort to try to change anything in the world or in ourselves.

Falling into this state of boredom is one of the worst things that can happen, because it destroys the very point of being alive. Our physical existence continues, our physiological needs are not silenced, but our psychic center is assailed and we helplessly witness its dissolution. The terrible thing is that the loss of self, of our individuality, is not caused by events, such as torture, from which we could perhaps recover, but by us. The perpetrator and the victim are one. Recovery seems hopeless, because what stands in the way is the very condition from which we are supposed to recover.

Boredom combines apathy and restlessness. In apathy nothing is interesting, because we are interested in nothing. The lack is in us, not in objects. We are disengaged from the world, alienated from other people, find all activities worthless, and our dominant feeling is emptiness. If this state persists, it becomes intolerable, because we crave stimulation, worthwhile activities, and objects that engage our interest. If the craving is unsatisfied, restlessness follows. We crave without knowing what might satisfy it, but nothing could, because we simultaneously seek something worth valuing and refuse to attribute value to anything. The unsatisfied craving compels us to keep searching, yet we have made its satisfaction impossible and thus doom the search for it. The restlessness, therefore, continues unabated. The incompatible states of apathy and restlessness collude in sabotaging whatever we try to do to relieve them. One or the other of them, however, becomes dominant. If it is apathy, the result is depression; if restlessness has the upper hand, we endlessly seek distractions. But the distractions are counterfeit. We would have to value them, but boredom makes us unable to value anything. If the distractions no longer engage us, if we cannot overcome apathy, and our restlessness persists unsatisfied, then the mixture, in whatever proportion, of these poisonous conditions makes us desperate for anything that would bring relief.

Serious, chronic boredom is a threat rather than a reality for many of us. It is a state into which we fall if we are reflective, eschew self-deception, and stalwartly face what we see as the truth. We reject evasions, and the loss of meaning and purpose follows. Most of us, however, sense the threat without being clear about what it is. In the current idiom, "we don't want to go there." We are bored, but we do not allow ourselves to be dominated by apathy. We seek distractions that would relieve the boredom and stand between us and the threat that clear-sightedness about boredom would make real.

Popular culture supplies the distractions we seek. Television, recreational drugs, pornography, surfing the Internet, health fads, garage sales, oriental cults, shopping in malls, and spectator sports are some of the familiar forms of distraction. They require little application and energy, give a modicum of pleasure, establish a lukewarm fellow feeling with others who are similarly engaged, and the distractions appear as justifiable forms of relaxation to which we are entitled after a day or week of hard work. Many of us become quite skillful in varying them, avoiding jadedness by overindulgence in any one distraction, and getting through life in this manner by earning a living and filling in the rest of the time. In our age, the distractions of popular culture are the opium of the people—and this is not always a metaphor.

There are some people who are bored, but do not fill their lives with distractions, because they see them for what they are. They may be reluctant to deceive themselves, or cannot silence their strong emotions, or have more time than even skillful manipulation can fill, or are alienated from their society, perhaps by a rebellious temperament. Such people have adequate comfort and possibilities and are more or less acutely aware of the threat of unassuaged boredom. They have moved beyond apathy and they restlessly seek some worthwhile activity that would relieve their boredom. They regard with indifference or contempt the large majority of their fellows who have succumbed to the distractions. They have, as we all do, an ambivalent nature, part of which inclines them toward cruelty, aggression, greed, envy, or selfishness. For such people, the thrill of evil is an attractive possibility.

9.2. The Thrill of Evil

Evil is far more thrilling than the soporific distractions poten-tial evil-doers scorn. Unlike the passivity of most distractions, evil-doing is active and energetic. It relieves the evil-doers' restlessness, because they have to plan, maintain secrecy, leave no clues, and outwit law enforcement agencies. Success gives them a feeling of accomplishment, because they have prevailed in difficult circumstances. Their independence and self-sufficiency are confirmed, and they can take pride in them. They can also express their contempt for the sheep-like herd who are duped by distractions. And their evil actions are authentic, because they express the part of their nature that truly motivates them. Their actions stem from their character, not from indoctrination, social conditioning, or external influences of some other kind. In doing evil, they increase their control of their lives and actions. Furthermore, evil-doing gives them pleasure in addition to what the exercise of authentic agency yields. It is the specific pleasure derived from their evil actions: profit from robbery; strength from mayhem; power from murder or rape. And to these must be added the pleasure of release from the restlessness that has led them to search for some worthwhile activity.

Evil-doing is attractive beyond the thrill and pleasure it yields, because it integrates the evil-doers' attitude to their lives and circumstances. They believe that morality and the law are arbitrary restrictions enforced by the authorities to protect their own interests. They see themselves as smart enough see through the hypocritical rhetoric employed to make the gullible conform. They think that all but fools seek their own advantage and that the only reason for conformity is to avoid punishment. They conform when the refusal is too costly, but they do as they please when they can get away with it. Such actions are not merely thrilling and pleasurable, they also demonstrate to the authorities that not everyone is deceived and that outwitting them is a game that can be won. Their emotions accompany these beliefs: pride at being one of the few who are not deceived and see things as they are; contempt for the herd that stupidly and slavishly conforms; satisfaction at being able to get away with violations; excitement during the planning and the execution of what the authorities call evil; and self-respect derived from a sense of independence and opposition to arbitrary authority. These beliefs and emotions lead to a strong disposition to act on them, to take risks when they seem worthwhile, to present a façade of conformity when it is advantageous; and, above all, through dissimulation, cunning, and calculation, to maintain independence and control in face of the menace of conformity.

Those who possess such an attitude are certainly not bored. Their beliefs, emotions, and motives form a coherent whole. They are fully and wholeheartedly alive. Their lives have meaning and purpose. But they derive these undoubted benefits from the evil they habitually and predictably do. Indeed, they are evil-doers precisely because it enables them to avoid boredom and the sickness of the soul with which it threatens.

Boredom thus may lead to evil, because evil can be thrilling and boredom is a symptom of an empty life lacking in meaning and purpose, a life that everyone wants to avoid. The distractions of popular culture are unlikely to satisfy those who are moderately intelligent and honest with themselves. For such people, the excitement of pitting themselves against moral and legal conventions, outwitting the authorities who try to enforce them, and the prospect of gaining from their evil actions money, or confirmation of their intelligence, strength, or power may prove attractive enough to override whatever scruples they may have.

A reason for evil-doing, then, is boredom and the thrill of evil that relieves it. But this reason is reinforced by the evil-doers' natural propensity for cruelty, aggression, greed, envy, or selfishness, and by the availability of ideologies that make evil-doing commendable by providing justification for it. Ideologies demonize victims as enemies of a fine ideal; free evil-doers from moral restraints; silence their benevolent or compassionate motives; and give free reign to their malevolent inclinations. It is, then, the combined motives of the desire to avoid boredom, the fatuity of the available popular distractions, the thrill of evil, the innate propensity for malevolence, and the availability of ideological justifications that provide strong enough reasons for doing evil.

The significance of this explanation of the connection between boredom and evil should not be either over- or underestimated. I do not claim that boredom always leads to evil. There are many bored people who do not become evil-doers. They may just continue to live boring lives, seek distractions, and do nothing as radical as rebelling against their society. They are much too bored, timid, resigned, or cowed for dramatic steps. There are also many evil-doers who have become what they are because of ideological indoctrination, strong resentment of supposed injustice, overpowering malevolence, or commitment to a flawed system of values, not because of boredom.

The explanation warrants only the more modest conclusion that boredom often leads to seeking thrills that would relieve it, and that evil-doing is one of the thrills that may do so. But when the explanation of evil-doing is that it relieves boredom, or that it is justified by ideological claptrap, or that it allows the expression of malevolent inclinations, then the explanation shows that evil-doers have reasons for doing evil. Not all evil-doers have reasons for what they do and those who have them may not have the reasons I have just described. But many do have those reasons and that explains why many ordinary people have become accomplices to mass murder and willingly caused the horrors of religious persecutions, Nazism, Communism, ethnic cleansing, and tribal and chauvinistic atrocities.

Modest as the significance of this explanation is, it should not be underestimated either. It reinforces the conclusion (reached in 6.5.) that the optimistic faith in the coincidence of the requirements of reason and goodness is mistaken. This faith is the secular version of religious faith in the existence of a God-given moral order in the scheme of things. Just as religious faith has permeated the sensibility of believers, so the secular faith is permeating the sensibility of post-Enlightenment liberals. Part of the significance of the explanation is that both versions of the faith are mistaken—and that is no small matter for it affects pervasive moral and political assumptions.

Another aspect of the significance of the explanation is that it points to what we can do to make evil less prevalent. As we have seen, there are reasons for doing evil. But there are also reasons against it. What we can obviously do is to strengthen the reasons against doing evil and weaken the reasons for doing it. The first involves clear, forceful, and widely publicized statement of the reasons against doing evil, including the credible warning that evil-doers will be held responsible for the evil they do. The second has to do with providing attractive alternatives to evil-doing.

Effective reasons against doing evil, of course, cannot be mere reminders of required conventions that prohibit the violation of basic requirements of human well-being, because evil-doers know perfectly well that their actions violate those requirements. Effective reasons must appeal to some consideration that would show evil-doers that it is unreasonable to violate required conventions. There are two such considerations.

The first is to point out that the well-being of evil-doers would be at serious risk if the required conventions of their society were not generally observed. It is, therefore, in their interest not to violate the required conventions on which everyone's well-being depends. It will be said against this that evil-doers may acknowledge that their well-being depends on general conformity to the required conventions, and still hold that particular violations, like their own, would not endanger their well-being. This, however, is not true. Even occasional violations threaten a society's general level of security and stability, and because of their threat everyone's well-being would be at risk, including the evil-doers' own. If evil-doers are reasonable, they will accept this, but they may still insist that the risk is negligible and it is reasonable for them to take it, especially because they have a much stronger countervailing reason for evil-doing, namely, their need to alleviate their boredom.

This first consideration can be strengthened further by adding to it a second one, namely, that others in their society have a strong reason to hold evil-doers responsible for the evil they do. And this will certainly jeopardize the well-being of the evil-doers.

Given the overwhelming power of their society and the authority's willingness to use it to enforce the required conventions, evil-doers will have stronger reason not to do evil than to do it. Although the reasons are stronger, they are still not conclusive, because evil-doers may reasonably accept great risks if they find boredom frustrating enough. But the reasons against evil-doing can be strengthened still more if they are conjoined with attractive alternatives to evil-doing.

If boredom is one reason why people become evil-doers, then alleviating their boredom will tend to weaken their reason for doing evil. The key is to encourage evil-doers to form reasonable conceptions of well-being. No more than encouragement is possible, however, because forming them depends on actions that only individuals can take. Only they can increase their control by reflecting critically on how they live, only they can make their attitudes less prone to mistakes, commitments better ordered, and conceptions of well-being more realistic. If they do not do it for themselves, no one can do it for them. But they can be encouraged to do it by the protection of the personal dimension of their system of values. This will provide them with the psychological space in which they can make what they will of their lives, once their basic needs are satisfied and their cultural identity provides sufficient attractive values. They can, then, choose some of these values, focus their attitudes and commitments on them, and form their conception of well-being on that basis.

I conclude that evil-doers, as everyone else, have reasons to form a reasonable conception of well-being. It will help them to avoid the frustrations of boredom and enjoy a better life. They will also have reasons not to do evil, provided their society enforces the required conventions that prohibit evil-doing and holds evil-doers responsible for the evil they do.

9.3. Unassuageable Boredom?

In the course of defending a version of the secular view of the human condition, I have rejected both the unsubstantial dream on which the religious view rests and the relativist conclusion that our values are arbitrary. I have argued against relativists that human, cultural, and personal values can be reasonable and against religious believers that it is not conformity to a supernatural moral order that makes them reasonable. If we have committed ourselves to reasonable values, we have good reasons to live according to them. If we do, we will not be evil-doers and our lives will not be boring. This conclusion will be rejected by both relativists and religious believers on the ground that it is shallow. They will say that deeper reflection on the human condition will lead reasonable people to recognize that the futility of our efforts and the meaninglessness of our lives are unavoidable if we cannot transcend the secular view. Relativists think that we cannot transcend it, and that is why we must accept the arbitrariness of our values. Religious believers conclude that we ought to transcend it, because only then can we avoid relativistic arbitrariness.

Nietzsche poses a question that challenges thoughtful people to reflect more deeply than the supposedly shallow secular view leads them to do. He asks: "What, if some day or night a demon were to steal after you into your loneliest loneliness and say to you: 'This life as you now live it and have lived it, you will have to live once more and innumerable times more. . . .' Would you . . . have answered him: . . . 'never have I heard anything more divine.' . . . How well disposed would you have to become to yourself and to life *to crave nothing more fervently* than this ultimate confirmation and seal."[9] Nietzsche's question invites us to reflect on whether we would welcome it if our present way of living continued into the indefinite future. Only if we answer sincerely in the affirmative, can we say that we have a reasonable conception of well-being and we are living according to it. Any other answer would indicate that for one reason or another well-being eludes us.

An ancient world-weary attitude involves the denial that a sincere affirmative answer can ever be given. The author of *Ecclesiastes* writes: "All things are full of weariness; a man cannot utter it. . . . What has been is what will be, and what has been done is what will be done; and there is nothing new under the sun. . . . All is vanity and striving after wind. What is crooked cannot be made straight. . . . In much wisdom is much vexation, and he who increases knowledge increases sorrow. . . . The fate of the sons of men and the fate of beasts is the same; as one dies, so dies the other. . . . The dead who are already dead [are] more fortunate than the living who are still alive; but better than both is he who has not yet been."[10]

The relativistic criticism of the secular view expresses the same attitude: if we reflect deeply enough, we will realize that we cannot give a sincere and affirmative answer to Nietzsche's question. My analysis of critical reflection on attitudes, commitments, values, and conceptions of well-being ultimately fails to improve our lives. Deeper reflection leads to this disheartening conclusion, because it shows that if we stop deceiving ourselves, we will realize that our boredom is unassuageable and our values are arbitrary.

Karel Capek, in his play, *The Makropulos Secret*, agrees: we cannot escape boredom.[11] Capek, probably ironically, calls the play comedy, but it is in fact as authentic a tragedy as any that has been written since those of ancient Greece. It is comic only in the sense that some of its lines are very funny. The same theme is treated in Leon Janacek's opera, *Makropulos*.[12] The theme, then, is taken up and discussed from a philosophical point of view by Bernard Williams in "The Makropulos Case: Reflections on the Tedium of Immortality."[13]

Capek's play is about a great opera singer, Emilia Marty. She has been 37 years old for 300 years. Her longevity and arrested aging is the result of an elixir, discovered by her father, Makropulos. One drop of the elixir prolongs life in its present state for 300 years. Emilia Marty has been perfecting her art for 300 years. When we encounter her she has achieved an unprecedented state of excellence. Her 300 years are just about up and she has to have another drop of the elixir, if she is to live on. She is asked about her state of mind and she describes it as "boredom. . . . Everything is so pointless, so empty, so meaningless. . . . One finds out that one cannot believe in anything. Anything. And from that comes this cold emptiness. . . . You realize that art is useless. It is all in vain. . . . People are never better. Nothing can ever be changed. Nothing, nothing, nothing really matters. If at this moment there were to be . . . the end of the world, or whatever, still nothing would matter. Even I do not matter." And she says to her quotidian interlocutors: "You disgust me. . . . You believe in everything: in love, in yourselves, in honor, in progress, in humanity . . . in pleasure . . . faithfulness . . . power . . . you fools." As for her, "everything tires me. It tires one to be good, it tires one to be bad. The earth itself tires me. . . . We . . . we old ones . . . we know too much . . . in us all life has stopped. . . . And it goes on, goes on, goes on. Ah, this terrible loneliness".[14] Janacek has her sing: "I've grown tired of good things,/I've grown tired of evil things./Tired of earth,/tired of the heavens!/And then one knows that the soul has died in him".[15]

Emilia Marty was forced by her extraordinary circumstances to put to herself Nietzsche's question. Her eventual answer is that she does not want to live on, because it would involve the endless repetition of familiar activities that have become boring. Such a life would be a tiresome burden that no reasonable person would want to bear. The suggestion is that if we understand what Emilia Marty had come to understand, we would arrive at the same conclusion as she did. We would see that lives committed to the pursuit of some conception of well-being only appear to be worthwhile, because self-deception prevents us from discovering how utterly boring they would prove to be in the long run. We would then do as Emilia Marty had done: refuse to take the elixir and, as a benefit to humanity, destroy the formula.

Let us ask, however, why it should be supposed that the indefinite prolongation of a life would have to involve endless repetition? If it did, it *would* become overwhelmingly boring, but why could it not involve an endless variety of different activities? Why would Emilia Marty have to remain a singer throughout her 337 years? Bernard Williams argues that this way of relieving the boredom of immortality is not open. If I would value quite different activities in the future from the activities I value now, then the I who performed the activities would also have to be different and the continuity necessary for immortality would be lost. If, on the other hand, my future activities would be the same as they now are, then I would soon find their endless repetition boring and I would no longer value the activities. In neither case is immortality worth having. Either it would not be I who lives on and then I have no reason now to value someone else living on, or it would be I who lives on, but my activities would lose the value they now have through endless repetition.

We should not dismiss the dilemma Williams has posed and let those who believe in immortality worry about it, because the same dilemma may be said to confront us as we live our mortal lives. If I go through life repeating the same valued activities, then the activities would lose their value and become boring through repetition. If I keep changing the activities I value, I would have to keep changing my attitudes, commitments, values, and conceptions of well-being, and that means that the self I now am would not be the same as the future self who is having quite different attitudes, commitments, values, and conception of well-being. If I do not change, my life becomes boring. If I do change, the resulting life is no longer the possession of the self I now am.

The dilemma Williams posed has been much discussed, but there is an obvious way out of it. There is no reason why part of me could not change in order to avoid the boring repetition of activities, while other parts of me remain unchanged and sustain the continuity of my body, memory, and many of my psychological dispositions. Of course, Emilia Marty would become bored with being even an excellent singer for 300 years. But when boredom threatens, she should stop singing and become an arctic explorer, learn to juggle, practice law, study astronomy, or become an expert at Chinese calligraphy. The possibilities of life are many and there is no reason why the same person could not stop pursuing possibilities that have become boring and start pursuing more interesting ones. The dilemma Williams poses would confront us in our mortal existence only if our identity were exhausted by our activities, but our activities constitute only a part of our identity. Our character traits, memory, sense of humor, talents and weaknesses, virtues and vices, sexual preferences, political views, musical tastes, and so forth may persist unchanged in the midst of even radically changing activities. Williams' supposed dilemma could not arise if the discredited assumptions of behaviorism were abandoned. I do not think, therefore, that our lives are permeated with unassuageable boredom. Many people can give a sincere affirmative answer to Nietzsche's question. I also think that the fine prose notwithstanding, the author of *Ecclesiastes* is simply mistaken: anesthesia, polyphony, printing, gun powder, Christianity, and one or two other things were new under the sun after these silly sonorous lines had been written.

The secular view, therefore, is not guilty of shallowness in not facing the abyss of unassuageable boredom that empties life of meaning, purpose, and enjoyment. If we are bored, we can overcome it, provided the contingencies of life do not prevent it, because our system of values is rich in possibilities of well-being. The secular view, however, may still be criticized for the shallowness of not facing what reflection reveals about the human condition.

9.4. The Burden of Reflection

Another line of thought that supposedly leads to a disheartening truth about the human condition begins with Isaiah Berlin's warm endorsement of Schumpeter's odd claim that "to realise the relative validity of one's convictions . . . and yet stand for them unflinchingly, is what distinguishes a civilised man from a barbarian." Berlin, then, adds that "to demand more than this is perhaps a deep and incurable metaphysical need; but to allow it to determine one's practice is a symptom of an equally deep, and more dangerous, moral and political immaturity."[16]

Readers not bowled over by Berlin's fine rhetoric will have questions. If our convictions have only relative validity, why should we stand for them unflinchingly? What should civilized people do when their unflinching convictions of relative validity about good and evil conflict? Why is it dangerous moral and political immaturity to believe in the objective validity of such convictions as that it is wrong to torture innocent people, to prostitute children, to burn people to death for their religious faith, to doom them to many years of forced labor for their political beliefs, or to murder them for being members of a hated group? Why does it make one a barbarian to be convinced that it is objectively, and not just relatively, better to settle international conflicts by negotiation than war, or that adequate nutrition is better than starvation, or that a society in which basic needs are satisfied is better than one in which they are not?

Berlin's response is that these questions are prompted by a deep and incurable metaphysical need that cannot be satisfied and whose satisfaction is the motivating force behind the religious and secular ideologies that are responsible for the familiar horrors of our history. He thinks that the questions are "rooted in the optimistic view—which seems to be at the heart of much meta-physical rationalism—that all good things must be compatible, and that therefore freedom, order, knowledge, happiness . . . must be at least compatible and perhaps even entail one another in a systematic fashion. But this . . . is perhaps one of the least plausible beliefs ever entertained by profound and influential thinkers."[17] The distinguishing mark of being civilized is to have reached by reflection the conclusion that the optimistic view is indefensible. We will see then that trying to satisfy the metaphysical need is a symptom of dangerous moral and political immaturity. Berlin would say that the secular view I have been defending is shallow, because it refuses to reflect deeply enough to reach this conclusion.

Now majesté I realize that to accuse Berlin of hedgehogery is lèse majesté, but I do so nevertheless. He is wrong to suppose that an unsatisfied metaphysical need lurks behind simple truths about good and evil. It is not an optimistic view, a symptom of metaphysical rationalism and of a dangerous ideological commitment to claim objective, and not just relative, validity for the conviction that it is better to satisfy basic needs than to frustrate them, or that ideologically motivated murder, torture, and enslavement are evil. Nor does it commit one to metaphysical rationalism to claim, as Berlin himself inconsistently does, that "no power, only rights can be regarded as absolute . . . that all men . . . have an absolute right to refuse to behave inhumanly . . . that there are frontiers, not artificially drawn, within which men should be inviolable."[18] Contrary to Schumpeter and to Berlin in one of his inconsistent moods, civilized people hold that such convictions have objective validity. The secular view I am defending is consistent in its commitment to such simple truths and to the rejection of politically and morally dangerous metaphysical rationalism. Berlin is mistaken in denying that these commitments are consistent.

Berlin's mistake follows from his failure to distinguish between pluralism and relativism about values. Pluralists accept that the validity of cultural and personal values is relative to societies and individuals, so they reject metaphysical rationalism. But they also hold that human values are objectively valid. They are basic requirements of human well-being and the simple truths I have listed above appeal to some of these values. Relativists hold that that no value has objective validity. Berlin veers between justified pluralism and unjustifiable relativism. That is his mistake and the source of his inconsistency.

Be that as it may with Berlin, perhaps relativists are right and secular pluralists are wrong. Bernard Williams has defended relativism and objected to shallow thinkers who fail to see that reflection unavoidably leads to the recognition of the relativity of all values. Williams says that "the modern world is marked by a peculiar level of reflectiveness" and "there is no route back from reflectiveness."[19] Reflection "destroy[s] knowledge, because thick ethical concepts that were used in a less reflective state might be driven from use by reflection, while the more abstract and general ethical thoughts . . . would not satisfy the conditions of propositional knowledge" (167). "The idea . . . of human beings . . . arriving at an objective foundation of ethical life they know to be objectively founded . . . [is] not a likely prospect" (171). "We would need, it seems to me, not only to be confident in [our] values . . . but also convinced that they were objective, which is a misguided thing to be" (173). We are, then, left with the conclusion that "the world has become *entzaubert*, in Max Weber's famous phrase: the magic has gone from it" (165). And so disenchantment (entzaubert), boredom, and relativism follow.

Williams thus agrees with the religious objections to the secular view I am defending, but he does not think of disenchantment, boredom, and relativism as problems. He rather laconically regards them as features of the modern world and resigns himself to living with the disheartening truths to which, he thinks, reflection leads those who are unwilling to deceive themselves.

Before we join Williams' resigned attitude, we should ask what reason does he give for the claims that there is no route back from reflection, that reflection destroys ethical knowledge, and that it is misguided to be convinced that some values are objective? Williams supposes that the reasons follow from what he calls genealogical reflection on social phenomena. He says that "genealogy is a narrative that tries to explain a cultural phenomenon by describing the way in which it came about, or could have come about, or might be imagined to have come about." And he goes on to say that genealogy "has particular importance in relation to our ethical life, the ethical life of modernity. Our ethical ideas are a complex deposit of many different traditions and social forces, and they have themselves been shaped by self-conscious representations of that history."[20] Genealogical reflection destroys ethical knowledge, because it shows that values are historically conditioned responses to particular circumstances and the histories and circumstances of different societies are different. If reflection brings us to understand this about values in general and about our values in particular, then we will see the correctness of Berlin's view that the validity of values is unavoidably relative to the historical circumstances of those who hold them. Williams' reason for thinking that the secular view I am defending is shallow is that it does not carry genealogical reflection far enough to recognize its relativistic consequences.

It seems to me, however, that Williams' attempt to show that genealogical reflection leads to relativism is wholly unpersuasive. I do not see how "a narrative that tries to explain a cultural phenomenon by describing the way in which it came about, or could have come about" has any bearing on the objective validity of the cultural phenomenon. Williams gives as examples of genealogical explanation Nietzsche on morality and religion and Hume on religion; to which may be added Hume on justice; various state of nature accounts of civil society by Hobbes, Locke, and Rousseau; Williams' own account of truthfulness; and Craig's account of knowledge. There are, of course, many other examples.

I agree that genealogical reflection may enhance our understanding of cultural phenomena; that it may show interestingly and surprisingly that the function of a cultural phenomenon is quite different from what participants in it believe or say that it is; and that all cultural phenomena bear the imprint of the historical and social context of their origin and subsequent development. But I do not agree that genealogical reflection can either vindicate or subvert cultural phenomena. Understanding a cultural phenomenon can be no more than a preliminary step, perhaps necessary, toward determining its validity.

Suppose for the sake of argument that the genealogical explanation of religion by either Hume or Nietzsche is correct. The perfectly reasonable response of a committed religious believer would be that the genealogy may reveal the venal motives of believers, but leaves untouched the truth or falsity of what they believe. Generally speaking, the motives people have, or suppose themselves to have, for holding a belief are one thing, the truth of the belief is quite another. Oddly enough, Williams explicitly recognizes this: "some will press a 'genetic fallacy' objection to the effect that the soundness of the belief must be an entirely separate question from its causation."[21] As far as I have found, however, he does not show how his view could be defended against what seems to me to be the fatally damaging implication of this objection.

Bearing this in mind, consider Williams' claims that there is no route back from reflection, that reflection destroys ethical knowledge, and that values have only relative, not objective, validity. It is certainly true that once we start to reflect and leave a prereflective state of innocence behind, we cannot return to it. But it is not true that reflection will make it impossible to hold the same beliefs as we have held prereflectively. Reflection may show that some of our pre-reflective beliefs were naïve, or it may reinforce some of them. Our pre-reflective beliefs that the murder, torture, or enslavement of innocent people is wrong may well be strengthened by a reflective understanding of human well-being and the perniciousness of ideology. Reflection, therefore, may strengthen rather than destroy ethical knowledge. It is true that reflection may show that some of our pre-reflective beliefs, say about humility, chastity, thrift, or homosexuality, are mistaken. Williams, however, supposes that genealogical reflection is bound to subvert all of our beliefs in the objectivity of all of our values. And in this, I think, he is mistaken.

Reflection may reveal that some, or even many, of our evaluations are the products of our cultural identity and individual conceptions of well-being. Or it may reveal that some other of our evaluations are derived from universal conditions of human well-being that are the products of our shared nature, not of any culture or conception of well-being. It seems to me that Williams' ingenious arguments show only what we knew all along, namely, that our beliefs are influenced by our context. But they do not show that the truth of all of our evaluations depends on our context.

9.5. Overview

I have argued that we should not deceive ourselves with the false hope derived from the unsubstantial dream of a supernatural moral order that guarantees that in the long run all will be well. Nor should we suppose that if we give up the dream, we must embrace relativism that denies the objectivity of all values. The alternative is the secular view I have defended. According to it, the key to our well-being is to increase our control by critical reflection. No amount of control will free us from the contingencies of life, but we can become less vulnerable to them if we construct and live according to a reasonable three-dimensional system composed of a wide plurality of human, cultural, and personal values. Each dimension has a standard of evaluation—the satisfaction of basic needs, the maintenance of cultural identity, and reasonable conceptions of well-being—and when values and evaluations conflict in particular situations, as they often do, the reasonable course of action is to opt for ones that are more important for our well-being in that situation at that time. Although reasonable conflict-resolutions vary with situations, there is usually one that is objectively the best and most reasonable in any particular situation.

Relativists rightly insist that cultural and personal values are relative to societies and individuals. But they wrongly suppose that the same is true of human values. Human values express objective requirements of human well-being that do not vary with societies and individuals. Religious believers are right to see that human values are not made by us and that the adequacy of our system of values depends on its conformity to objective conditions that exist independently of our hopes, fears, and evaluations. But they are wrong to suppose that the objective conditions are dependent on a supernatural order that permeates the scheme of things.

Although each dimension of our system of values has the means to protect conditions of our well-being, each faces a major problem. For the human dimension, the problem is the prevalence of evil; for the cultural dimension, it is widespread disenchantment with modern life; and for the personal dimension, it is boredom that pervades many lives once their comforts have been secured. These problems are intimately connected. Part of the reason why boredom is a pervasive psychological condition is that disenchantment is a widespread social condition. Part of the reason why evil is prevalent is that the thrill of evil-doing is a welcome relief from boredom and an alternative to disenchantment. Religious critics claim that these problems are unavoidable consequences of abandoning commitment to a supernatural moral order. My response has been that the problems arise, because of our failure to make better use of the resources our system of values provides.

If we enforce required conventions more strictly, hold evil-doers responsible more reliably, and encourage people to take advantage of attractive alternatives to evil-doing more strongly, then evil will be less prevalent. If we learn from and adapt to our circumstances the inspiring exemplars embedded in the classic works of art, literature, morality, philosophy, politics, and religion, then disenchantment will be less widespread. And if we make better use of the rich possibilities of life that our system of values provides, then boredom will be alleviated. I state these remedial measures in general terms, but their force derives from the particular details I have endeavored to provide in the preceding chapters.

The chief obstacles in the way of doing all this is our ambivalent nature and fallibility, both of which are ineradicable parts of the human condition. We become disenchanted, bored, and evil-doers, because our attitudes are mistaken, our commitments are incoherent, and our conceptions of well-being are unreasonable. We need to rely on critical reflection to correct, insofar as we can, our tendencies to go wrong in these ways. The extent to which we succeed is the extent to which we diminish evil, disenchantment, and boredom. Complete success will unavoidably elude us, because we are ambivalent and fallible, and because we cannot entirely free ourselves from the contingencies of life. But partial success is greatly preferable to the misery that follows if we fail to do what we can to succeed.

10

Secular Hope

Religious critics have argued that the secular view cannot sustain hope for the betterment of the human condition. Without hope disillusion follows and it exacerbates the adversities we already face. Since the secular view rejects the possibility of supernatural help that might give us hope, it is left with the forlorn wish that we will be

> From too much love of living,
> From hope and fear set free.

It remains for us to

> . . . thank with brief thanksgiving
> Whatever gods may be
> That no life lives for ever;
> That even the weariest river
> Winds somewhere safe to sea.[1]

I think, however, that a deeper understanding of the human condition permits defenders of the secular view to have more reasonable hope.

10.1. Depth

I will concentrate on depth that is an admirable, highly desirable, and yet rare quality of some exceptional people. Its opposites are shallowness and superficiality, and profundity is its first cousin. Penetrating understanding, profound emotions, exceptionally creative imagination, and a wise philosophical outlook are some indications of depth. Understanding is especially important for it, because emotions, imagination, or outlooks lack depth if they involve a failure of understanding. If strong and passionate emotions are directed toward trivial or non-existent objects, if exceptionally lively imagination is mingled with fantastic impossibilities seriously entertained, if a philosophical outlook ignores relevant facts, they will lack depth. Depth has an essential connection with truth. Understanding is important to it, because it bridges the gap between appearance and reality. Misdirected emotions, fanciful imagination, and a cavalier attitude to facts cannot do that.

Depth, however, is more than bare understanding. Scholars, pedants, and experts lack depth if their minds are cluttered with accurate information about trivia. Depth involves understanding what is important and explaining why. Those who have it are able to discern the connection between apparently unrelated phenomena, to see below their surface and understand the underlying structure which accounts for the appearances. Depth provides a chiasmic view that illuminates what was previously problematic, even if no one was aware that there was a problem in need of illumination. It often raises penetrating questions no one asked before.

Yet depth is not merely a cognitive excellence. It concerns important matters, and it is natural if understanding them exerts formative influence on our emotions, imaginations, and how we see the world. Sophocles and Euripides on tragedy, Hobbes and Machiavelli on politics, Augustine and Montaigne on self-understanding, Sextus and Hume on skepticism, Nietzsche on the death of God, Darwin on evolution, Einstein on relativity, and Wittgenstein on language are some notable examples of views that have influenced our attitude toward the world, and consequently how we respond to it. Their influence is felt even by those who do not understand or disagree with them. It is best to think of depth as having cognitive, emotive, imaginative, and motivational *aspects*, rather than as a cognitive achievement to which other aspects of our inner lives are irrelevant.

Depth occurs in many forms: artistic, literary, moral, philosophical, political, religious, scientific, and historical among others. All forms of depth are important for us, but I will concentrate on the form the secular view may yield of the human condition. The first step toward it is the sort of descriptive account I have been teasing out of the tradition that extends from Euripides to our days. Part of it is the recognition that we are beset by our ubiquitous mistakes and by the contingencies, limits, evil, disenchantment, and boredom that so often stand between us and our well-being. The understanding we reach prompts emotional reactions: optimism or pessimism, resignation or resentment, romantic rebellion or a quest for certainty, distrust of reason or search for an infallible method, and so forth. It may provoke imaginative efforts to formulate an ideal theory to save us from our predicament, or to design a blueprint for improving human nature, or to retreat into romantic aestheticism as an escape from the sordidness of everyday life. And it may spur us to formulate a philosophical outlook by searching for the laws of history, society, or psychology that would enable us to explain, predict, and control the tendency of our affairs to get out of hand and redound to our detriment.

The dismal failures of many of these reactions to the descriptive understanding of the human condition are central features of the secularization of life that began with the secular faith of the Enlightenment, a faith that, I believe, is an aberration of the secular view. The faith promised that once we are freed from the burden of tradition and authority and become well enough educated to rely on our native reason and good will, there will remain no obstacle to the improvement of the human condition. But the promise was not kept, could not be kept, because it failed to recognize the no less native unreason and ill will that also motivate us. The familiar wars, revolutions, murderous ideologies, pervasive nihilism, mindless pleasure-seeking, cynicism, search for oriental cults, and widely shared yearning for more certainty, security, and

210 THE HUMAN CONDITION

meaning than we have are so many dangerous reactions to the failures of the secular faith. Religious critics point to these failures as the effects of the poverty of secularism and the rejection of religion.

These critics are right about the failures, but wrong about their cause. The failures are not symptoms of the bankruptcy of the secular view. They are the effects of the misguided faith that ought not to have been held in the first place. Part of depth is to understand that the secular faith is untenable and an obstacle to a realistic view of the human condition. One main reason for the persistence of the faith and its hold on the minds of so many people who ought to know better is that it is partly true. The true part holds that reason and good will are basic parts of our nature. The false part ignores that unreason and ill will are also basic parts of our nature. The faith is reinforced by the all-too-familiar stratagem of focusing on confirming and ignoring disconfirming evidence. It is easy to find people and actions motivated by reason and good will, but it is just as easy to find ones with contrary motives. If the first strengthen the faith, then the second ought to weaken it. What ought to happen, however, does not happen, because the faith reinforces the illusions of those who hope for a steady progress toward a forever improving future. But the failures show that the faith, the illusion, and the hope are unreasonable.

Part of depth is to face the fact that we are one of the main sources of the adversities that stand in our way. Reason and unreason, good and ill will are ineradicable parts of our nature. At different times and places, in different circumstances, and in different individuals sometimes one, sometimes the other part dominates. It is certainly true that reason and good will ought to be strengthened and the unreason and ill will weakened. But the strengthening and weakening can only be done by us, and the doing of it also depends on which tendencies of our ambivalent nature are temporarily dominant or recessive. We endeavor to lift ourselves by frayed bootstraps. The secular faith is unreasonable, because it refuses to face this fact. Religious faith, to its credit, faces it, but it has nothing better to offer in response than an unsubstantial dream. There are, however, strong reasons for believing that if the secular view is freed from the incubus of this misguided faith, it has the resources to sustain a modest reasonable hope for the future.

The news depth gives us is not upbeat. The understanding we gain from it of the human condition and of the shallowness of the secular faith is somber and disillusioning. It easily provokes the dangerous emotive, imaginative, and philosophical reactions I have pointed at earlier. What should we do, then, if we have a realistic view of the human condition and resist the blandishments of both secular and religious faith?

10.2. Modest Hope

We should live without illusions and we should hold on to the modest but reasonable hope that the system of values that has provided the human, cultural, and personal requirements of our well-being in the past will continue to do so in the future. An illusion is a false or misleading view of some aspect of reality. It may allow us to cope with some unbearable facts, but in the ordinary course of events, in everyday life, when we are engaged in more or less important practical activities, an illusion sooner or later leads to an inappropriate response and to the failure to accomplish whatever we set out to do. This makes it unreasonable to allow illusions to guide our actions, especially when something important is at stake. It is an illusion that truth and justice must prevail, that our beloved children cannot come to a bad end, that villains could not get away with it, that luck will not desert us, or that reason and good will guarantee well-being. Such illusions prevent us from facing unpleasant facts and trying to avoid consequences we could not reasonably want. It is true that even our best efforts may fail, but that is not a reason against making them. On the contrary, it is a reason for making them, because if we do not, we increase the chances of the failure we want to avoid. All this is plain common sense. But it takes depth, not just common sense, to respond appropriately if we abandon illusions.

One seductive response is to allow disillusion to overpower us. This may take a variety of unwholesome forms: despair; cynicism; instant gratification; consoling ourselves with mysticism, oriental cults, or religious fanaticism; misanthropy; fervent ideological moralizing; numbing ourselves with work or physical exertion; and so forth. Disillusion in all these and other forms is an unreasonable overreaction to having given up illusions. If we no longer believe that things will turn out for the best, we need not conclude that everything is going to hell. To recognize that we are fallible and vulnerable does not mean that we are bound to be mistaken, nor that calamity lurks just around the corner. We are at risk, but we are not doomed. The contingencies of life do not just threaten, but may actually favor us. And although the attitudes, commitments, and conceptions of well-being we have formed on the basis of critical reflection may be mistaken, they may also be reasonable and contribute to our well-being. Living with disillusion, therefore, is no better than living with illusions. Illusions lead us to believe falsely that the world is better than it is; disillusion involves the equally false belief that the world is worse than it is. Part of depth is to see that they are obverse sides of a counterfeit coin.

We can go deeper still if we consider why abandoning illusions so often leads to disillusion. The answer is, I think, that illusions give rise to an expectation and when the illusions are abandoned, the expectation persists and is often disappointed. The expectation is that if we do what we reasonably can toward our well-being, then we will have it. If fallibility and contingencies frustrate this expectation, we become bitter, outraged, and indignant at what we see as the unfairness of the scheme of things. How, we ask the unresponsive heavens, could this happen to us, or to those we love, or to the cause dear to our heart? When we get no answer, we eventually realize, provided we are reasonable enough, that the heavens are silent, because they cannot speak, and if they could, they would have nothing to say. Then the frustrated expectation, which we should have given up together with the illusions that have sustained it, shocks us into the overreaction of disillusion.

If we understand this, we have reached greater depth, and the obvious remedy follows from it. The same reasons that prompted us to abandon the illusions give us reasons to abandon the expectation as well. If we give up the expectation, we will not be shocked if it is not met, and, then, we will not overreact to its disappointment and succumb to disillusion. We will allow the realization we have gained from greater depth to sink in and affect not only our understanding, but also our emotions, imagination, and outlook. We will accept, then, that the world was not made for us and we will not conclude that it was made against us. We will realize that it could not have been made either way, because it had not been made. It just is in its indifferent, ever-changing immensity. How we fare in it matters a great deal to us, but not at all to it. Nothing matters to it, not even its own dissolution, if that were possible, because nothing could matter to an insentient mass, regardless of its size.

To have reached this stage of depth is to have gone far, but there is still farther to go. For we cannot fail to ask what the reasonable attitude is for those who have given up illusions and the misguided expectation that goes with them, and avoided the perfervid passions of disillusion. The reasonable attitude is realism about the human condition, and that is the attitude that follows from the secular view I have been defending throughout the book. What is this attitude?

It is to pursue our well-being with the acknowledgment that our success depends on external and internal conditions. Among these conditions are limits to what we can do to achieve well-being. They are not removable or circumventable obstacles in our way, but inhospitable conditions that we cannot overcome, such as the finite capacity of our brain, the permutations and combinations allowed by human DNAs, the scarcity of the Earth's resources, and our helplessness in the face of natural disasters. Both internal and external limits constrain the efforts we can make and how we can make them. One of the internal limits I have stressed is our fallibility, and among external limits I have emphasized the significance of contingencies. The distinction between internal and external limits is no more than an expository convenience. We are natural beings, part of the natural world, the only world we know of, and this makes the limits both inside and outside of our skin the effects of the space-time-causal network of the natural world, and thus not sharply separable.

The external and internal conditions in which we pursue our well-being, however, not only limit its pursuit but also make it possible. For it is natural conditions, first external and eventually internal as well, that enable us to reduce our vulnerability to the vicissitudes of evolution and acquire some control over how we live. And it is natural conditions again that enable us to increase the control we have. Our control is much less than complete, and our ability to increase it is weaker than we might hope, but we have some and we could have more if we conduct our affairs as reasonably as fallibility and contingencies permit.

The evolutionary process that our natural conditions have made possible is the interposition of a protective system of values between the human and the non-human parts of the world. Reason guides us to use the control we have, and to increase it as much as we can, in accordance with the system of values we have constructed. We humanize the minute segment of the world we imperfectly control by our system of values. And that is the key to our well-being. Of course, our efforts at control and at increasing control are limited by our fallibility and vulnerability to contingencies. But normally, which is most of the time, our limits and possibilities coexist.

A realistic secular view of the human condition involves recognizing this. It is a view that acknowledges our limits and encourages the pursuit of our possibilities as the only means we have for bettering our condition. This acknowledgment and encouragement are the constructive aspects of the realistic secular view. But it has also a critical aspect that guards against both the illusion that our condition is better than it is and the disillusion that it is worse.

Secular realism lies between these stultifying extremes, between the unsubstantial dreams of illusions and the corrosive nihilism of disillusion. And realism gives us the modest hope that the secular view allows us to have.

The human condition is a convenient abstraction we can use to refer collectively to the shared conditions of individual human beings. A general description, whose details vary greatly from person to person, is that we pursue our well-being, given our characters and circumstances, by drawing on the resources of our society's system of values, especially on the cultural identity embedded in that system. We consciously or otherwise make some values our own. We try to live, more or less reasonably, with greater or lesser success, according to a conception of well-being we have formed out of human, cultural, and personal values.

A fine thinker has called this process self-enactment, and described it in a way I wholly accept. "This disposition . . . received its classic expression in the *Essais* of Montaigne: . . . a reading of the human condition in which a man's life is understood as an adventure in personal self-enactment. Here there was no promise of salvation for the race or prevision that it would late or soon be gathered into one fold, no anticipation of a near or distant reassemblage of a 'truth' fragmented at the creation of the world or expectation that if the human race were to go on researching long enough it will discover 'the truth', and no prospect of a redemption in a technological break-through providing a more complete satisfaction of contingent wants; there was only a prompting not to be dismayed at our own imperfections and a recognition that 'it is something almost divine for a man to know how to belong to himself' and to live by that understanding."[2]

Depth, then, may be said to consist in a descriptive understanding of the human condition that engages our emotion, imagination, and motivation; in the rejection of both religious and secular faith; in the recognition that our nature includes the contingencies that beset us; in the abandonment of illusions and the expectation they prompt; in resistance to disillusion; and in the acceptance of a realistic view of our possibilities and limits. The secular view is that if depth is understood in this way, it allows us to have modest hope.

Critics of the secular view will say that this is pretty thin gruel for souls that hunger for more substantial nutrition. I think I have said enough in response to religious critics, but I have not considered defenders of the secular faith who agree with religious critics, although of course not with their constructive alternatives. I will discuss Mill and Kant, who derive much more robust hope than I think is reasonable from the ideal of autonomy. They hold that autonomy is the key to individual well-being, and they have made its pursuit the widely accepted aim of much contemporary moral and political thought. I think that the hope they derive from autonomy is another illusion, sustained by the untenable but flattering secular faith that human beings are basically motivated by reason and good will.

10.3. The Illusion of Autonomy

The ideal of autonomy is that individuals should choose how they want to live and then live that way. Their choices should be uncoerced by threats, manipulation, or emergencies; informed by understanding both the circumstances and the likely consequences of the various available alternatives; and based on the evaluation of the alternatives as good, bad, better, worse, indifferent, or irrelevant. Autonomous individuals, then, should act on the alternative they have chosen in this manner. The closer they come to meeting these conditions, the closer they come to choosing reasonably for themselves how they should live. All normal human beings have the capacity to make such choices and their well-being depends on making them reasonably. The aim of morality and politics ought to be to create the conditions in which they can do so. The robust hope autonomy is supposed by Mill to provide is that in principle nothing stands in the way of creating these conditions and thereby enabling individuals to pursue their own good in their own way. When they do so, they have "an improving state of the human mind" and "the influences are constantly on the increase which tend to generate in each individual a feeling of unity with all the rest; which, if perfect, would make him never think of, or desire, any beneficial condition for himself in the benefits of which they [i.e. all the others] are not included."[3] Here is the secular faith in its full glory!

A great deal has been written about the history, analysis, and interpretation of this ideal of autonomy in general,[4] but I will be concerned for the moment only with individuality in particular, which Mill considers to be an essential feature of the ideal. I concentrate on Mill, because he is the pivotal figure in one of the two most influential contemporary approaches to morality and politics. I think that Mill's view is deeply flawed.

Mill starts out with his famous simple principle: "the sole end for which mankind are warranted, individually or collectively, in interfering with the liberty of action of any of their numbers is . . . to prevent harm to others. His own good, either physical or moral is not a sufficient warrant. He cannot rightfully be compelled to do or forbear because it will be better for him to do so, because it will make him happier, because . . . to do so would be wise or even right."[5] And he goes on: "there should be different experiments in living; that free scope should be given to varieties of character, short of injury to others; and that the worth of different modes of life should be proved practically. . . . It is desirable, in short, that in things which do not primarily concern others individuality should assert itself. . . . The free development of individuality is one of the leading essentials of well-being."[6]

Reasonable contemporary readers of Mill's impassioned rhetoric will call to mind those spoilers: the facts. Robert Whitaker estimates in *Ethical Human Psychology and Psychiatry* 7 (Spring 2005), that the number of people in the US disabled by mental illness in 2005 was about 6,000,000. The International Adult Literacy Survey, reported by the Plain Language Network, puts the number of absolute illiterates in the US at 14,680,000. A bill introduced to the 107th Congress estimates that in 2002 there were 14,800,000 alcoholics and 4,000,000 drug addicts in the US. The report of the Suicide Prevention Resource Center says that in 2003 there were 787,000 suicide attempts in the US. And it is common knowledge that there is widespread unwanted pregnancy; an epidemic of AIDS; generations of families none of whose members ever held a job; untold number of unemployable high school dropouts; and so forth. No one here and now could reasonably believe that "each [of these people] is the proper guardian of his own health, whether bodily *or* mental and spiritual," or that their free development of individuality is "the leading essentials of well-being," or that "their own good, physical or moral, is not a sufficient warrant" for interference, even though the actions of such people harm primarily themselves, not others. In Mill's time, similar facts were readily available. They make his simple principle absurd.

Mill could not have been unaware of such unfortunate facts. It was perhaps because of them that he qualified, and qualified again, the simple principle, although he did not inform his readers that he was doing so and he did not seem to have noticed that the qualifications were inconsistent with the original principle. He wrote: "it would be absurd to pretend that people ought to live as if nothing whatever had been known in the world before they came into it; as if experience had as yet done nothing toward showing that one mode of existence, or of conduct, is preferable to another. Nobody denies that people should be so taught and trained in youth as to know and benefit by the ascertained results of human experience."[7] He claimed, speaking of the "passionate love of virtue and the sternest self-control," that "it is through the cultivation of these that society both does its duty and protects its interests," and he added that a person has character if his "desires and impulses are his own—are the expressions of his own nature, as it has been developed and modified by his own culture."[8] He said that "the honor and glory of the average man is . . . that he can respond internally to wise and noble things, and be led to them.'"[9] Thus Mill giveth, and thus he taketh away.

If individuality consists in conducting one's experiment in living without interference from others, then it may well involve going to hell in one's own way, and that is hardly a leading essential of well-being. If it is accepted that well-being depends on one's character being modified and cultivated by one's culture and on being taught virtue and self-control, then well-being excludes the free development of individuality. And since individuality is an essential feature of autonomy, Mill cannot reasonably suppose that the pursuit of autonomy creates "an improving state of human mind" and provides robust hope for the betterment of the human condition, since, as the facts show, it often leads to the opposite.

Human well-being requires that the development of autonomy be done in the right way, and that includes, even on Mill's showing, the interference of society and culture with the autonomy of individuals. There is no simple principle that determines how intrusive that guidance should be. It depends on how reasonable the prevailing system of values is, how benevolent or malevolent particular individuals are, on what form the guidance should take, and on how serious are the internal and external dangers that threaten the society and culture at a particular time. These are complicated matters of judgment that vary from case to case. Mill's rhetoric is an obstacle to making reasonable judgments.

10.4. The Illusion of the Categorical Imperative

The realistic secular view of the human condition I am defending allows only for a modest hope, because we are fallible and vulnerable to contingencies. Kant says, however, that fortune and fate, which are pretty much what I mean by contingencies, are "usurpatory concepts . . . allowed to circulate by almost universal indulgence," and he plainly disapproves of them.[10] If we have no reason to believe in contingencies, then we have no reason to believe that they stand in the way of a more robust hope than I think is reasonable. If we understand why Kant thinks this about fortune and fate, then we get to the core of his approach to reason and morality.

According to Kant, we can be self-legislators and give ourselves a moral and rational law that commands our will. If we do that, and only then, contingencies will not stand in our way, and we will be free, rational, and moral. He says that "will is a kind of causality belonging to living beings so far as they are rational. *Freedom* would then be a property this causality has of being able to work independently of alien causes." If we are free of alien causes, that is, of contingencies, we will act rationally and morally, and thus autonomously. The "freedom of the will . . . [is] autonomy—that is, the property which the will has of being a law to itself." We are rational self-legislators if the law we give ourselves is the categorical imperative: "Act only on that maxim through which you can at the same time wish that it should become a universal law."[11] The categorical imperative requires us to act as we would want everyone to act independently of all contingent differences in our characters, circumstances, and preferences. To act that way is a universal and impersonal requirement of reason and morality. It is an absolute requirement that allows no exceptions, because making an exception for any person or any action, including oneself or one's action, would be inconsistent with the requirement of universality and impersonality, and thus at once irrational and immoral. The test of the morality and rationality of an act of self-legislation, therefore, is whether one could wish the law we have given ourselves to be universally and impersonally applicable. Only if we could consistently wish that would the law conform to the formal and pure requirements of reason and morality. Being formal and pure, they free one from all contingencies, from the usurpation of fortune and fate, and it is thus the key to a robust hope for the human condition. Kant confidently says "that the hindrances to universal enlightenment . . . are gradually becoming fewer."[12] In a tone more restrained than Mill's, here, once more, is the secular faith. But Kant's version of it, I will now argue, is no more persuasive than Mill's.

Consider the place of self-legislation and reason in Kant's moral thought. Self-legislation is rational and moral only if the law one gives oneself is universally and impersonally applicable. Kant recognizes, of course, that in non-moral contexts one may be guided by what he calls the hypothetical imperative, which allows for particular and personal considerations. But in moral contexts one must either follow a universal and impersonal principle or be immoral and irrational. From this absurd consequences follow.

One is that personal relationships involving, for example, love and friendship are excluded by Kant's view from morality. For what those obligations are depends on the identity and the character of the people involved and on the history of their relationships. Kant's view cannot be rescued from the absurdity of excluding from morality one of the most important moral relationships by saying that love and friendship have obligations that are universally and impersonally applicable to all those who love and have friends. Whether I should forgive my beloved or friend for an insult, thoughtlessness, or disloyalty depends on how serious the offense was, how the other had treated my own past offenses, how much pressure the offender was under, how close the relationship is, how important it is in both of our lives, and so forth. There is no universal and impersonal answer to such questions.

Furthermore, genuine love and friendship by their very nature are guided by affection, not obligation. Lovers and friends have obligations toward one another, but they routinely go beyond them. If they start thinking in terms of obligations, their relationship is already in trouble. Personal relationships are certainly moral, if anything is, but universal and impersonal principles have only a negligible place in them. Because Kant makes following universal and impersonal principles an absolute and exclusive requirement of reason and morality, the absurdity follows that personal relationships cannot be rational and moral.

The existence of moral conflicts points to another indefensible consequence of Kant's view. It often happens that one's genuine moral obligations conflict. Obligations toward family and work, parents and children, law and morality, public and private life, truthfulness and kindness, justice and loyalty often conflict. Such conflicts are routine features of moral life. If we suppose with Kant that obligations are dictated by the universal and impersonal requirements of the categorical imperative, then conflicting obligations force us to acknowledge that the categorical imperative may place on us incompatible requirements. Regardless which of the conflicting obligations reason and morality prompt us to fulfill, we will have violated the other. And that, according to Kant, is irrational and immoral. Thus the absurdity follows that in case of moral conflicts reason and morality require us to act irrationally and immorally. The alternative is to deny that genuine moral conflicts can occur, but that leads to the no less absurd denial of facts of moral life we all routinely experience.

If autonomy requires self-legislation, and if self-legislation can be freed from contingencies only by following the supposed requirements of reason and morality to act on the universal and impersonal principles dictated by the categorical imperative, then we must conclude that autonomy cannot be freed from contingencies. Since Kant's robust hope was based on that possibility, we have no reason to accept it and good reasons to doubt it.

In the foregoing criticisms I have not questioned Kant's view of reason, but I will now do so. Kant is emphatic that the reason involved in autonomy is practical. It is like theoretical reason in being universally and impersonally applicable, but it is unlike it in commanding actions, not beliefs. Autonomy, then, is to follow the universal and impersonal commands of practical reason.

To make this less abstract, consider the command that prohibits lying. Kant says that "to be *truthful* (honest) in all declarations is therefore a sacred command of reason prescribing unconditionally, one not to be restricted by any conveniences."[13] He explains that the categorical imperative commands truth telling, because no one could rationally suppose that telling a lie when it is convenient should become a universal law. No one, then, could believe what anyone say, and that would make communication impossible. This is not something that anyone could reasonably wish.[14] He says elsewhere, a bit hysterically, that "by a lie a human being throws away and, as it were, annihilates his dignity as a human being. A human being who does not himself believe what he tells another . . . has even less worth than if he were a mere thing . . . such a speaker is a mere deceptive appearance of a human being, not a human being himself."[15]

I forgo laboring the absurd consequences of these *obiter dicta*: a human being cannot tell a lie, because if he did he would not be one; lying to a terrorist to save thousands of innocent lives is to throw away one's dignity and humanity; and, contrary to Kant's claim, communication goes on even though politicians, advertisers, job candidates, students, and adulterers, among others, lie with great frequency. I will concentrate instead on the supposed universality and impersonality of practical reason. Let us accept for the moment that lying is as horrendous an immoral and irrational act as Kant says it is. The fact remains that it is not as simple as it seems to tell what a lie is. Are polite inquiries about a detested person's well-being or a pretended yawn lies? Is it a lie to encourage a stupid child's efforts by praising him for doing what he should have been able to do a year earlier or to read out a particularly silly passage from a solemn metaphysical work in an ironic tone obviously at odds with its intended meaning? Is it a lie for an atheist to pray? Do egalitarians lie when they avow their principles, but do not distribute their wealth? Is Wallace Stevens lying when he has mountains talk to each other?

Even if one takes deadly seriously the injunction of practical reason that prohibits lying, one needs to know how to tell what a lie is. That, however, a universal and impersonal principle does not and cannot tell us. For the question is not what the principle says, but how to apply what it says to particular cases. One can be firm in holding a principle and be at a loss to apply it. Kant recognizes this. He says that the application of universal and impersonal principles requires judgment. "Judgment is a peculiar talent which can be practiced only, and cannot be taught. . . . For although an abundance of rules borrowed from the insight of others may indeed be proffered to, and as it were grafted upon, a limited understanding, the power of rightly employing them must belong to the learner himself. . . . He may comprehend the universal *in abstracto*, and yet not be able to distinguish whether a case *in concreto* comes under it."[16]

This has a disastrous implication for Kant's view of practical reason. For practical reason is supposed to command what we ought to do, but it now transpires that it only gives us a principle for whose application we need judgment. But the judgment must always be made *in concreto*, in particular cases. As Aristotle rightly observes, judgment is to know how to act toward "the right person, to the right extent, at the right time, with the right aim, and in the right way, *that* is not for everyone, nor is it easy; that is why goodness is both rare and laudable and noble."[17] If practical reason is universal and impersonal, its command cannot tell us what we ought or ought not to do in a particular situation, such as whether saying or leading others to believe something would be a lie. If it is supplemented with judgment, it will tell us what we ought or ought not to say or lead others to believe in a particular situation, *in concreto*, but it would, then, lose its universality and impersonality, because in other situations the reasonable judgment may be different. If autonomy cannot just be to act according to the categorical imperative, if it must be combined with judgment, then judgment brings back all the contingencies that Kant supposed himself to be avoiding when he stressed the formality and purity of practical reason. He is thus stuck with a dilemma: if practical reason is merely formal and pure, it cannot tell us what action would be good or bad, moral or immoral, rational or irrational. If it is combined with judgment, it can tell us those things, but it loses its universality and impersonality. Contingencies and our fallibility, then, come flooding back and they stand in the way of the robust hope that Kant supposes and the realistic secular view denies that we can reasonably have.

I conclude that neither Mill nor Kant has managed to make his faith reasonable. They have been seduced by the Enlightenment and ignored the endarkenment that our history so amply demonstrates.

10.5. Secular Hope without Illusions

Influential as Mill and Kant are, they have not said the last words on the subject of autonomy. Numerous subsequent defenders of autonomy as a moral and political ideal have made strenuous efforts to avoid the absurd consequences of the theories of Mill and Kant. Nevertheless, all such attempts face the following dilemma. They must either deny or acknowledge that reasonable individual choices about how one should live or act are based on the prevailing system of values. If they deny it, they deny plain facts of moral life, and that makes them absurd. If they acknowledge it, they must acknowledge that reasonable individual choices are not autonomous.

Consider the first alternative. A newly married young couple must choose whether they should have a child. Since they are neither celibate nor sterile, they either use or do not use contraception. Suppose they are reasonable, think and talk about it, and ask themselves whether and how a child would fit into the life they want to have. They will answer, if at all, on the basis of their upbringing, education, religious beliefs or unbeliefs, the examples of people they have known, the books or articles they have read, the television programs they have seen, the advice or example of their parents, relatives, and friends, and so forth. These influences are laden with the prevailing system of values. They seek the answer by evaluating and accepting or rejecting what has influenced them. But whatever they choose, they cannot ignore the prevailing values, because they force choices on them.

Defenders of autonomy may acknowledge this and insist that if the couple is reasonable, they will look within themselves to evaluate the value-laden influences to which they are willy-nilly subject. Being reasonable, they will not evaluate them arbitrarily. They will think about the influences and struggle to choose whether they should follow or resist them. But, if they are to avoid arbitrariness, they can choose only by evaluating the influences on the only basis available to them, namely, other influences. And all influences reflect the prevailing values. This is how we all make reasonable choices about how we live. Our choices are, thus, inseparably connected with the prevailing system of values, even if we go against them.

Defenders of autonomy may grant that this is how we in fact proceed, and insist that we ought not to proceed in this way. We ought to ignore the prevailing system of values and choose autonomously by turning inward. The question, then, defenders of autonomy must answer is what a reasonable choice would be based on. It must be based on something, otherwise it would be unreasonable. It cannot be based merely on a preference, because preferences may be unexamined, trivial, self-destructive, inconsistent, ignorant, or otherwise flawed. If our choice is reasonable, it must appeal to a preference we have reason to have. Defenders of autonomy must recognize eventually that preferences are made reasonable by something outside of them. And that brings the argument in a full circle back to what defenders of autonomy say we ought not do, namely, take into account the prevailing system of values. That does not mean that we must accept the values. But even if we choose to act on preferences that go against them, we cannot avoid taking them into account. That is why opting for the first alternative of the dilemma commits defenders of autonomy to absurdity.

Consider, then, the second alternative that acknowledges the obvious facts I have just adduced. Why could not defenders of autonomy say that the decisions reached the way I have just described are in fact autonomous decisions? Because it would be inconsistent with their original claim. They claimed that autonomy requires us to choose freely in the light of our understanding and evaluation of the available alternatives. But we have now seen that the choices presuppose the prevailing system of values. They are our own choices only in the sense that it is we rather than someone else, who make them. However, we make them in the light of the values of the system. We may make the values our own, but we do not make them. It is contrary to the originally intended meaning of autonomy to say that it consists in following values one has not made. Defenders of autonomy could opt for the second alternative only by abandoning the claim with which they have started out.

I labor this point not to quarrel about the meaning of a word, but to make clear that the robust hope derived from the ideal of autonomy is illusory. The robust hope, it will be remembered, is based on the secular faith that by becoming more and more autonomous, we will become less and less at the mercy of fallibility and contingencies, that there is in principle no obstacle to our doing this, and that we can make the human condition better and better. But if we have no option and must rely on the prevailing system of values, then we remain as fallible and as subject to contingencies as we have always been. For the system of values has been formed and is maintained by human beings like us, who are as ambivalent about good and ill will, reason and unreason as we are. Our inner lives are not so many impregnable citadels into which we can retreat and from which we can view the world as spectators. We have no choice but to live in the world and our inner lives are inseparable from what lies outside of them. These outside influences may be limiting, evil, disenchanting, or boring, and may carry with them the contingencies from which we cannot free ourselves. Robust hope, therefore, is unreasonable.

Hope, however, can also be modest and reasonable if it is based on increasing the control we have by critical reflection. We can direct it inward and examine our attitudes, commitments, and conceptions of well-being, and we can direct it outward to examine the human, cultural, and personal values and the

conventions embedded in the prevailing system of values. And
we can improve both inwardly and outwardly directed critical
reflection by trying to recognize and avoid mistakes we are likely
to make. Reasonable hope derives from the possibility we normally
have to do this. This possibility is limited, because we remain
fallible and vulnerable to contingencies, and they may handicap
our attempts to improve our critical reflection. But we may avoid
some mistakes and contingencies may not assail us. We have no
guarantees, but we have possibilities. I have endeavored throughout
the book to describe what they are. They do not permit robust
hope, but they are enough to stave off disillusion.

Critical reflection is a key element of reasonable hope. It is like
autonomy in some ways and unlike it in others. Both are ideals that
require us to try to have as much control over our lives as possible
and to try to increase, within reasonable limits, whatever control
we have. Unlike autonomy, critical reflection does not require
that the ideal must be followed by everyone; nor that following it
requires a unilateral declaration of independence from our society's
system of values; nor that we must retain for ourselves the final
authority over how we live. By way of concluding this chapter,
I will comment briefly on these differences between the ideals of
autonomy and critical reflection.

Autonomy is supposed to be a requirement of reason and
morality. Failure of autonomy, therefore, is failure in reason and
morality. Or, to express it slightly differently, autonomy is a
necessary condition of being reasonable and moral, and that is what
makes autonomy an ideal. Critical reflection is also an ideal, but it
is not required by either reason or morality. Reason and morality
certainly allow critical reflection, but it is possible to live reasonably
and morally without critical reflection having a significant part in
how we live. Critical reflection is an ideal for those who live
in fortunate circumstances, in comfort, in a stable, law-governed
society, have considerable leisure, are tolerably well-educated and
given to introspection and contemplation, want to see life steadily
and as a whole, and prefer private life to the hurly-burly of public

engagement. I acknowledge that this is my ideal. But it is just one ideal of how one should live, and there are others. Critical reflection need not have an important place in lives dedicated to service, adventure, social reform, testing one's physical limits, or exploring the unexplored; nor in lives involving voluntary participation in a hierarchical institution (religious, military, tribal, ethnic, and the like) where there are clear rules and strict discipline; nor in the lives of creative or performing artists. We know that such lives can be reasonable and moral, because many have been. Part of what is wrong with the ideal of autonomy is that its claims are much too exclusive and dismissive of no less reasonable and moral ideals.

Another difference between autonomy and critical reflection has to do with how their defenders regard the prevailing system of values. Both recognize that we live in a society and we are inevitably influenced by its values. But autonomy is supposed to involve leaving these influences behind and living by values we give ourselves. The development of autonomy is assumed to be the development of independence, of becoming a more and more sovereign ruler over how we live. Critical reflection, by contrast, takes for granted that the values by which we live are inextricably connected with our society's system of values. We are enabled by the prevailing values to live as we want, we derive our personal values from them, and we criticize or justify our own and other people's values by appealing to some of the prevailing values. The conventions and values that form our cultural identity are not obstacles to our well-being, but means to it. We should strive to reflect on them critically and to adapt them to us and us to them, rather than try to leave them behind and free ourselves from them. The question is not whether we should or should not do this. We have no alternative to doing it. But we can do it more or less reasonably, and critical reflection enables us to do it more reasonably.

The last difference between autonomy and critical reflection I will mention concerns our authority of choosing how to live.

Others may advise or persuade us, but, defenders of autonomy claim, we ought to have ultimate authority to make the relevant choices. Given fallibility, limited experience, and unclarity about how we want to live, it is hard to see why it would be always more reasonable to trust ourselves than to trust others who are less fallible, more experienced, and have clearer understanding of what is involved in living in a way we merely grope toward. It is not unreasonable for real or metaphorical apprentices to surrender their authority to masters, students to teachers, patients to physicians, clients to lawyers, actors to directors, and so forth. We all do this frequently, and, as far as I can see, we may do it quite reasonably. The claim that we should have ultimate authority to choose how we live appears plausible only because it is imprecise. We do not choose how we should live. We choose whether and how we should do something that is involved in how we think we should live. We are unreasonable if we do not recognize that some people may know better than we whether and how we should do that particular thing. And if we recognize it, and yet do not follow their advice when we need it, then, once again, we are unreasonable. Critical reflection does not commit us to the epistemological hubris of claiming final authority when our well-being depends on accepting the authority of those who know better.

Defenders of autonomy want to free us from outside influences, because they rightly see that they unavoidably limit the control we have over how we live. What they fail to see is that we are natural beings and we cannot free ourselves from the conditions of our lives. The attempt to do so is doomed, and that is why autonomy is an untenable ideal, even if its defenders avoid the absurdities with which Mill and Kant have saddled themselves. Of course, the ideal of autonomy may be reformulated so as to recognize that reason and morality allow other ideals of life beside autonomy, that, although we cannot be free of contingent influences, we can examine the ones to which we are subject, and that we may reasonably accept the authority of others. If it were reformulated in this way, then the differences between autonomy and critical reflection would disappear and whether we call the ideal autonomy or critical reflection becomes merely a verbal difference that makes no real difference.

Conclusion

Wallace Stevens writes:

> To say more than human things with human voice,
> That cannot be; to say human things with more
> Than human voice, that, also, cannot be;
> To speak humanly from the height or from the depth
> Of human things, that is acutest speech.[1]

This stanza expresses perfectly both what I have tried to do in this book, speaking humanly of human things, and what I think of as a misguided effort to say human things with more than human voice. We have the voice we have, our only voice, and if we speak, we must use it. But it is important to speak reasonably about important matters, and I have tried to do that about our well-being. The secular view is that our well-being largely depends on the values of the human world we have created in the midst of the vast indifferent world of facts.

The human world is a world of customs, meanings, and conventions; languages, works of art, traditions, and histories; puns, insults, games, and sports; laws, governments, and trials; ideals, obligations, and punishments; love, grief, shame, gratitude, guilt, and pride; kitsch, pornography, addiction, and advertising; bribery, flattery, fraud, and failure; courage, justice, wisdom, and truthfulness; concentration camps, wars, and torture; books, concerts, museums, rodeos, and quiz shows; and of a multitude of other artifacts, practices, institutions, glories, and depravities that jointly form the system of values that many generations inhabiting a society have constructed throughout its history. Human well-being largely, but not entirely, depends on living and acting according to the values of this system.

The human world may be considered from two points of view.[2] One is *sub specie aeternitatis*; God's or the Universe's view, if either had one; a view of the world in which the human world with its values appears as a collection of facts among a multitude of other facts. This is the *synoptic* view. The other is *sub specie humanitatis*; a historically and culturally conditioned view; the world viewed from within the human world, through our system of values. This is the *humanist* view. The synoptic view motivates persistent attempts "to say human things with more than human voice," but these attempts cannot succeed. The humanist view prompts us to speak humanly of human things, and the secular view I have been defending is a version of it.

According to the synoptic view, the human world and its values are a minute segment of the world and subject to its order. The key to our well-being is to acquire knowledge of this order and derive our values from it. If well-being eludes us, it is because we are ignorant of the order or fail to make our values conform to it. If we know the order, what we should do in pursuit of well-being will become clear. The great religions, most metaphysical systems, and scientific views are synoptic, but there are two basic types of synoptic views. One regards the order of the world as God-given and benign. Religious views are of this type. The other holds that the order is constituted of facts and the laws of nature, and it is indifferent to our well-being. Nevertheless, our well-being depends on conforming to it, because attempts to do otherwise are futile and doomed to fail. Scientific views are of this type. Metaphysical systems typically develop either religious or scientific types of synoptic views. Synoptic views differ in details essential to them, but, their differences notwithstanding, they are committed to the claim that our well-being depends on knowing and conforming to the order, whether benign or indifferent, that governs everything, including the human world.

Thomas Nagel has written most interestingly about the relation between the synoptic and the humanist views. He writes: "The wish to live so far as possible in full recognition that one's position in the universe is not central has an element of the religious impulse about it, or at least an acknowledgment of the question to which religion purports to supply an answer. A religious solution gives us borrowed centrality through the concern of a supreme being. Perhaps the religious question without the religious answer amounts to antihumanism, since we cannot compensate for the lack of cosmic meaning with a meaning derived from our own perspective."[3] Nagel does not say why the meaning we derive from our perspective could not compensate for the lack of cosmic meaning. The humanist view I am defending is precisely that the meaning derived from the human world and its system of values is a reasonable alternative to the search for cosmic meaning.

Nagel is right in this: according to the synoptic view our position in the universe is not central and has no more value than anything else, since from that point of view nothing has value. But from the humanist point of view our position in the universe is central, because we care about our values in an indifferent universe. It would be, then, the height of folly for us to adopt the synoptic rather than the humanist view. Yet Nagel thinks that we should strive to do that especially in morality and politics, and he acknowledges that his position "amounts to a strong form of antihumanism: the world is not our world."[4] Perhaps he thinks so because he is misled by the great success of science that is made possible by proceeding, insofar as it is humanly possible, from the synoptic view.

Humanists can accept that questions of fact are best approached scientifically. Questions of value, however, are not questions of fact. They are questions about how to think about the human value of facts. We have no reason to approach questions of value from the synoptic view, especially since the answer is the foreordained one that our values are deluded. Nagel sees this. He concludes his fine essay on the absurd by saying that "if *sub specie aeternitatis* there is no reason to believe that anything matters, then that does not matter either."[5] But he does not believe that nothing matters. On the contrary, he goes on to write impassioned works about what reason and morality require us to do to make the world a better place. Part of the reason for preferring the humanist to the synoptic view is that synoptic attempts to derive our values from something outside the human world cannot succeed. For such attempts presuppose the values of the human world, which are much richer and more various than what could be derived from the facts and laws that constitute the order of the world. Defenders of synoptic views, intentionally or not, are antihumanists, because, by seeking to derive our values from what lies outside the human world, they jeopardize our efforts to construct the values we need for our well-being.

Consider first the synoptic claim that our well-being depends on acquiring knowledge of the facts and the laws of world's order. It is certainly true that our well-being depends on having such knowledge, but it is not true that this requires leaving the human world behind. For, if we seek knowledge of the order to further our well-being, we must already have some values and some conceptions of well-being that enable us to distinguish between facts and laws that are and those that are not relevant to our well-being. The order contains all the facts and laws, but not all of them are relevant to our well-being. Defenders of synoptic views must recognize that our well-being depends only on some of them. We must be able to distinguish between components of the order that are and those that are not relevant to our well-being. We can do this, however, only if we already have some values and conceptions of well-being, and that is just what the human world provides for us.

The facts we come to know in this way may lead us to revise the values and conceptions of well-being with which we have started, but we must begin with some values and some conceptions of well-being, because if we did not, we would not know which of the countless facts and laws we should conform to in order to pursue our well-being. The synoptic view, therefore, presupposes the humanist view that contains the conception of well-being and the values out of which it is formed. That is why defenders of synoptic views cannot reasonably aim at our well-being by going beyond the values of the human world. Their efforts are self-defeating, because if they succeeded, we would not know how to pursue our well-being.

The synoptic claim that the values of the human world must be derived from the order of the world is true of some values, but not of others, and it is not true of any reasonable conception of well-being. We have seen that there is a great plurality of human, cultural, and personal values, and we form conceptions of well-being out of them. Human values are derived from the fact that well-being requires the satisfaction of our basic needs. Defenders of synoptic views are right that our basic needs are dictated by facts and laws external to the human world. But they are wrong to suppose that the same is true of cultural and personal values. Ballet, chamber music, civility, depth, diplomacy, faith, friendship, integrity, marriage, puns, trial by jury, wisdom, and countless other cultural and personal values are our constructions and form parts of the human world.

In constructing these values, we must, of course, draw on facts and recognize the laws that govern them. But it is the essence of human values that they are richer than these components. For the values humanize the facts by ascribing to them what we take to be their significance for our well-being. The facts are transformed into values by our cognitive, emotive, imaginative, and volitional responses to them. If we concentrate merely on the facts, as defenders of synoptic views say we should, we render ourselves incapable of recognizing their significance for our well-being. To see a dance as the motion of middle-sized material object governed by the laws of kinetics, or chamber music as the production of a sequence of sounds within the range audible to human ears is to miss their essence.

Moreover, once we have constructed values, we find that they often conflict with one another, because human limitations and scarce resources make it impossible to pursue them fully and simultaneously. We need to have some way of judging which of the conflicting values is more important in a particular cultural or personal context. There are no facts or laws external to the human world from which reasonable judgments of this sort could be derived. We derive the judgments we make from our system of values, which we form partly out of some of the many cultural and personal values available in our part of the human world.

Our cultural and personal values, conflict-resolutions, and conceptions of well-being partly constitute the human world's system of values. Defenders of synoptic views are right to claim that there is an order in the world that exists independently of the values of the human world and that our well-being partly depends on conforming to it. But they are wrong to conclude that all our values are derived from that order. Our well-being requires much more than conformity to the order and the satisfaction of basic needs. It requires participation in the human world with its cultural and personal values. And that is why synoptic views face a dilemma: if they leave behind the human world, they cannot give a reasonable account of our well-being; if they give a reasonable account of our well-being, they must rely on rather than go beyond the human world.

The synoptic response is that if humanists do not recognize a standard outside of the human world by which our values can be reasonably judged, then they cannot avoid arbitrariness. Our well-being depends on distinguishing between reasonable and unreasonable values. But we can do this, defenders of synoptic views say, only by going beyond the values themselves and appealing to some standard that does not rely on the values. If there is such a standard, it necessarily goes beyond our values; if there is not, we cannot reasonably rely on our values, and we have no reason to believe that the conceptions of well-being formed out of them will actually lead to our well-being.

Defenders of synoptic views are right to hold that arbitrariness is a serious danger and that some humanists, namely, relativists, have failed to avoid it. Relativists agree that we must choose between relying on a standard external to the human world and accepting the arbitrariness of our values. But unlike defenders of synoptic views, relativists choose arbitrariness. This, however, is a false choice. A pluralistic conception of practical reason allows us to avoid both arbitrariness and the futile search for an external standard.

According to this conception, one central aim of practical reason is to promote human well-being. This is a substantive, not a formal, aim. And, since conceptions of well-being vary with times, places, and persons, the requirements of practical reason cannot be universal and impersonal. Conceptions of well-being are alike in being formed out of the values embedded in the human world and in being formed by individuals who more or less consciously, more or less reflectively, more or less critically commit themselves to trying to realize some of the possibilities of life the prevailing system of values represent. But conceptions of well-being also differ, because they are formed out of different values and the values must be pursued within limits set by different conventions.

As we have seen, some of the values are universally human. The conventions that protect them are required by human well-being, because they consist in the satisfaction of basic needs we all have. Some other values are cultural. They are protected by conventions that vary with societies and are derived from the institutions, practices, and modes of evaluation that have become traditional in the course of a particular society's history and form the shared cultural identity of its members. Some further values are personal. They are protected by conventions that vary with individuals. We derive our personal values from the prevailing cultural values, and we shape our character and adjust to our circumstances in accordance with the conceptions of well-being we have formed out of our personal values.

Values and conventions may or may not be reasonably held. If the humanist view is to avoid arbitrariness, it must show how a pluralistic conception of practical reason can distinguish between reasonably and unreasonably held values and conventions. The first step toward showing this is to recognize that whether human, cultural, and personal values and required and variable conventions are reasonably held depends on different considerations. A value is held reasonably if it provides a component of individual well-being and a convention is held reasonably if it enables individuals to pursue a reasonably held value. But each type of value is intended to provide a different component of well-being, and that is why different values and conventions are held reasonably, if they are, for different reasons.

Human values are reasonably held if they consist in the satisfaction of basic needs. They are basic, because their satisfaction is a requirement of well-being regardless of what cultural or personal values we have. A required convention is reasonably held if it protects a reasonably held human value. It does not make a value human, nor a convention required, if it is strongly held or if it is thought to be required for well-being only because some cultural and personal values depend on it. Everyone may think that belief in God is a universal requirement of human well-being, but if there is no God, whatever value the belief has, it is not universal, and a convention protecting it is not required.

Human values and required conventions, therefore, depend on facts and relativists are mistaken in regarding these values and conventions as arbitrary. They are universal and impersonal requirements of human well-being, regardless of cultural and personal differences. But these requirements are prima facie, not absolute, because they allow for reasonable exceptions in case of conflicts or if human well-being in general depends on it.

Our well-being also depends on cultural and personal values and on variable conventions. Cultural values are reasonably held if they are components of the cultural identity of the people of a society. As Clifford Geertz puts it: "man is an animal suspended in webs of significance he himself has spun. I take culture to be those webs, and the analysis of it to be therefore not an experimental science in search of law but an interpretive one in search of meaning."[6] These webs of significance are complex and intricate. Their components at once overlap and conflict, reciprocally support and cast doubt on one other. They are formed of aesthetic, historical, legal, literary, moral, philosophical, political, religious, and scientific values; of active or passive participation in commerce, medicine, sports, travel, and work; of customs about crafts, education, etiquette, fashion, grooming, holidays, humor, law enforcement, and style; of the institutions of elections, graduation, law courts, marriage, museums, opera, prisons, and theater; of the activities of climbing mountains, giving dinner parties, going to concerts, jogging, paying taxes, and telling jokes; and so on and on. A society's culture is composed of such elements. They constitute its form of life and the cultural identity of those living in it, and we all derive from the surrounding culture our personal values and conceptions of well-being.

These values, activities, customs, and institutions are guided, regulated, and enabled by expressed or tacitly understood conventions we have been taught in the course of growing up. And when we are grown-up, normally intelligent, and under no great stress, we know what is expected of us and what we can expect of others. We recognize each other as sharing a cultural identity. It makes us belong and it is what we lack when we find ourselves in a foreign society.

Cultural values and the variable conventions protecting them are in constant flux. The conditions to which they respond change; internal and external criticisms lead to further changes; as do conflicts, crises, and new interpretations of traditional values and conventions. Cultural identity changes as its components change. The change of components may be dramatic, but the change of cultural identity itself is normally slow. What usually happens is that when some values and conventions change, the change slowly spreads over to other values and conventions. This is just what is happening to our cultural identity now as a result of dramatic changes in traditional attitudes to communication, sex, technology, warfare, and much else.

There are no comparable changes in human values and required conventions, because basic human needs do not change. That is why it makes good sense to say that the satisfaction of these needs is a universal and impersonal requirement of practical reason. Cultural identity, however, does change, because the ways in which we interpret the facts we encounter and the experiences we have depend on constantly changing circumstances. How, then, does the pluralistic conception of practical reason make it possible to distinguish between reasonable and unreasonable cultural values and variable conventions at any particular time, especially since they are apt to change?

On the basis of our allegiance to them. Our allegiance is reasonable if we maintain it voluntarily and because we rightly believe that our well-being depends on them. Voluntary allegiance does not require explicit choice. It requires only that we should accept most of the prevailing cultural values and variable conventions, even though we could question and reject them. Many people in our society have been doing just this about traditional aesthetic, religious, and sexual values and conventions. As a result, allegiance to them has been considerably weakened. This is part of the process that leads to changes in our cultural identity. But the values and conventions of physical security, private property, social mobility, uncensored press, freedom of employment, political equality, access to education, peace, and public health have not changed much. Continuing allegiance to them forms part of our continuing cultural identity.

Voluntary allegiance also depends on the possibility of leaving the society if we find its cultural values and variable conventions unacceptable. We may think that political corruption, the abuse of freedom, and rampant commercialism are deeply objectionable and incorrigible tendencies, and then we may switch our allegiance to another society, which we hope is better. But if we stay when we could leave, if our criticisms of the prevailing cultural identity call only for piecemeal, rather than fundamental, changes, then our allegiance to them is voluntary.

We may maintain our allegiance voluntarily, but for the wrong reasons. We may be afraid of changes emigration would involve, or be ignorant of other societies, or we may be resigned to alienation from our society, or suffer from a failure of nerve, self-doubt, or infirmity of purpose. Voluntary allegiance is reasonable only if we maintain it, because we rightly see that our well-being is intimately connected with our cultural identity. We conceive of our well-being in terms of living according to the prevailing values, participating in some of the institutions and practices, and following some of the customs. We feel we belong to our society and we share our sense of belongingness with others who feel the same way. This is an ideal condition that few actual lives enjoy. We are all more or less dissatisfied with the prevailing cultural identity. But if our dissatisfactions are not too deep, we have reason to maintain our allegiance to it voluntarily. The pluralistic conception of practical reason thus makes it possible to avoid both the arbitrariness of relativism and the futile synoptic search for a standard external to the human world.

There remains the problem presented by the ubiquitous conflicts among reasonably held human, cultural, and personal values and conventions. A conception of practical reason is defensible only if it provides some non-arbitrary way of resolving their conflicts. According to the pluralistic conception, the conflicts should be resolved in favor of the value and convention that we have reason to regard as more important for the protection of the prevailing system of values as a whole. That system is always more important for the well-being of people in a society than any of the particular values or conventions.

It is, of course, often a very difficult question which of the conflicting values is more important from that point of view. But we should not look to practical reason for a canonical principle that tells us authoritatively which of the conflicting values is more important. What practical reason provides is a guide to how we should go about seeking reasonable conflict-resolutions. It does not tell us what we should do. It tells how we should think about what we should do. Eventually we have to make a judgment, and our judgment may be mistaken. Practical reason enables us to say that it is mistaken, if it is, because we got wrong the relative importance of the conflicting values. And, of course, the judgment may also be correct, because the value we preferred over another is indeed more important to the protection of the whole system of values by which we live.

Relativists correctly insist that practical reasoning ends in fallible judgments, but they incorrectly conclude that the judgments are not merely fallible but also arbitrary. They are not arbitrary, because reasons for or against them can be given and the reasons are not arbitrary either, because their relative weight depends on their importance for the well-being of the people in a society at a particular time. Defenders of synoptic views rightly insist that reasonable conflict-resolutions depend on the availability of some standard, but they are wrong to suppose that the standard must be external to the human world.

It is not the least reason for rejecting both synoptic and relativist views and accepting humanism that when we speak to ourselves or to our friends, children, or neighbors, we speak humanly, not synoptically or relativistically. Who indeed makes decisions about divorce, suicide, abortion, career change, or loyalty to friends, causes, or institutions on the basis of considering what everyone should decide about such matters or on the basis of the fact that in Teheran, Timbuctu, or Tianjin people do things differently? If we decide reasonably, we do it on the basis of reflection on what we should do, given our history, character, relationships, and circumstances, rather than on the basis of trying to figure out what other people with different histories, characters, relationships, and circumstances should do.

Our situatedness is an essential feature of the human condition. Defenders of synoptic views go wrong because they think that practical reason requires us to transcend the local values that have become customary in the particular situation in which we find ourselves. Relativists go wrong, because they think that the requirements of practical reason are no more than customary local values themselves. One underestimates, the other overestimates the significance of our situatedness. Each is partly true and partly false, and because of the half-truth they contain, each appears to be initially plausible, until its false half is brought to mind.

The half-truth of the synoptic view is that practical reason requires us to go beyond our situatedness and ask whether our evaluations of the local values are reasonable. Its false half is the assumption that we can do this only if we transcend our situatedness and appeal to some standard external to it. The half-truth of relativism is that many of our values are local and our evaluations of them depend on the conditions prevailing in our situation. Its false half is that this makes all our evaluations ultimately arbitrary. Defenders of synoptic views try to say human things by borrowing a voice external to the human world, and that cannot be done. Relativists speak of human things, but they stay on their surface and underestimate the resources of practical reason.

Practical reason enables us to judge whether our evaluations of customary values are reasonable. This judgment is external to the customary values, but internal to the human world. We do not judge by appealing to a standard external to the human world, but by endeavoring to identify and correct the mistakes we make in our evaluations. We are fallible and we often make mistakes in forming our attitudes and commitments to customary values, in recognizing available possibilities and limits, and in constructing our conceptions of well-being. Practical reason in this context involves critical reflection directed inward, toward our psychological states. Its method is self-correction. And its aim is to remove obstacles to our well-being.

Practical reason does not guarantee our well-being. Much can go wrong, even if the prevailing cultural identity is as close to ideal as possible. The personal values and variable conventions out of which we form our conceptions of well-being may be faulty, because our critical reflection on the available possibilities may be mistaken, and because the contingencies of life, evil, disenchantment, and boredom may prevent us from living according to our conceptions of well-being even if they are not faulty. Assume, however, that nothing goes wrong and we live as we want. When does practical reason allow us to say that what we are enjoying is genuine, rather than counterfeit well-being?

When we are satisfied with how life is going, we do not regret major decisions we have taken; we wish our life to go on in the same way; we enjoy our more important activities and relationships; we are not lastingly enraged, resentful, ashamed, or humiliated; we feel that if we could do it again, we would live by and large as we are doing; we have a general sense that we are succeeding in living as we want. When these attitudes are thoughtful, sincere, and genuine expressions of how we feel, not just the face we put on in public, but what we say to ourselves privately, in the middle of a sleepless night, then we speak to ourselves humanly of human things.[7]

Notes

Chapter 1

1. Euripides, *Hecuba*, in *The Complete Greek Tragedies: Euripides III*, trans. William Arrowsmith (Chicago: University of Chicago Press, 1958), 489–92.

2. The number of books on this subject is great. The bibliography would itself fill a book. I merely mention four recent works: Daniel C. Dennnett, *Breaking the Spell: Religion as a Natural Phenomenon* (New York: Viking, 2006); my own *Moral Wisdom and Good Lives* (Ithaca: Cornell University Press, 1995); Philip Kitcher, *Living with Darwin* (New York: Oxford University Press, 2007); and Erik J. Wielenberg, *Value and Virtue in a Godless Universe* (New York: Cambridge University Press, 2005).

3. Bernard Williams, *Shame and Necessity* (Berkeley: University of California Press, 1993), 166, 163, 164. I have changed the original order of the quoted lines.

4. The conflict between these two points of view is the theme of Thomas Nagel's distinguished body of work, especially of *Mortal Questions* (Cambridge: Cambridge University Press, 1979) and *The View from Nowhere* (New York: Oxford University Press, 1986). It is no doubt my fault, but I have not been able to understand why he thinks that it is of great importance to take what he calls the objective view of the world. I can see why it is important for the physical and biological sciences to attempt to do this, but not why it is important for ethics, about which he says much, and aesthetics, about which he says very little.

5. David Hume, "The Sceptic" in *Essays, Moral, Political and Literary*, ed. Eugene F. Miller (Indianapolis: Liberty Press, 1985/1777), 178, 180.

6. Oscar Wilde, *The Picture of Dorian Gray* (Harmondsworth: Penguin, 1949/1891), 29.

7. G. E. Moore, "Some Judgments of Perception" *Philosophical Studies* (London: Routledge, 1922), 228.

8. Michel de Montaigne, *The Complete Works of Montaigne*, trans. Donald M. Frame (Stanford, CA: Stanford University Press, 1943/1588), 856–7.

9. Wallace Stevens, "Chocorue to Its Neighbor" in *The Collected Poems* (New York: Vintage, 1982), 300.

Chapter 2

1. Virtually all the works I refer to below stress the difficulty of making clear the meaning of freedom. One good example is Robert Kane, *A Contemporary Introduction to Free Will* (New York: Oxford University Press, 2005).

2. For a recent defense of libertarianism, see John Martin Fischer, *The Metaphysics of Free Will* (Oxford: Blackwell, 1994); Robert Kane, *The Significance of Free Will* (New York: Oxford University Press, 1998). For a general survey and bibliography, see Timothy O'Connor, "Free Will" *Stanford Encyclopedia of Philosophy*, http:/plato.Stanford.edu/.

3. For recent defenses of determinism, see Ted Honderich, *A Theory of Determinism* (Oxford: Clarendon Press, 1988); Galen Strawson, *Freedom and Belief* (Oxford: Oxford University Press, 1986). For a general survey and bibliography, see Carl Hoefer, "Determinism" *Stanford Encyclopedia of Philosophy*, http:/plato.Stanford.edu/.

4. For recent defenses of compatibilism, see Daniel Dennett, *Elbow Room* (Cambridge, MA: MIT Press, 1984); Harry Frankfurt, *The Importance of What We Care About* (New York: Cambridge University Press, 1988); Stuart Hampshire, *Thought and Action* (London: Chatto & Windus, 1960); Peter Strawson, "Freedom and Resentment" in *Freedom and Resentment*

(London: Methuen, 1974); and Charles Taylor, *Human Agency and Language* (Cambridge: Cambridge University Press, 1985), essays 1, 2, and 4. For a general survey and bibliography, see Michael McKenna, "Compatibilism" *Stanford Encyclopedia of Philosophy*, http:/plato.Stanford.edu/.

5. For an excellent introductory account of these disputes, see Kane, *A Contemporary Introduction to Free Will*. A more advanced account is Robert Kane, ed., *The Oxford Handbook of Free Will* (New York: Oxford University Press, 2002).

6. For some concurring opinions, see "My present opinion is that nothing that might be a solution [of the problem of free will] has yet been described. This is not a case where there are several possible candidate solutions and we don't know which is correct. It is a case where nothing believable has . . . been proposed by anyone in the extensive public discussion of the subject." Thomas Nagel, *The View from Nowhere* (New York: Oxford University Press, 1986), 112. "The question, then, of whether determinism is true or of whether men have free will is no longer regarded as a simple or even a philosophically sophisticated question by many writers. Concealed in it is a vast array of more fundamental questions, the answers to which are largely unknown." Richard Taylor, "Determinism" in *Encyclopedia of Philosophy*, ed. Paul Edwards (New York: Macmillan, 1967), vol. 2, 372. "Although the terms of the debate have been considerably sharpened, it is fair to say that the basic issue . . . still lives. . . . It is hard to say where this argument will go, or even where it should go. . . . Either free agency is ineffable, free agency . . . is illusory, or compatibilism is true. Take your pick (if you can)." Gary Watson, "Free Action and Free Will" *Mind* 96 (1987): 145–72.

7. Frankfurt, *Importance of What We Care About*, 16.

8. Hampshire, *Thought and Action*, 177.

9. Strawson, *Feeling and Resentment*, 25.

10. Taylor, *Human Agency*, 16.

Chapter 3

1. One notable exception is Harry G. Frankfurt's fine essay "Rationality and the Unthinkable" in *The Importance of What We Care About* (Cambridge: Cambridge University Press, 1988). I agree with much of Frankfurt's argument, but not with one of his central claims, namely, that the unthinkable is primarily a matter of the will. I see no reason why people may not be led primarily by their beliefs, emotions, imagination, or experience to regard some actions as unthinkable as far as they are concerned.

2. C. P. Cavafy, "Che Fece . . . Il Gran Rifiuto" in *C.P. Cavafy Collected Poems*, trans. Edmund Keeley & Philip Sherrard, ed. George Savidis (Princeton: Princeton University Press, 1975).

3. This is the theme of tragedy. The literature on it is immense. For a recent work close to my view about the human condition, see George W. Harris, *Reason's Grief: An Essay on Tragedy and Value* (New York: Cambridge University Press, 2006).

4. On this point, see Williams on integrity in J. J. C. Smart & Bernard Williams, *Utilitarianism: For and Against* (Cambridge: Cambridge University Press, 1973) and his "Persons, Character and Morality" in *Moral Luck* (Cambridge: Cambridge University Press, 1981).

5. "I have argued that the states universally accounted bad and to be avoided and prevented have a clear priority in practical thinking and morality. When one is identifying ends of actions that are common to all humanity, one thinks first of the great natural and man-made disasters against which both prudence and morality are required as protection and as shields. . . . The great evils are those states of affairs which are to be avoided for reasons that are independent of any reflective thought and of any specific conception of evil." Stuart Hampshire, *Innocence and Experience* (New York: Allen Lane, 1989), 106.

6. "He explains himself to himself by his history, but by the history as accompanied by unrealised possibilities . . . . His individual

nature and the quality of his life, do not depend only on the
bare log-book of events and actions. His character and the
quality of his experience emerge in the possibilities that were
real possibilities for him, which he considered and rejected
for some reason or other. From the moral point of view, it
is even a significant fact about him as a person that a certain
possibility, which might have occurred to him as a possibility,
never did occur to him." Hampshire, *Innocence and Experience*,
101. In following this approach I have learned much from this
book of Stuart Hampshire, as well as from *Thought and Action*
(London: Chatto & Windus, 1959), *Freedom of the Individual*
(London: Chatto & Windus, 1965), and *Morality and Conflict*
(Cambridge: Harvard University Press, 1983). I have also been
influenced by Charles Taylor's *Human Agency and Language:
Philosophical Papers 1* (Cambridge: Cambridge University Press,
1985), especially essays 1, 2, and 4, and *Sources of the Self*
(Cambridge: Harvard University Press, 1989).

7. Aristotle, *Nicomachean Ethics*, trans. W. D. Ross, rev. J. O.
Urmson, in *The Complete Works of Aristotle*, ed. Jonathan Barnes
(Princeton: Princeton University Press, 1984), 1094a. For an
excellent account of Aristotle's moral thought, see Richard
Kraut, *Aristotle on the Human Good* (Princeton: Princeton
University Press, 1989).

8. For two very good historical accounts, see, Julia Annas, *The
Morality of Happiness* (New York: Oxford University Press,
1993) and Martha C. Nussbaum, *The Therapy of Desire* (Princeton: Princeton University Press, 1994).

Chapter 4

1. Harry G. Frankfurt, *The Importance of What We Care About*
(Cambridge: Cambridge University Press, 1988).

2. Stuart Hampshire, *Thought and Action* (London: Chatto &
Windus, 1960); *Freedom of the Individual*, expanded edition

(Princeton: Princeton University Press, 1975); *Morality and Conflict* (Cambridge: Harvard University Press, 1983).

3. Martha C. Nussbaum, "Narrative Emotions" in *Love's Knowledge* (New York: Oxford University Press, 1990).

4. Charles Taylor, *Human Agency and Language* (Cambridge: Cambridge University Press, 1985) and *Sources of the Self* (Cambridge: Harvard University Press, 1989).

5. See Richard Wollheim, "On Persons and Their Lives" in *Explaining Emotions*, ed. Amelie Rorty (Berkeley: University of California Press, 1980); *The Thread of Life* (Cambridge: Harvard University Press, 1984); and *The Mind and Its Depths* (Cambridge: Harvard University Press, 1993).

6. Alasdair MacIntyre, *After Virtue* (Notre Dame: University of Notre Dame Press, 1981), especially Chapter 15. References in the text are to the pages of this edition.

7. Dissent from the narrative approach is decidedly a minority view. For a very interesting form of it, quite different from my own, see Galen Strawson's "A Fallacy of Our Age" in *Times Literary Supplement* October 15, 2004, 13–15; *The Self?* (Oxford: Blackwell, 2005); and *Selves: An Essay in Revisionary Metaphysics* (Oxford: Clarendon Press, 2009).

8. Michel de Montaigne, *Essays* in *The Complete Works of Montaigne*, trans. Donald M. Frame (Stanford: Stanford University Press, 1958/1588), 220.

9. Friedrich Nietzsche, *Human, All Too Human*, trans. R. J. Hollingdale (Cambridge: Cambridge University Press, 1996/1879–80), no. 517, 182.

Chapter 5

1. *Apocrypha*, 2 Maccabees 6, 18.

2. Stuart Hampshire, "Two Theories of Morality" in *Morality and Conflict* (Cambridge: Harvard University Press, 1983/1977), 38–9.

3. Immanuel Kant, *Groundwork of the Metaphysics of Morals*, trans. H. J. Paton (New York: Harper, 1964/1785), 60, 79, 84, 88.

4. Friedrich Nietzsche, *On the Genealogy of Morals*, trans. Walter Kaufmann (New York: Modern Library, 1966/1887), 453, 456.

5. I should not leave Kant without noting that there have been numerous contemporary attempts to recast his views so as to avoid this and other problems with it. This is not the place for a detailed discussion of them. I merely note that if the recast Kantian views remain absolutist, they do not avoid the problem of ignoring two of the three dimensions of value. If they give up absolutism, then my criticisms do not apply to them. See, e.g., Marcia Baron, *Kantian Ethics (Almost) without Apology* (Ithaca: Cornell University Press, 1995); Barbara Herman, *The Practice of Moral Judgment* (Cambridge: Harvard University Press, 1993); Thomas E. Hill, Jr. *Autonomy and Self-Respect* (Cambridge: Cambridge University Press, 1991), *Dignity and Practical Reason in Kant's Moral Theory* (Ithaca: Cornell University Press, 1992), *Respect, Pluralism, and Justice: Kantian Perspectives* (Oxford: Oxford University Press, 2000), and *Human Welfare and Moral Worth: Kantian Perspectives* (Oxford: Clarendon Press, 2002); and Christine M. Korsgaard, *Creating the Kingdom of Ends* (Cambridge: Cambridge University Press, 1996) and *The Sources of Normativity* (New York: Cambridge University Press, 1996).

6. For some contemporary defenses of relativism, see Michael Krausz, ed. *Relativism: Interpretation and Confrontation* (Notre Dame, IN: University of Notre Dame Press, 1989); John L. Mackie, *Ethics: Inventing Right and Wrong* (Harmondsworth: Penguin, 1977); Gilbert Harman & Judith Jarvis Thomson, *Moral Relativity and Moral Objectivity* (Cambridge, MA: Blackwell, 1996); and David B. Wong, *Moral Relativity* (Berkeley: University of California Press, 1984). A very different approach to relativism is followed by people who have been influenced by the post-*Tractatus* work of Wittgenstein. Among them are Stanley Cavell, ''The Availability of Wittgenstein's Later

Philosophy" in *Must We Mean What We Say?* (Cambridge: Cambridge University Press, 1969/1962); Alice Crary, *Beyond Moral Judgment* (Cambridge: Harvard University Press, 2007); Cora Diamond, "Having a Rough Story about What Moral Philosophy Is" in *New Literary History*, 15 (1983): 155–69; Sabina Lovibond, *Ethical Formation* (Cambridge: Harvard University Press, 2002); John McDowell, "Virtue and Reason" in *Mind, Value and Reality* (Cambridge: Cambridge University Press, 1998); and Bernard Williams, "Internal and External Reasons" in *Moral Luck* (Cambridge: Cambridge University Press, 1981/1980). In fairness to this latter approach, I should add that its defenders refuse to accept the relativist label on the odd ground that no alternative to it is conceivable.

7. Classic statements of individualism are Thomas Hobbes, *Leviathan* (London: J. M. Dent, 1914/1651); Henry Sidgwick, *The Methods of Ethics* (Indianapolis: Hackett, 1981/1874); Max Stirner, *The Ego and His Own* (New York: Harper & Row, 1971/1845). Some contemporary treatments are David Gauthier, *Morals by Agreement* (Oxford: Clarendon Press, 1986) and David Gauthier, ed., *Morality and Rational Self-Interest* (Englewood Cliffs, N.J.: Prentice-Hall, 1970).

8. Isaiah Berlin, "Two Concepts of Liberty" in *Four Essays on Liberty* (Oxford: Oxford University Press, 1969/1958), 154.

Chapter 6

1. Stuart Hampshire, "Morality and Pessimism" in *Morality and Conflict* (Cambridge: Harvard University Press, 1983), 89.

2. Some further examples are discussed in detail in my *The Roots of Evil* (Ithaca: Cornell University Press, 2005), Part One. For other examples, see, e.g., Jonathan Glover, *Humanity: A Moral History of the Twentieth Century* (New Haven: Yale University Press, 1999); Stephanie Courteous et al. *The Black Book of Communism* (Cambridge: Harvard University Press,

1999); Martin Gilbert, *The Holocaust* (New York: Henry Holt, 1985).

3. Jean-Jacques Rousseau, *Discourses on the Origin and Foundation of Inequality Among Man*, trans. Donald A. Cress (Indianapolis: Hackett, 1988/1754), 89 and *Letter to Beaumont* in *Oeuvres complètes*, 5 vols. (Paris: Gallimard, 1959–95), 935; trans. Timothy O'Hagan in *Rousseau* (London: Routledge, 1999), 15.

4. Immanuel Kant, *Religion within the Bounds of Reason Alone*, trans. Theodore M. Greene and Hoyt H. Hudson (New York: Harper & Row, 1960/1794), 39, 31.

5. John Stuart Mill, *Utilitarianism* (Indianapolis: Hackett, 1979/1861), 3, 31–2.

6. John Rawls, *A Theory of Justice* (Cambridge: Harvard University Press, 1971), 506, 561, 476, 245.

7. Philippa Foot, *Natural Goodness* (Oxford: Clarendon Press, 2001), 5, 9, 14.

8. Annette Bayer explicitly refers to it as such in her "Secular Faith" in *Postures of the Mind* (Minneapolis: University of Minnesota Press, 1985) and John Rawls in the last four sentences of *A Theory of Justice* clearly avows it, although he does not say that it is a faith.

9. Rawls, *A Theory of Justice*, 311–12.

10. Susan Wolf, *Freedom Within Reason* (New York: Oxford University Press, 1991), 79.

11. For an interesting historical account of this explanation, see Susan Neiman, *Evil in Modern Thought* (Princeton: Princeton University Press, 2002).

12. This, of course, is one of the themes of Hannah Arendt's work on evil. See especially *Eichmann in Jerusalem: A Report of the Banality of Evil* (New York: Viking, 1963) and also *The Origins of Totalitarianism* (New York: Harcourt, 1941). Arendt would have avoided a great deal of controversy and vituperation directed at her if instead of the banality of evil, she talked about the banality of most evil-doers.

13. I owe this point to Joel J. Kupperman's *Ethics and the Qualities of Life* (New York: Oxford University Press, 2007), Chapter 1, where he discusses, among other topics, the significance of the Milgram experiments. This is the best response I know of in the voluminous literature provoked by these experiments.

14. For the detailed study of this mentality, see Norman Cohn's *The Pursuit of the Millennium* (London: Secker & Warburg, 1957) and *Europe's Inner Demons* (London: Heinemann, 1975).

Chapter 7

1. Stuart Hampshire, *Thought and Action* (London: Chatto & Windus, 1960), 178.

2. Harry G. Frankfurt, *The Importance of What We Care About* (New York: Cambridge University Press, 1988), 24.

3. H. L. A. Hart, *Punishment and Responsibility* (New York: Oxford University Press, 1968), 114–15.

4. Thomas E. Hill, Jr., *Autonomy and Self-Respect* (New York: Cambridge University Press, 1991), 92.

5. Robert Kane, *A Contemporary Introduction to Free Will* (New York: Oxford University Press, 2005), 129, 128.

6. The discussion that follows is based on Chapter 4 of *The Roots of Evil* (Ithaca: Cornell University Press, 2005), where I treat this case in much greater detail.

7. Gitta Sereny, *Into that Darkness* (London: Pimlico, 1995). First published (London: André Deutsch, 1974). Parenthetical references in the text are to the pages of the Pimlico edition.

8. Bernard Williams, "How Free Does the Will Have To Be?" in *Making Sense of Humanity* (Cambridge: Cambridge University Press, 1995/1985), 16.

9. Gary Watson, "Responsibility and the Limits of Evil" in *Responsibility, Character, and the Emotions*, Ferdinand Schoeman, ed. (New York: Cambridge University Press, 1987), 276.

10. Susan Wolf, "Asymmetrical Freedom" in *Moral Responsibility*, John M. Fischer, ed. (Ithaca: Cornell University Press, 1986), 233.

11. This way of thinking about responsibility is indebted to and follows several writers, such as Joseph Butler, "Upon Resentment" in *Fifteen Sermons* (London: Bell, 1953/1726); Peter Strawson, "Freedom and Resentment" in *Freedom and Resentment* (London: Methuen, 1974); Jonathan Bennett, "Accountability" in *Philosophical Subjects*, Zak van Straaten, ed. (Oxford: Clarendon Press, 1980); Gary Watson, "Responsibility and the Limits of Evil" op. cit.; and R. Jay Wallace, *Responsibility and the Moral Sentiments* (Cambridge: Harvard University Press, 1996), especially Chapter 2.

12. Much has been written about them under the labels of dirty hands and double effects. For reviews of the literature and bibliography, see C. A. J Coady, "Dirty Hands" and William D. Solomon, "Double Effect" both in *Encyclopedia of Ethics*, second edition, Lawrence C. Becker & Charlotte B. Becker, eds. (New York: Routledge, 2001).

13. David Hume, *A Treatise of Human Nature*, L. A. Selby-Bigge, ed. (Oxford: Clarendon Press, 1960/1739), 535.

Chapter 8

1. Max Weber, "Science as a Vocation" in *Essays in Sociology*, trans. & eds. H. H. Gerth and C. Wright Mills (New York: Oxford University Press, 1946/1919), 155.

2. See, for instance, "The argument of this book has been that . . . we cannot create our own values, and we cannot achieve meaning just by inventing goals of our own; the fulfillment of our nature depends on . . . faith in the ultimate resilience of the good; we need to live in the light of hope. Such faith and hope, like the love that inspires both . . . is available to us through cultivating the disciplines of spirituality." John

Cottingham, *On the Meaning of Life* (London: Routledge, 2003), 103–4. "A common conception of what it is for a human life to mean something other than the personal satisfaction of its possessor finds its most adequate justification in the supposition that there is a God who is on our side, and that we have reason to believe this chiefly because He has promised that it is so." Gordon Graham, *Evil and Christian Ethics* (Cambridge: Cambridge University Press, 2001), 227. "The stable and systematic moral universe for which the ethical philosopher asks is fully possible only in a world where there is a divine thinker with all-enveloping demands . . . his way of subordinating the demands to one another would be the finally valid casuistic scale." William James, "The Moral Philosopher and the Moral Life" in *The Will to Believe, and Other Essays* (New York: Dover, 1956/1896), 211. For a detailed discussion, see Leszek Kolakowski, "The Revenge of the Sacred in Secular Culture" in *Modernity on Endless Trial* (Chicago: University of Chicago Press, 1990). References in the text are to the pages of Kolakowski's essay. "People lived in an 'enchanted' world", their experience was "of peace or wholeness . . . of integrity or generosity or abandonment or self-forgetfulness . . . [they had] moments of experienced fullness, of joy and fulfillment", but in our disenchanted lives "we experience above all a distance, an absence, an exile . . . an absence of power; a confusion, or worse, the condition often described . . . as melancholy, ennui. . . . What is terrible in this latter condition is that we lose a sense of . . . fullness . . . even of what fullness would consist in." Charles Taylor, *A Secular Age* (Cambridge: Harvard University Press, 2007), 29, 5, and 6.

3. Gustave Caillebotte, *The Orange Trees or the Artist's Brother in His Garden*, 1878, Museum of Fine Arts, Houston, Texas/Bridgeman Art Library.

4. Herman Melville, *Billy Budd, Sailor*, published posthumously in 1924. There are many editions, see, e.g., *Billy Budd and Other Stories* (New York: Penguin, 1986).

5. For a biography, see J. M. S. Allison, *Lamoignon de Malesherbes, Defender and Reformer of the French Monarchy* (New Haven: Yale University Press, 1938).

6. David Hume, *Enquiries concerning Human Understanding and concerning the Principles of Morals*, ed. L. A. Selby-Bigge, second edition (Oxford: Clarendon Press, 1902/1777), 9.

7. David Hume, *The Natural History of Religion* (Stanford: Stanford University Press, 1957/1757), 74, 73.

8. All quoted passages are cited from Ernest Campbell Mossner, *The Life of David Hume* (Oxford: Clarendon Press, 1970/1954), 598–600.

9. A fascinating account of their deliberations is in Ian Kershaw's *Fateful Decisions* (New York: Penguin, 2007).

10. Winston S. Churchill, *The Second World War, vol. 1: The Gathering Storm* (Boston: Houghton Mifflin, 1958/1949), 601.

11. See Note 2 above.

Chapter 9

1. Bertrand Russell, *The Conquest of Happiness* (London: Routledge, 1993/1930), 44.

2. Martin Heidegger, "What is Metaphysics?" in *Existence and Being*, ed W. Brock (Chicago: Regnery, 1949), 364, 366.

3. Karl E. Scheibe, *The Drama of Everyday Life* (Cambridge: Harvard University Press, 2000), 19.

4. O. E. Klapp, *Overload and Boredom* (Westport, CT: Greenwood, 1986), 11–12.

5. Reinhard Kuhn, *The Demon of Noontide* (Princeton: Princeton University Press, 1976), 331.

6. Jacques Barzun, *From Dawn to Decadence* (New York: HarperCollins, 2000), 801.

7. William James, *The Varieties of Religious Experience* in *Writings 1902–1910* (New York: The Library of America, 1987/1902), 128, 135–6.

8. Kuhn, *Demon of Noontide*, 40, 45, 52.

9. Friedrich Nietzsche, *The Gay Science*, trans. Walter Kaufmann (New York: Vintage, 1974/1882), 341. Nietzsche asks the same question in "Why I Am So Clever?" in *Ecce Homo*, trans. Walter Kaufmann (New York: Modern Library, 1966/1908).

10. *Ecclesiastes*, 1,1–18, 3.16, 4.2–3.

11. Karel Capek, "The Makropulos Secret" in *Toward the Radical Center*, trans. Yveta Sinek & Robert T. Jones (Highland Falls, N.J.: Catbird Press, 1990), 110–77.

12. Michael Evans, *Janacek's Tragic Operas* (London: Faber & Faber, 1977), 168–203.

13. Bernard Williams, "The Makropulos Case: Reflections on the Tedium of Immortality" in *Problems of the Self* (Cambridge: Cambridge University Press, 1973), 82–100.

14. Capek, 173–5.

15. Evans, 44b.

16. Isaiah Berlin, "Two Concepts of Liberty" in *Four Essays on Liberty* (Oxford: Oxford University Press, 1969/1958), 172.

17. Isaiah Berlin, " 'From Hope and Fear Set Free' " in *Concepts and Categories*, Henry Hardy, ed. (London: Hogarth, 1978), 198.

18. Berlin, "Two Concepts of Liberty", 165.

19. Bernard Williams, *Ethics and the Limits of Philosophy* (London: Fontana/Collins, 1985), 163. Parenthetical references in the text are to the pages of this work.

20. Bernard Williams, *Truth and Truthfulness: An Essay in Genealogy* (Princeton: Princeton University Press, 2002), 20.

21. Ibid. 224.

Chapter 10

1. Algernon Swinburne, "The Garden of Proserpine" in *The Complete Works of Algernon Charles Swinburne*, eds. Edmund Gosse and Thomas Wise (London: Heinemann, 1925–27).

2. Michael Oakeshott, *On Human Conduct* (Oxford: Clarendon Press, 1975), 241.

3. John Stuart Mill, *Utilitarianism* (Indianapolis: Hackett, 1979/1861), 32.

4. For its history, see J. B. Schneewind, *The Invention of Autonomy* (New York: Cambridge University Press, 1998). For reliable surveys of the analyses and interpretations, as well as bibliographies, see the articles on autonomy by Sarah Buss and John Christman in *Stanford Encyclopedia of Philosophy,* http://plato.Stanford.edu/.

5. John Stuart Mill, *On Liberty* (Indianapolis: Bobbs–Merrill, 1956/1859), 13.

6. Ibid. 68–9.

7. Ibid. 70.

8. Ibid. 73.

9. Ibid. 81.

10. Immanuel Kant, *The Critique of Pure Reason*, trans. Norman Kemp Smith (London: Macmillan, 1953/1787), A84, B117.

11. Immanuel Kant, *Groundwork of the Metaphysics of Morals*, trans. H. J. Paton (New York: Harper, 1964/1785), 114.

12. Immanuel Kant, "An Answer to the Question: What is Enlightenment?" in *Practical Philosophy*, trans. Mary J. Gregor (Cambridge: Cambridge University Press, 1996/1784), 21.

13. Immanuel Kant, "On a Supposed Right to Lie from Philanthropy", op. cit. 613.

14. Kant, *Groundwork*, 70–1.

15. Immanuel Kant, *The Metaphysics of Morals*, trans. Mary Gregor (Cambridge: Cambridge University Press, 1996/1797), 182.

16. Kant, *Critique of Pure Reason*, A134.

17. Aristotle, *Nicomachean Ethics*, 1109a23–9, trans. W. D. Ross, rev. J. O. Urmson, in *The Complete Works of Aristotle*, ed. Jonathan Barnes (Princeton: Princeton University Press, 1984).

Conclusion

1. Wallace Stevens, *The Collected Poems* (New York: Vintage Books, 1982), 300.

2. Much has been written about this. Here is a sample of excellent contemporary works on the subject: David E. Cooper, *The Measure of Things* (Oxford: Clarendon Press, 2002); Edward Craig, *The Mind of God and the Works of Man* (Oxford: Clarendon Press, 1987); Christine M. Korsgaard, *The Sources of Normativity* (Cambridge: Cambridge University Press, 1996); John McDowell, *Mind, Value, and Reality* (Cambridge: Harvard University Press, 1998); Thomas Nagel, *The View from Nowhere* (New York: Oxford University Press, 1986); and Bernard Williams, *Truth and Truthfulness* (Princeton: Princeton University Press, 2002).
3. Nagel, *View from Nowhere*, 210.
4. Ibid. 108.
5. Thomas Nagel, "The Absurd" in *Mortal Questions* (Cambridge: Cambridge University Press, 1979), 23.
6. Clifford Geertz, *The Interpretation of Cultures* (New York: Basic Books, 1973), 5.
7. This, of course, is a very large subject about which much more needs to be said. I have said what I could in *Enjoyment: The Moral Significance of Styles of Life* (Oxford: Clarendon Press, 2008).

Works Cited

Allison, J. M. S., *Lamoignon de Malesherbes, Defender and Reformer of the French Monarchy* (New Haven: Yale University Press, 1938).

Annas, Julia, *The Morality of Happiness* (New York: Oxford University Press, 1993).

Apocrypha.

Arendt, Hannah, *The Origins of Totalitarianism* (New York: Harcourt, 1941).

———— *Eichmann in Jerusalem: A Report of the Banality of Evil* (New York: Viking, 1963).

Aristotle, *Nicomachean Ethics*, trans. W. D. Ross, rev. J. O. Urmson, in *The Complete Works of Aristotle*, ed. Jonathan Barnes (Princeton: Princeton University Press, 1984).

Baier, Annette, "Secular Faith" in *Postures of the Mind* (Minneapolis: University of Minnesota Press, 1985).

Baron, Marcia, *Kantian Ethics (Almost) without Apology* (Ithaca: Cornell University Press, 1995).

Barzun, Jacques, *From Dawn to Decadence* (New York: HarperCollins, 2000).

Bennett, Jonathan, "Accountability" in *Philosophical Subjects*, ed. Zak van Straaten (Oxford: Clarendon Press, 1980).

Berlin, Isaiah, "Two Concepts of Liberty" in *Four Essays on Liberty* (1958; Oxford: Oxford University Press, 1969).

———— " 'From Hope and Fear Set Free' " in *Concepts and Categories*, ed. Henry Hardy (London: Hogarth, 1978).

Butler, Joseph, "Upon Resentment" in *Fifteen Sermons* (1726; London: Bell, 1953).

Caillebotte, Gustave, *The Orange Trees or the Artist's Brother in His Garden* 1878, Museum of Fine Arts, Houston, Texas/Bridgeman Art Library.

Capek, Karel, "The Makropulos Secret" in *Toward the Radical Center*, trans. Yveta Sinek & Robert T. Jones (1922; Highland Falls, N.J.: Catbird Press, 1990).

Cavafy, C. P., "Che Fece . . . Il Gran Rifiuto" in *C.P. Cavafy Collected Poems,* trans. Edmund Keeley & Philip Sherrard, ed. George Savidis (Princeton: Princeton University Press, 1975).

Cavell, Stanley, "The Availability of Wittgenstein's Later Philosophy" in *Must We Mean What We Say?* (Cambridge: Cambridge University Press, 1962).

Churchill, Winston S., *The Second World War, vol. 1: The Gathering Storm* (1949; Boston: Houghton Mifflin, 1958).

Coady, C. A. J., "Dirty Hands" in *Encyclopedia of Ethics,* second edition, eds. Lawrence C. Becker & Charlotte B. Becker (New York: Routledge, 2001).

Cohn, Norman, *The Pursuit of the Millennium* (London: Secker & Warburg, 1957).

_____ *Europe's Inner Demons* (London: Heinemann, 1975).

Cooper, David E., *The Measure of Things* (Oxford: Clarendon Press, 2002).

Cottingham, John, *On the Meaning of Life* (London: Routledge, 2003).

Courteous, Stephanie et al. *The Black Book of Communism* (Cambridge: Harvard University Press, 1999).

Craig, Edward, *The Mind of God and the Works of Man* (Oxford: Clarendon Press, 1987).

Crary, Alice, *Beyond Moral Judgment* (Cambridge: Harvard University Press, 2007).

Dennett, Daniel, *Elbow Room* (Cambridge, MA: MIT Press, 1984).

_____ *Breaking the Spell: Religion as a Natural Phenomenon* (New York: Viking, 2006).

Diamond, Cora, "Having a Rough Story about What Moral Philosophy Is" in *New Literary History* 15 (1983): 155–69.

Ecclesiastes.

Euripides, *Hecuba,* in *The Complete Greek Tragedies: Euripides III,* trans. William Arrowsmith (Chicago: University of Chicago Press, 1958).

Evans, Michael, *Janacek's Tragic Operas* (London: Faber & Faber, 1977).

Fisher, John Martin, *The Metaphysics of Free Will* (Oxford: Blackwell, 1994).

Foot, Philippa, *Natural Goodness* (Oxford: Clarendon Press, 2001).

Frankfurt, Harry, *The Importance of What We Care About* (New York: Cambridge University Press, 1988).

Gauthier, David, ed., *Morality and Rational Self-Interest* (Englewood Cliffs, N.J.: Prentice-Hall, 1970).

_____ *Morals by Agreement* (Oxford: Clarendon Press, 1986).

Geertz, Clifford, *The Interpretation of Cultures* (New York: Basic Books, 1973).

Gilbert, Martin, *The Holocaust* (New York: Henry Holt, 1985).

Glover, Jonathan, *Humanity: A Moral History of the Twentieth Century* (New Haven: Yale University Press, 1999).

Hampshire, Stuart, *Thought and Action* (London: Chatto & Windus, 1960).

_____ *Freedom of the Individual* (London: Chatto & Windus, 1965).

_____ *Morality and Conflict* (Cambridge: Harvard University Press, 1983).

_____ *Innocence and Experience* (New York: Allen Lane, 1989).

Harman, Gilbert & Judith Jarvis Thomson, *Moral Relativity and Moral Objectivity* (Cambridge, MA: Blackwell, 1996).

Harris, George W., *Reason's Grief: An Essay on Tragedy and Value* (New York: Cambridge University Press, 2006).

Hart, H. L. A., *Punishment and Responsibility* (New York: Oxford University Press, 1968).

Heidegger, Martin, "What is Metaphysics?" in *Existence and Being,* ed. W. Brock (Chicago: Regnery, 1949).

Herman, Barbara, *The Practice of Moral Judgment* (Cambridge: Harvard University Press, 1993).

Hill, Thomas E. Jr., *Autonomy and Self-Respect* (Cambridge: Cambridge University Press, 1991).

_____ *Dignity and Practical Reason in Kant's Moral Theory* (Ithaca: Cornell University Press, 1992).

_____ *Respect, Pluralism, and Justice: Kantian Perspectives* (Oxford: Oxford University Press, 2000).

_____ *Human Welfare and Moral Worth: Kantian Perspectives* (Oxford: Clarendon Press, 2002).

Hobbes, Thomas, *Leviathan* (1651; London: J. M. Dent, 1914).

Hoefer, Carl, "Determinism" *Stanford Encyclopedia of Philosophy,* http:/plato.Stanford.edu/.

Honderich, Ted, *A Theory of Determinism* (Oxford: Clarendon Press, 1988).

Hume, David, *A Treatise of Human Nature*, ed. L. A. Selby-Bigge (1739; Oxford: Clarendon Press, 1960).

Hume, David, *The Natural History of Religion* (1757; Stanford: Stanford University Press, 1957).

——— "The Sceptic" in *Essays, Moral, Political and Literary,* ed. Eugene F. Miller (1777; Indianapolis: Liberty Press, 1985).

——— *Enquiries concerning Human Understanding and concerning the Principles of Morals*, ed. L. A. Selby-Bigge, second edition (Oxford: Clarendon Press, 1902/1777).

James, William, "The Moral Philosopher and the Moral Life" in *The Will to Believe, and Other Essays* (1896; New York: Dover, 1956).

——— *The Varieties of Religious Experience* in *Writings 1902–1910* (1902; New York: The Library of America, 1987).

Kane, Robert, *The Significance of Free Will* (New York: Oxford University Press, 1998).

——— ed., *The Oxford Handbook of Free Will* (New York: Oxford University Press, 2002).

——— *A Contemporary Introduction to Free Will* (New York: Oxford University Press, 2005).

Kant, Immanuel, "An Answer to the Question: What is Enlightenment?" in *Practical Philosophy* trans. Mary J. Gregor (1784; Cambridge: Cambridge University Press, 1996).

——— *Groundwork of the Metaphysics of Morals*, trans. H. J. Paton (1785; New York: Harper, 1964).

——— *The Critique of Pure Reason* trans. Norman Kemp Smith (1787; London: Macmillan, 1953).

——— *Religion within the Bounds of Reason Alone,* trans. Theodore M. Greene & Hoyt H. Hudson (1794; New York: Harper & Row, 1960).

——— "On a Supposed Right to Lie from Philanthropy" *The Metaphysics of Morals,* trans. Mary Gregor (1797; Cambridge: Cambridge University Press, 1996).

Kekes, John, *Moral Wisdom and Good Lives* (Ithaca: Cornell University Press, 1995).

——— *The Roots of Evil* (Ithaca: Cornell University Press, 2005).

——— *Enjoyment: The Moral Significance of Styles of Life* (Oxford: Clarendon Press, 2008).

Kershaw, Ian, *Fateful Decisions* (New York: Penguin, 2007).

Kitcher, Philip, *Living with Darwin* (New York: Oxford University Press, 2007).

Klapp, O. E., *Overload and Boredom* (Westport, CT: Greenwood, 1986).

Kolakowski, Leszek, "The Revenge of the Sacred in Secular Culture" in *Modernity on Endless Trial* (Chicago: University of Chicago Press, 1990).

Korsgaard, Christine M., *Creating the Kingdom of Ends* (Cambridge: Cambridge University Press, 1996).

_____ *The Sources of Normativity* (New York: Cambridge University Press, 1996).

Krausz, Michael, ed., *Relativism: Interpretation and Confrontation* (Notre Dame, IN: University of Notre Dame Press, 1989).

Kraut, Richard, *Aristotle on the Human Good* (Princeton: Princeton University Press, 1989).

Kuhn, Reinhard, *The Demon of Noontide* (Princeton: Princeton University Press, 1976).

Kupperman, Joel J., *Ethics and the Qualities of Life* (New York: Oxford University Press, 2007).

Lovibond, Sabina, *Ethical Formation* (Cambridge: Harvard University Press, 2002).

McDowell, John, "Virtue and Reason" in *Mind, Value and Reality* (Cambridge: Cambridge University Press, 1998).

MacIntyre, Alasdair, *After Virtue* (Notre Dame: University of Notre Dame Press, 1981).

McKenna, Michael, "Compatibilism" *Stanford Encyclopedia of Philosophy*, http:/plato.Stanford.edu/.

Mackie, John L., *Ethics: Inventing Right and Wrong* (Harmondsworth: Penguin, 1977).

Melville, Herman, *Billy Budd, Sailor*, in *Billy Budd and Other Stories* (New York: Penguin, 1986).

Mill, John Stuart, *On Liberty* (1859; Indianapolis: Bobbs-Merrill, 1956).

_____ *Utilitarianism* (1861; Indianapolis: Hackett, 1979).

Montaigne, Michel de, *The Complete Works of Montaigne,* trans. Donald M. Frame (1588; Stanford, CA: Stanford University Press, 1943).

Moore, G. E., "Some Judgments of Perception" *Philosophical Studies* (London: Routledge, 1922).

Mossner, Ernest Campbell, *The Life of David Hume* (1954; Oxford: Clarendon Press, 1970).

Nagel, Thomas, *Mortal Questions* (Cambridge: Cambridge University Press, 1979).

Nagel, Thomas, *The View from Nowhere* (New York: Oxford University Press, 1986).

Neiman, Susan, *Evil in Modern Thought* (Princeton: Princeton University Press, 2002).

Nietzsche, Friedrich, *Human, All Too Human,* trans. R. J. Hollingdale (1879–1880; Cambridge: Cambridge University Press, 1996).

—— *The Gay Science,* trans. Walter Kaufmann (1882; New York: Vintage, 1974).

—— *On the Genealogy of Morals,* trans. Walter Kaufmann (1887; New York: Modern Library, 1966).

—— "Why I Am So Clever?" in *Ecce Homo,* trans. Walter Kaufmann (1908; New York: Modern Library, 1966).

Nussbaum, Martha C., "Narrative Emotions" in *Love's Knowledge* (New York: Oxford University Press, 1990).

—— *The Therapy of Desire* (Princeton: Princeton University Press, 1994).

O'Connor, Timothy, "Free Will" *Stanford Encyclopedia of Philosophy,* http:/plato.Stanford.edu/.

Oakeshott, Michael, *On Human Conduct* (Oxford: Clarendon Press, 1975).

Rawls, John, *A Theory of Justice* (Cambridge: Harvard University Press, 1971).

Rousseau, Jean-Jacques, *Discourses on the Origin and Foundation of Inequality Among Men,* trans. Donald A. Cress (1754; Indianapolis: Hackett, 1988).

—— *Letter to Beaumont* in *Oeuvres complètes* 5 vols. (Paris: Gallimard, 1959–95), trans. Timothy O'Hagan in *Rousseau* (London: Routledge, 1999).

Russell, Bertrand, *The Conquest of Happiness* (1930; London: Routledge, 1993).

Scheibe, Karl E., *The Drama of Everyday Life* (Cambridge: Harvard University Press, 2000).

Schneewind, J. B., *The Invention of Autonomy* (New York: Cambridge University Press, 1998).

Sereny, Gitta, *Into that Darkness* (1974; London: Pimlico, 1995).

Sidgwick, Henry, *The Methods of Ethics* (1874; Indianapolis: Hackett, 1981).

Smart, J. J. C. & Bernard Williams, *Utilitarianism: For and Against* (Cambridge: Cambridge University Press, 1973).

Stevens, Wallace, "Chocorue to Its Neighbor" in *The Collected Poems* (New York: Vintage, 1982).

Stirner, Max, *The Ego and His Own* (1845; New York: Harper & Row, 1971).

Strawson, Galen, *Freedom and Belief* (Oxford: Oxford University Press, 1986).

_____ "A Fallacy of Our Age" in *Times Literary Supplement* October 15, 2004, 13–15.

_____ *The Self?* (Oxford: Blackwell, 2005).

_____ *Selves: An Essay in Revisionary Metaphysics* (Oxford: Clarendon Press, 2009).

Strawson, Peter, "Freedom and Resentment" in *Freedom and Resentment* (London: Methuen, 1974).

Swinburne, Algernon, "The Garden of Proserpine" in *The Complete Works of Algernon Charles Swinburne,* eds. Edmund Gosse and Thomas Wise (London: Heinemann, 1925–27).

Taylor, Charles, *Human Agency and Language* (Cambridge: Cambridge University Press, 1985).

_____ *Sources of the Self* (Cambridge: Harvard University Press, 1989).

_____ *A Secular Age* (Cambridge: Harvard University Press, 2007).

Taylor, Richard, "Determinism" in *Encyclopedia of Philosophy,* ed. Paul Edwards (New York: Macmillan, 1967).

Wallace, R. Jay, *Responsibility and the Moral Sentiments* (Cambridge: Harvard University Press, 1996).

Watson, Gary, "Free Action and Free Will" *Mind* 96 (1987): 145–72.

_____ "Responsibility and the Limits of Evil" in *Responsibility, Character, and the Emotions*, ed. Ferdinand Schoeman (New York: Cambridge University Press, 1987).

Weber, Max, "Science as a Vocation" in *Essays in Sociology,* trans. & eds. H. H. Gerth and C. Wright Mills (1919; New York: Oxford University Press, 1946).

Wielenberg, Erik J., *Value and Virtue in a Godless Universe* (New York: Cambridge University Press, 2005).

Wilde, Oscar, *The Picture of Dorian Gray* (1891; Harmondsworth: Penguin, 1949).

Williams, Bernard, "The Makropulos Case: Reflections on the Tedium of Immortality" in *Problems of the Self* (Cambridge: Cambridge University Press, 1973).

_____ "Persons, Character and Morality" in *Moral Luck* (Cambridge: Cambridge University Press, 1981).

Williams, Bernard, "Internal and External Reasons" in *Moral Luck* (Cambridge: Cambridge University Press, 1981).

—— *Ethics and the Limits of Philosophy* (London: Fontana/Collins, 1985).

—— *Shame and Necessity* (Berkeley: University of California Press, 1993).

—— "How Free Does the Will Have To Be?" in *Making Sense of Humanity* (1985; Cambridge: Cambridge University Press, 1995).

—— *Truth and Truthfulness: An Essay in Genealogy* (Princeton: Princeton University Press, 2002).

Wolf, Susan, "Asymmetrical Freedom" in *Moral Responsibility*, ed. John M. Fischer (Ithaca: Cornell University Press, 1986).

—— *Freedom Within Reason* (New York: Oxford University Press, 1991).

Wollheim, Richard, "On Persons and Their Lives" in *Explaining Emotions,* ed. Amelie Rorty (Berkeley: University of California Press, 1980).

—— *The Thread of Life* (Cambridge: Harvard University Press, 1984).

—— *The Mind and Its Depths* (Cambridge: Harvard University Press, 1993).

Wong, David B., *Moral Relativity* (Berkeley: University of California Press, 1984).

Index

[Italicized entries in the index refer to character studies that are concrete illustrations of the argument]

absolutism 103–7, 177–84
Adolf 27–30, 39–43
Aristotle 6, 63
attitudes 15–16, 19–22, 34–8,
   47–66, 67–8
autonomy 216–25

Berlin 110–11, 199–201
boredom 185–206

Caillebotte 171
Capek 196–7
Churchill 175
conception of well-being 59–66,
   67–87
coherence 72–81
commitments 56–63, 72–4, 81–6
  conditional 58–63
  unconditional 57–63
contingency 4, 12–15, 19–23
control 16–19, 26–46
critical reflection 26–46, 52–3, 63–6,
  228–31
conflicts 88–9, 97–113
conventions 89–95
cultural identity 94–95, 162–84

depth 207–11
disenchantment 2, 162–84

Eleazar 100–1
Euripides 7–8, 12, 23
evaluations 10–12
  modes of 93, 166–71

evil 114–37, 189–94
  adequate explanation of 127–35
  inadequate explanations of
   122–7
  reflexivity of 139–46
  responsibility for 138–61
  secular problem of 119–22
excuses 153–60
exemplars 171–7

Fecund 69–74, 77–8, 80
Flaubert 101–3
Foot 120
Frankfurt 74, 76
freedom 26–46
  and compatibilism 26, 30–3,
   38–40, 43–6
  and determinism 26, 28–33,
   38–42
  and libertarianism 26, 28–33,
   38–42
  variable approach to 33–46
Freud 18

Geertz 239–40

Hampshire 74, 76, 101–3, 114–15,
  140
Hart 140
Hill 140
hope 207–31
humanist view 233–45
Hume 6, 23, 158, 173–4

ideologies 131–7
indifference 8–10
individualism 103–7, 109–10
intention 146–9

James 186–7

Kane 140–1
Kant 44, 106–7, 120, 136, 179,
    219–23
Kolakowski 163–6, 176, 179

limits 53–6

MacIntyre 75–6
Makropulos 196–9
Malesherbes 172–3
Melville 171–2
Mill 120, 136, 217–19
Montaigne 6, 25, 83–4, 215
Moore 18

Nagel 234–8
narratives 74–81
Nietzsche 86, 195
Nussbaum 74, 76

optimism 2, 121–7, 135–7

Rawls 120–1, 179
realism 2–3, 81–6
reason 3–4, 110–13, 160–1, 183–4,
    232–45
    practical 19–23, 183–4
relativism 103–8, 201–4, 243–4
religious point of view 1–3

responsibility for evil 138–61
    and excuses 153–60
    and intention 146–9
    standard of 149–53
Rousseau 120, 136

Sarah 53–5, 57, 61–2
Schumpeter 199–201
scientific view 3
secular faith 121–7, 135–7
synoptic view 233–8
secular view 1–2. 4–5, 194–9,
    207–31
Socratic view 110–13
standard of responsibility 149–53
Stangl 141–5, 148–9
Stevens 25, 232

Taylor 74, 76

unsubstantial dream 7–8, 12, 67
unthinkable 53–63

values 14–16, 23–5, 47–53, 82–6,
    88–113, 114–37, 238–45
    commitments to 56–63
    cultural 49–50, 91–5, 162–84
    human 49–50, 89–91, 114–37
    personal 96–7, 185–206
value pluralism 88–113, 182–4,
    201–4
variable approach 33–46

Watson 146–7
Wilde 17
Williams 9, 145, 147, 196–9, 201–4
Wolf 121, 146–7
Wollheim 74, 76